D1519511

Understanding
Written Language

Understanding Written Language

Explorations of Comprehension Beyond the Sentence

A. J. Sanford

and

S. C. Garrod

Both of the University of Glasgow

JOHN WILEY & SONS

Chichester · New York · Brisbane · Toronto

Copyright © 1981 by John Wiley & Sons Ltd.

British Library Cataloguing in Publication Data:

Sanford, A.J.
   Understanding written language.
   1. Reading, Psychology of
   I. Title   II. Garrod, S.C.
   428′.4′019   BF456.R2   80-40849

   ISBN 0 471 27842 4

Phototypeset by Dobbie Typesetting Service, Plymouth, Devon, England
and printed in the United States of America

To our daughters
Bridget and Nicola

Acknowledgements

A number of colleagues and friends are due a debt of gratitude for their help and support during the writing of this book. Particularly useful comments on earlier drafts were given by Phil Johnson-Laird and Ivana Markova, and many valuable and salutary discussions were had with Derek Corcoran and Keith Stenning. In addition, our students, and members of the Watt Society, provided a useful sounding-board both for our theories and the general layout of the book. In particular, thanks are due to Anne Anderson, James Boyle, Liz Boyle, June Hamilton, Robert Henderson, and Jim Mullin. Seemingly endless drafts were deciphered with patience by Sheena Bryson, who also typed the final manuscript. Finally, our largest debt of gratitude is to our wives, Valerie and Celia, who provided continued encouragement throughout.

Credits for figures and tables

We wish to thank the following individuals and organizations for permission to reproduce material published elsewhere:

Figure 2.2	From Collins, A. and Quillian, M. R. (1972a), by permission of Academic Press and the authors.
Figure 2.6	From Minsky, M. (1975) by permission of McGraw-Hill and the author.
Table 3.3	From Shafto, M. (1973) by permission of Academic Press and the author.
Table 3.5 and Table 3.6	From Schank, R. and Abelson, R. (1977) by permission of Lawrence Erlbaum Associates and the authors.
Figure 3.3	From Rumelhart, D. E. and Ortony, A. (1976) by permission of Academic Press and the author.
Table 4.1, Figure 4.4, and Figure 4.5	From Thorndyke, P. W. (1977) by permission of Academic Press and the author.
Figure 4.2	From Kintsch, W., et al (1975) by permission of Academic Press and the authors.
Figure 4.3	From Kintsch, W. and Keenan, J. (1973) by permission of Academic Press and the authors.

| Table 9.1 and Figure 9.2 | From Kieras, D. (1978) by permission of Academic Press and the author. |
| Figure 9.1 | From Gilliland, J. (1975) by permission of Hodder and Stoughton and the author. |

Contents

Preface

The written word provides a major means of transmitting ideas and feelings freely throughout the human community. As such, it has been explored widely by linguists, anthropologists, philosophers, and educationalists each from their own particular orientation. Our approach is psychological — to analyse those processes by which the written word comes to be understood by the reader. In Part I of the book, we have tried to provide an introduction to the kinds of issues which are of central importance, and at the same time to lay a foundation for Part II. Part II itself presents a theory of the processes by which comprehension takes place.

Because the approach is psychological, we have paid much attention to empirical observation and experimentation. Indeed, most of the analyses presented in Part II are based on explicitly described experimental studies. At the same time, we have tried to relate our views to a range of discursive issues, such as good and poor writing styles, good paragraph structure, and good and poor readers. In short, we have attempted to present an integrated framework through which diverse aspects of language use may be brought together.

Apart from this empirical characteristic, a second feature is that the exposition is problem-oriented. Rather than discuss the broad range of issues to be found in the relation of psychology to language, from the outset we have been driven by the question: *how do readers come to understand written text*? In seeking answers to this question, many problems have been highlighted by recent developments in the computing science discipline of artificial intelligence. Inevitably, in writing computer programs which can understand natural language and paraphrase or answer complex questions about a discourse, workers in artificial intelligence come face-to-face with problems similar to those encountered by psychologists trying to describe how humans carry out these functions. After all, an important part of the venture in both psychology and artificial intelligence is to discover what understanding *means* in practical terms. However, as a practical discipline, artificial intelligence leads to specific problems which may have more than one (viable) solution. So although a particular solution may provide a good hypothesis of how humans process information, the psychological reality of the hypotheses can only be established by empirical observation.

The first part of the book comprises material which we have found appropriate for psycholinguistic and memory courses at the advanced under-graduate and postgraduate levels. It has been our experience that our students prefer a problem-oriented approach to cognitive psychology rather than one in which a more descriptive approach is taken. Furthermore, we hope that the book will be of interest to researchers in all disciplines having any contact with understanding the written word, and to this end we have attempted to provide sufficient discussion of psychological terms to enable the interested non-psychologist to come to grips with the argument.

The nature of language has interested enquiring minds almost as far back as the appearance of the earliest texts. Our contribution to its understanding is offered in the belief that the answer to many questions is to be found in the psychological processes underlying the use of language. Written language does not live in books — the squiggles on the page can live only through the agency of the minds of readers.

Glasgow, January 1980   A. J. SANFORD
S. C. GARROD

Part 1

CHAPTER 1

The Nature of the Problem

In this book we shall be discussing how a reader comes to understand what is written in a piece of discourse. The reader is confronted with words and sentences on the page, and by applying the appropriate mental machinery ends up with something in his mind which captures the gist of what has been written. Our aim is to describe what is known of the operation of this machinery.

This chapter is introductory, and is intended to provide a sample of some of the interesting problems which are encountered when the comprehension of discourse is examined. It will be shown how knowledge of the world and the process of comprehension are inextricably bound together. Such a dependence on knowledge leads to the question of how knowledge itself can be characterized, and a fuller discussion of this is presented in Chapter 2. Chapter 3 continues the story by describing in detail the way in which knowledge relates to comprehension at all levels — words, sentences, and complete tracts of discourse. While it may sound a truism to say that understanding depends on knowledge, we hope to show in Chapter 3 that the details of this dependency are in fact very varied and complex.

If the reader usually ends up with the 'gist' of a passage in his mind then a fairly obvious question is what it is that gist might be. Psychologists have approached this question by looking at what people actually remember of texts and relating the results to theories of gist. A description of this approach forms the basis of Chapter 4, where certain theories of memory for text are critically evaluated.

These four chapters form the first section of the book and represent a selective review of the background literature, which by its very nature originates in research from a number of different disciplines. Perhaps the most important of these is the still inchoate study of Artificial Intelligence, a branch of computer science whose aim is to simulate complex human behaviour. A number of people working in this area have been able to construct computer programs capable of taking in natural discourse and 'understanding' it. A program can be said to have understood if it can type out a paraphrase or summary of what has been put into it, or produce a translation into a foreign language, or give 'intelligent' answers to questions about the discourse.

Inevitably, any program which can do this will incorporate useful ideas about how to characterize comprehension. While these ideas may lead to a working model, they need not reflect the way in which human beings actually comprehend — but nevertheless they should not be ignored in any analysis of the process. For the psychologist, Artificial Intelligence provides a useful fund of ideas. For this reason, in the present book we shall often allude to such work, although it is not strictly concerned with *human* understanding.

Psychologists, by contrast, are directly concerned with how humans process information. Ultimately, psychological theories stand or fall on empirical data, be it obtained in laboratory experiments or in everyday observation. This is true of our own work, and much of the book is concerned with developing theories which depend upon various kinds of empirical work which will be described at some length. However, for many researchers, the test of a good theory is not simply that it explains the data, but that it is sufficiently complete to work in novel situations if it could be implemented in some way. This is the second attraction of the computer. Any theory which is sufficiently explicit can be written as a computer program, and the behaviour of the system tested in novel situations.

Work from other disciplines enters into our discussions. Linguistics, with its aim of describing the structure of language, obviously plays a role. So too does philosophy, with its emphasis on analytic processes and problems of adequate description. Finally, anthropologists, whose concern is in part with universals of human knowledge, have also made contributions to which we shall allude. However, the primary aim is to produce an account of the comprehension process within the confines of the psychological approach, basing our claims on empirical observation, or at least relating them to empirical work.

The major thrust on the working detail of a psychological account of discourse comprehension begins in Part 2 of the book. Three chapters on different aspects of this detail lead up to a general summary and expansion of a psychological account in Chapter 8. Chapter 9 is more discursive, being concerned with a wide variety of issues from good and poor writing to good and poor readers.

A. The Isolated Sentence and Beyond

Let us begin by considering just what a written discourse is. Looked at in one way, it is a number of sentences, each made up of words put together using the appropriate rules of syntax and semantics. Looked at in another, it could be a description or a story designed to convey a message to the reader. Accordingly, comprehension can refer both to the processes whereby the component sentences are understood and to the way in which the message itself is understood. Much of psycholinguistics is concerned with the former problem — discovering the processes whereby a person comes to interpret isolated sentences in the language. Reasons for this bias are not hard to find. Many linguists would assume that the sentence is the largest clearly definable entity in a language (cf. Lyons, 1968, p. 172) and thus forms a natural unit of analysis. Sentences can be grammatical or ungrammatical, and meaningful or meaningless, depending upon whether they are constructed in accordance with the appropriate linguistic rules. A proper aspect of the study of psycho-linguistics is therefore the way in which knowledge of grammar is applied to sentences in order to parse them into an appropriate representation. Thus, the sentence is a seemingly tractable and relatively simple entity to work with, because it is easily defined. On the other hand, full discourse is not. A discourse can take many forms — a legal document, a short story, a description of how to mend a car engine, a newspaper article — and all have different structures, different styles, and so on. All they have which is obviously in common is that they are made up of sentences.

One way of tackling comprehension is thus to suppose that a discourse consists of sentences, and that the meaning of the discourse is a sum of the meanings of all of the sentences making it up.

The problem with this approach is that, in all but perhaps legal discourse, the message conveyed goes far beyond the individual sentences which make up a text. This is true in even the shortest examples. For instance, consider the two sentences below:

(1) Jill came bouncing down the stairs.
(1′) Harry rushed off to get the doctor.

Most readers would interpret this in terms of Jill falling on the stairs, injuring herself, and as a result of this Harry calling a doctor. Notice how different the interpretation is when (1) is followed by a slightly different sentence.

(1) Jill came bouncing down the stairs.
(1″) Harry rushed over to kiss her.

What this suggests is that far from being tied to the literal content of the component sentences, the message in a text is dependent on the reader bringing in additional knowledge in an attempt to come up with a coherent interpretation of the passage as a whole.

One way of characterizing this additional component of text meaning is in terms of the inferences which the skilled reader must make in order to connect the meanings of the various sentences in a sensible way. Thus, in reading sentences (1) and (1′) above it could be argued that the reader is drawing a variety of inferences, such as 'Jill fell down the stairs', 'Jill hurt herself', 'people who hurt themselves consult doctors', etc., each of which enables the reader to form a link between the events described. There are, in fact, a wide range of such textual inferences, and Trabasso, *et al.* (1977) have suggested that they fall into four basic categories.

The first and most straightforward type they describe as the *lexical inference*. This type of inference is called for in solving problems of lexical ambiguity or nominal reference. If you consider the following pair of sentences, both forms are called for:

(2) Mary had worked in the hospital for years.

(3) *The woman* was truly outstanding in *the theatre*.

In order to understand these, the reader will have to infer that the *the theatre* is used in the unusual sense of operating theatre. If (3) had been read in isolation this particular interpretation would be most unlikely, in fact in this case *the woman* would be seen as an actress. The other form of lexical inference is illustrated in interpretation of *the woman* as referring to *Mary*. This second type of lexical inference is called for very often, since it is usual to refer to only a limited number of individuals within any text and commonly to do so with different expressions. Such references are termed anaphoric.

The second class of inferences which Trabasso *et al.* describe comprise *inferences of space and time*. To understand any narrative text the reader has to be able to anchor the events and episodes described in some sort of spatio-temporal framework. Even in the simplest narratives, like that shown below, one finds oneself doing this.

(4) Thomas went to the theatre on Wednesday.

(5) He bumped into an old friend of his.

Readers will automatically infer that the event described in (5) occurred *on Wednesday* and in *the theatre*. In other words, sentence (4) seems to serve as a setting in which sentence (5) may be interpreted.

The two classes of inference mentioned so far are relatively straightforward in that it is possible, at least in principle, to describe the conditions under which a reader will have to make them. In fact there will be some discussion of these in subsequent chapters of the book. For the moment let us consider the other two types of inference, which are not nearly so straightforward. These are the so-called *extrapolative* and *evaluative inferences*.

As we have pointed out with our initial example of 'Jill bouncing down the stairs and Harry calling the doctor', most readers would extrapolate beyond the two events described in order to come up with some link between them. In a sense we could think of this text as elliptical, representing a shortened version of something like the following:

'Jill bounced down the stairs. In doing so she hurt herself. It is common for people to call a doctor in these circumstances. Harry, who had seen her doing this, therefore went out to call the doctor.'

To the extent that this is true, the reader must have inferred the sequence of intervening events which link the two sentences. In other words, he will have extrapolated beyond what is actually given in the text. Hence the term extrapolative inference.

The final type of inference that Trabasso *et al.* describe they call evaluative. This type of inference arises because the value or significance of an event depends upon the context in which it is presented and readers will often have to determine this in order to understand what the text is about. An example may help to illustrate the point. If a reader encountered sentence (6) in the context of a description of someone having completed a substantial and expensive meal in a restaurant, it would have a very different significance from the same sentence in the context of someone who wanted to buy a packet of cigarettes.

(6) Harry could only find one pound in his wallet.

This is simply because the reader would infer, in the former case, that Harry might have trouble paying the bill. The significance of the event described depends upon our knowledge of what may happen in a certain context.

The fact that one can describe such a wide range of text inferences indicates the inadequacy of any theory of text comprehension based solely on processes operating at the level of the isolated sentence. But will a taxonomy of inferences, such as that attempted above, help in determining a more credible approach to the psychology of comprehension? For instance, would it be adequate to say that the meaning of text is constituted by the meaning of each sentence in isolation plus the various types of inference which a reader will have to draw in order to relate these sentences? There are a number of problems which arise. In the first place, it would be foolish to assume that the processes underlying one type of inference could be described adequately without reference to the others. This is illustrated in the example given below (from Schank, 1975):

(7) John wanted to go to Hawaii.
(7′) He called his travel agent.
(7″) *He* said they took cheques.

In order to interpret *he* in (7″) a lexical inference is called for. While under most circumstances this pronoun would be taken as a reference to *John*, in this case it refers to the *travel agent*. However, in coming to the correct conclusion, the reader will have had to draw an extrapolative inference to the effect that it is the travel agent who will require payment and that it is he who would determine whether or not a cheque was acceptable. Thus what started as a lexical inference ends up requiring an extrapolative one.

What is striking about examples like (7) is the way in which the sentences seem to evoke in the mind of the reader a situation to which the discourse refers. In fact one only need go as far as a single sentence to demonstrate the discrepancy between its meaning (in the isolated sense) and what it seems to refer to in the mind of the average reader. Consider for instance the sentence below, which is borrowed from Collins and Quillian (1972b):

(8) The policeman held up his hand and stopped the car.

Such a sentence could be interpreted in a variety of ways. The policeman could have physically stopped the car through his own strength, for example. But most readers would not interpret it in that way. Rather, it seems to evoke some sort of mental scenario in which there is *a driver* who *steps on a brake*, and *who does this in response to seeing the policeman's hand*. Such an interpretation or evoked scenario incorporates much information which is absent from the text itself. But the example indicates more than this; it also suggests that the reader uses his knowledge of *typical* situations to help in developing this scenario. In this case, it shows a use of knowledge of a policeman's role in traffic control for instance. With a different sentence, but of comparable linguistic format, such as (9), a different scenario is evoked.

(9) The wicket-keeper held up his hand and stopped the ball.

In this case, it is of *a man dressed in protective gloves*, who *catches a ball coming from the hand of the bowler*, etc. In other words, this scenario depends upon the reader's knowledge of what typically happens in a game of cricket.

The fact that discourse often and characteristically refers to some situation which the reader already knows about allows him to construct some sort of mental scenario, which will incorporate much of the additional information needed to draw the various types of inference which we have described above. Thus, although at times it may be helpful to consider different types of inference in terms of the conditions under which they may be required, it is also most likely that they derive from a single source, namely the reader's attempt to discover some unique mental model of what the writer is talking about.

The discussion above exemplifies the problem of saying what a discourse is. On the one hand, it *is* only the sentences themselves. On the other hand, the sentences only have a significance because of knowledge in the mind of the reader which was there before the text was encountered. Rather than simply describe a text as a linguistic object, it therefore seems more appropriate to describe it as a series of instructions which tell the reader how to utilize the knowledge he already has, and contingently modify this knowledge in the light of the literal content of the discourse itself. The problem of text comprehension then becomes more than one of the interpretation of isolated sentences: it becomes a question of the processes whereby language calls forth appropriate knowledge, and of how wording, stress, and grammatical construction alter the specific knowledge brought to bear in any given case. This is the essence of a psychological account of discourse comprehension.

B. Discourse as a Contract

It might seem strange to suggest that a reader constructs a complex situational model to which he assumes the text refers. After all, what happens if this model turns out to be completely inappropriate? We would suggest that the modelling process is no accident, but derives from the function of a discourse itself. The basis on which discourse is produced and understood is essentially contractual. A writer wishes to convey an idea to his readers. In essence, this means that he must establish in the mind of his reader a situational model which is the same as (or closely similar to) the one in his own mind. He can then refer to this model as his discourse unfolds and be reasonably certain that what he says will be intelligible. In the absence of such a common model, a discourse *will* be unintelligible, even if every sentence in it is coherent and grammatical. Dooling and Lachman (1971) produced a very neat illustration of this in the following passage:

> (10) With hocked gems financing him, our hero bravely defied all scornful laughter that tried to prevent his scheme. 'Your eyes deceive', he had said. 'An egg, not a table, correctly typifies this unexplored planet'. Now three sturdy sisters sought proof. Forging along, sometimes through calm vastness, yet more often over turbulent peaks and valleys, days became weeks as many doubters spread fearful rumours about the edge. At last, from nowhere, welcome winged creatures appeared signifying momentous success.

Although each sentence within this passage is grammatical and meaningful in isolation, the passage as a whole is virtually incomprehensible and very hard to remember. As a piece of discourse, the writer has not honoured his contract to elicit a situational model in the mind of the reader. Such a model is immediately accessible given a title: to reread it knowing that it is about 'Christopher Columbus's discovery of America' is to guarantee its intelligibility.

This passage is of course rich in metaphor, making it hard to understand without a quite explicit statement of theme to bring to mind the appropriate background model. Without a key to the theme, discourse would be at best very long-winded and more often than not impossible to understand. Consider the following example:

> (11) John Smith got ready to go to the theatre.
> (11′) He tied his hair into a top-knot with a huge velvet bow.

(11′) seems strange. It does not fit the idea of a man going to the theatre. However, it would pass as reasonable if the discourse had been preceded by an orienting statement:

> (12) John Smith was playing the 'old dame' in the small-town pantomime.

The point with this last example is that while it is intelligible, it is awkward in the extreme. Readers may have had various theories about it:
- It doesn't make sense.
- John is going to a fancy-dress ball at the theatre.
- John is a transvestite.
- The bow is part of his costume.

In the absence of a thematic model, no interpretation is possible.

These examples illustrate what happens when a writer fails to honour his part of the contract. For the reader's part, his problem is somewhat different: he has to assume that the writer is in fact writing about a coherent situation and that it is his task to discover what this situation is. The utility of the mental model which we suggest the reader generates is that it will allow for unique representations of what is being said. While any sentence may be ambiguous in isolation, once it is interpreted with respect to a particular scenario it takes on a unique meaning. Thus sentence (8) about a policeman stopping a car is seen as portraying some particular situation rather than an optional series of different situations. From a psychological standpoint, this would suggest that the mental representation of a text is some combination of information in the text itself and its interpretation in terms of the reader's own knowledge. One aspect of this is illustrated in the interpretation of the following sentences:

(13) John was on his way to school last Friday.
(13′) He was really worried about the maths lesson.

On reading this, most readers assume John to be a schoolboy. Thus it seems rather bizarre if the discourse continues:

(14) Last week he had been unable to control the class.

Now, while there is nothing in (13) and (13′) to explicitly indicate that John is a schoolboy, anyone finding (14) strange must admit to having imported situational knowledge of some sort into their interpretation of the two sentences. Such specific interpretations can have a rather disturbing effect:

(15) John was on his way to school last Friday. He was really worried about the maths lesson. Last week he had been unable to control the class. It was unfair of the maths master to leave him in charge. After all, it is not a normal part of a janitor's duties.

To the extent that such an example is disturbing, it illustrates the fact that the text evokes a model of a situation which is based on the knowledge the reader already has. The problem is to characterize the interplay between background knowledge and those words on the page which bring it into the reader's mind.

Most readers find example (15) quite striking. But the point is not restricted to such unusual examples. Let us consider a further case, taken from Charniak (1972):

(16) Jane was invited to Jack's birthday party. She wondered if he would like a kite. She went to her room and shook her piggy-bank. It made no sound.

The meaning which a reader extracts from this paragraph is more than just a list of the propositions it contains. It is understood as a set of statements related by a central theme which the reader must assume forms the basis on which the writer produced the paragraph. The theme revolves around purchasing a present to take to a birthday party, even though there is no explicit statement of this in the passage itself. But without the use of such a central theme it is difficult to imagine how a reader could draw the appropriate inferences to relate *a kite* to a birthday present, *her piggy-bank* to its purchase, and the significance of the piggy-bank making no sound to the meaning of the passage as a whole. In other words, the various inferences which the reader seems to draw derive in a relatively straightforward way from the scenario which he assumes forms the basis of the passage.

If we accept that a discourse produces models of situations in the mind of the reader, and that readers are under some sort of psychological contract to relate all discourse to such models, then the various forms of inference can all be handled within this common framework.

C. Towards a Process-Model of Comprehension

Where do such models come from? Obviously, knowledge of situations, objects, and simple events, knowledge of social significance and of typical actions, come from long-term memory. Consequently, one of the issues which is discussed in the next chapter is the nature and organization of various kinds of knowledge. But knowledge in isolation is of no use — it has to be made accessible through the sentences of the discourse. This brings us face to face with the question of how a piece of text can be described in such a way as to enable it to make contact with knowledge. This question is addressed directly in Chapter 3. Needless to say, although the exposition up to this point has paid little heed to the problem of how individual sentences are understood, such understanding is an essential part of comprehension. In fact, it is difficult to separate discourse comprehension from individual sentence comprehension in natural situations, but there is a difference in emphasis in the processes involved.

A sentence can be thought of as a standard grammatical structure with a verb relating noun-phrases to one another in some way. The verb serves to indicate the action or state itself, and to specify the roles played by the noun-phrases. So, for instance,

(17) John loves Mary

means that John has certain feelings for Mary. Syntactic convention makes this very different from

(17′) Mary loves John

in which the roles of Mary and John are reversed. In this way, syntax and semantics both play a role in conveying meaning. However, even a sentence as simple as this raises the question of the mental model. *Loves* carries certain implications, and implies certain behaviour patterns. Even at this level, understanding a sentence requires understanding a situation, and so requires the sentence to be interpreted in terms of situational knowledge. The problem of how to characterize these operations and determine the extent of the model is a recurrent theme in the book, and is tackled fairly directly in the next two chapters.

If the individual sentence is a conventional way of configuring the words which make it up, then there are also rules determining the ways in which

12

individual sentences are dovetailed into one another in a more complete discourse. These rules are less well explored than within-sentence rules, and we are not proposing to try to produce a complete list here. However, one or two examples are in order.

Two conventions relate to anaphoric reference. Consider the sentence pair below:

>(18) John took a train to Manchester.
>(18') The train was ten minutes late getting there.

In (18'), use of the definite article is called for. It would not make sense to say, instead of (18'):

>(19) *A* train was ten minutes late getting there.

The 'rule' appears to be that when an entity is *given* in the discourse, later references to it have to be made through the definite noun-phrase, otherwise the reader has trouble appreciating that the anaphoric reference is to the same entity.

Another rule is that things being mentioned are usually specified fairly fully initially, and then referred to in a less specific way. Consider the sentence pair:

>(20) A donkey carried the faggots up the mountainside.
>(20') The animal was tired of being a beast of burden.

Most people find this format preferable to:

>(21) An animal carried the faggots up the mountainside.
>(21') The donkey was tired of being a beast of burden.

Furthermore, it is quite conventional to use a pronoun for second mentions:

>(22) Mary went to meet John at the station.
>(22') She took the green Ford.

And it seems to violate some rule if this is not done:

>(23) Mary went to meet John at the station.
>(23') Mary took the green Ford.

We shall not elaborate other examples of rules governing suprasentential constructions. In many cases, violation of them does not make a discourse incomprehensible in the way that violations of sentential grammar would make sentences incomprehensible. Rather, they seem to reflect some sort of strain imposed on the reader. For this reason, it is better to think of these rules as *rules of considerate discourse construction*.

The basic view which is adopted in this book is that these rules reflect psychological constraints in the reader, and that a theory of discourse comprehension is therefore a theory which relates conventions of language to these constraints. One intuitively obvious example will serve to show what is meant by a psychological constraint. It is everyone's experience that pronouns (*he*, *she*, *it*) can be badly used, so that it is not always clear to which entities or events they are referring. This is true under some circumstances even when the reference is logically unambiguous:

(24) Mary took the car to the station, to pick up her husband.
She had trouble starting it, and had to have the neighbour's wife give her a jump-start. He was not pleased that she was late.

The *he* in the last sentence is hard to relate to Mary's husband, although no other singular, masculine entity has been mentioned. A psychological constraint operating seems to be that all entities mentioned are not equally easy to refer to. A psychological model must explain why.

The second part of this book is concerned with the description of psychological constraints in the reader, and the way in which these constraints govern the mental models developed during reading. Our approach is essentially experimental. After all, in this chapter all we have done is appeal to the reader's intuitions through single examples in order to make certain points. But such is not the nature of psychology. A phenomenon must be demonstrated experimentally in such a way that it is shown to be general, and in such a way that it can be sensibly related to accounts of its occurrence. The aim is to provide such demonstrations, and to produce elements of an account which describe the detail of the comprehension process at work.

CHAPTER 2

Approaches to the Knowledge-Base

The term 'knowledge-base' is used here to refer to all of the information stored in memory which is brought to bear in understanding a piece of discourse. While it would be quite impossible to describe the knowledge-base fully, especially in the present circumstances where understanding of it is limited, the objective of this chapter is to discuss various views of the knowledge-base which have had an impact on psychological theories and computer implementations of programs for understanding natural language. An equally important aim is to lay a foundation for discussions in the chapters which follow.

At the linguistic end, much of the problem has been seen as one of characterizing the meanings of words — what could be termed 'semantic' knowledge. Theories developed in semantics have focused, in part, on very important formal problems — for instance, explaining why certain sentences are self-contradictory, ambiguous, or anomalous (e.g. Bierwisch, 1970). From the psychological and computational point of view, the main focus of interest has been in the problem of how to store semantic information efficiently, and more recently in how this information is used in sentence or discourse processing.

As workers in Artificial Intelligence became more adventurous in constructing programs aimed at discourse comprehension, so it became more and more apparent that a very great deal of mundane, everyday knowledge was necessary to carry out the task (e.g. Charniak, 1972; Norman, et al., 1975; Schank and Abelson, 1977). Furthermore, as the extent of the required knowledge-base increased, so the problem of how to organize and arrange it into manageable partitions became steadily more pressing. These two aspects of the problem of how knowledge relates to text comprehension guide much of the chapter. Ultimately, it is probably fruitless to try to isolate these problems from the details of how the knowledge-base is to be used. Although little direct reference to text-processing is made in the present chapter, the ideas presented have evolved through efforts to try to produce workable models of the understanding process which are capable of being used in more and more complex linguistic environments. Indeed, it should be appreciated that the most recent attack on the scope and organization of knowledge results directly from concern with the whole spectrum of cognitive operations, including perception, classification, labelling, and language-processing, amongst others.

The chapter will be broken up into three main sections. The first will deal with the theoretical approaches to word meaning, and might be viewed as an attempt to characterize the knowledge-base at the level of individual concepts. The second section is less theoretical, but looks at psychological investigations of knowledge storage and the extent to which these investigations would support organization along the lines suggested by the semanticists. In fact, the conclusions drawn from these studies give only partial support for such organization, conceptual knowledge appearing to be more intrinsically bound up with our knowledge of the situations in which things commonly occur than in terms of the semantic relationships between the concepts. This leads to the third section, which is reserved for discussing some of the recent theories of situation knowledge organization which have emerged in the field of Artificial Intelligence. But let us first turn to theories of word meaning.

It is a platitude that the message conveyed in any discourse depends upon the meanings of the words of which it is comprised, and this has led to literally thousands of years of speculation about the nature of word meanings. This study has come to be called the study of *semantics*.

Although we have been at pains to argue that the mental representation of a piece of discourse is ultimately dependent on context well beyond the level of the sentence, this does not mean that word-level semantics is of no consequence. Any language-processing system, man or machine, must possess some kind of internal dictionary whereby words provide access to meaning representation.

There are two aspects to word meaning: an *intensional* and an *extensional* aspect. Intension refers to the intrinsic meaning of a word and its relation to the meaning of other words, whereas the extension of a word is the entire class of entities to which it can refer, in any real or imagined world. So the extension of the word *table* is every real or imaginary table. Until recently, most studies of semantics have emphasized the intensional aspect, usually called the *sense* of the word. Extension becomes more obviously important when words are considered *in use* in either written discourse or conversation. However, whichever aspect of word meaning one considers, one of the most important premises of current semantics is the proposal that a word's meaning may be broken down into independent components.

A. Word Meaning

1. Semantic components

It is now almost universally accepted that the sense of a word can be represented as a bundle of semantic components, which describe its underlying semantic structure. These components can be thought of as propositions which a given word entails. Suppose, for example, that the word *boy* is used in a text. Part of the meaning of the word *boy* entails other elements:

(1) A boy: is a male, non-adult, human, etc. . . . . .

This can be written in the symbolic form:

(2) Boy (x) → male (x) & non-adult (x) & human (x).

The arrow indicates 'can be written as', and (x) is any particular boy.

Componential analysis is essentially a search for the components appropriate to the adequate description of the meaning of the word. The hope is that all words can be represented in this way, that the number of components required should be less than the total number of words, and that these components should encompass all words in all languages. In practice, componential analysis begins with the selection of a *semantic field* for investigation. A semantic field is difficult to define (c.f. Miller and Johnson-Laird, 1976), but corresponds roughly to a field of words which is bounded in number, among which there is some intuitively obvious relationship. Examples which have been investigated include: kinship terms (Goodenough, 1965), terms for containers (Lehrer, 1970), and verbs of motion (Miller, 1972).

Components are identified by examining the relationships amongst the words in the domain selected, usually by means of finding analogies amongst pairs of words. So, for example, the intuitively related set *man, woman, boy, girl* would yield:

Man	*Woman*	*Boy*	*Girl*
+ Male	— Male	+ Male	— Male
+ Adult	+ Adult	— Adult	— Adult

This matrix consists of two features, which might be expressed as *male* and *adult*. The introduction of other words into the domain of enquiry reveals other features. For example, putting in *son* would reveal a *parent* feature. *Parent* is not like *male* and *adult* in that it is relational. While in male (x), *male* is a predicator taking one argument, x, meaning x is male, it is necessary to write parent (x, y), meaning x is the parent of y; *parent* is a predicator taking two arguments which relates x and y. A comparison of this set with still other words would reveal other components: introducing *bull* would reveal a *human* feature; introducing *brick* would reveal an *animacy* feature; and so on. With this handful of components, *father* would be written as:

(3) Father (x, y) → parent (x, y) & male (x) & human (x) & human (y) & adult (x) & animate (x) & animate (y).

Even such an expanded structure as this does not convey everything about father (x, y). For instance, it does not say that a father has to be older than his natural child. But such features can emerge from fuller analyses.

Several interesting and important points can be made on the basis of these straightforward illustrations. First, the sense of a word can often be decomposed into components which seem somehow more primitive than the word itself. The word is really a shorthand label for the fuller statement made up of the necessary propositions which underlie it. Furthermore, the decomposition of a particular word may contain features which could themselves be rewritten as other words. For instance, man (x) could be rewritten as:

(4) Man (x) → male (x) & human (x) & adult (x) & animate (x).

Notice that the right-hand side of this expression is an element of the expression for father (x, y) given above. Thus, father (x, y) could have been written as:

(5) Father (x, y) → parent (x, y) & man (x).

In other words, viewed in this way, *father* is simply a greater specification on the sense of *man*. Such observations can serve to group words together in a convenient way.

The second point is related to this. Attempts at modelling meaning in computers, and at producing psychological models of meaning, have often made use of some variant of the feature approach. (Two of these will be described in the next chapter.) The attraction of the approach is obvious: for one thing, at least some of the information conveyed by a word can be captured by components, so that if it is assumed that the components form part of the explicit knowledge-base, a discourse-processor can make use of this information. A trivial example would be the use of a pronoun like 'he', which could be written as:

(6) He (x) → singular (x) & male (x) . . . .

If 'he' is used to refer back to 'my father' in a previous sentence, then textual connectivity could be achieved by matching the *male* feature in both 'he' and 'father'.[1]

Thirdly, for some semanticists, such as Katz (1972), the sense of a word is simply a listing of all the necessary properties of the entity the word can refer to, the list being its semantic components. However, there are a number of problems with the isolation of primitives in the way shown above, which are revealed when more subtle aspects of meaning are considered. For example, 'spinster' might be broken down by componential analysis into adult (x), woman (x), never married (x). However, in common usage, 'spinster' generally, but not necessarily, has come to carry the features *middle-aged or elderly* as well. Similarly, the term 'girls' can sometimes refer to adult women, as in 'the girls in the typing pool' (Clark and Clark, 1977). Although such usages of these terms are essential to our everyday understanding, there is some danger that they might be overlooked in any simple componential approach.

Another serious problem is with certain category names. For instance, Wittgenstein (1953) claimed that there are no properties in common amongst all games — card games, ball games, children's games, Olympic games, etc.

The argument is that although some 'games' have certain things in common, there are no things which provide a unique basis for calling a specific example 'a game'. Ryle (1949) has made similar claims for actions such as working, thinking, and trading, amongst others. This argument implies that a search for truly necessary and distinctive features may be fruitless for some terms.

These three points show at once the attraction of the componential approach and some of the problems associated with it. Perhaps the most important single contribution the approach makes is that sense can be represented as a set of conditions for the applications of a word. Of course, the detailed analyses carried out within the framework of the approach throw much light on the meanings of certain words, despite its inadequacies as an all-embracing technique and form of description.

2. The nature of primitives and procedural semantics

While the intensional side of meaning is at the heart of the featural analyses described above, in practice words relate to objects and events in the world. When a person produces an utterance like:

(9) Bring me the book that is on the table

the listener must be able to relate the word 'table' to the physical object to which it refers. This leads to an important way of thinking of the meaning of a word: as the operational procedure for identifying objects as exemplars of it. This approach is a species of so-called *procedural semantics*. An example for *table* might look something like this:

Table: Is it a physical object?
: Does it have a flat surface?
: Does it have a leg or legs at right angles to the flat surface?

Provided satisfactory tests can be devised, and the procedures can actually be realized, then this appears to be an excellent way of handling the extensional meaning of the word table. The lists of tests are at one level very much like the semantic components discussed above. However, each of the tests has to have its roots in primitive *perceptual* tests rather than in lists written in natural language. For instance, 'flat surface' describes a range of complex perceptual phenomena. Procedures for recognizing objects at this level are described in Winston (1975) and Miller and Johnson-Laird (1976).

Of course, not all words can be completely defined perceptually. For instance, *father* cannot, *animal* cannot, *game* cannot, and so on. Indeed, even the definition of reasonably specific objects cannot be handled adequately by perceptual procedures. Words do in fact have a conceptual aspect as well as possible perceptual routines for matching them to objects. The conceptual side of meaning must contain descriptions of function, and how a concept is linked to other concepts. For instance, a table may be considered (conceptually) as:

Table: Man-made object
Typical materials: wood, metal, plastic

Used for eating, working, playing games, putting things on
Has flat top when in use
etc.

Miller and Johnson-Laird (1976) argue that the perceptual characteristics *follow from* the way in which a table is used, and that any identification procedure is therefore guided by the concept. A further point is that words seem to be related to other words — the 'semantic field' idea mentioned above. They argue that if definitions were made entirely in terms of perceptual procedures, then the meanings of words would be essentially independent of one another.

Miller and Johnson-Laird suggest that some of the relations amongst procedural descriptions of things can be expressed as a *key* which describes tests to apply to objects and on the outcome of these tests determines what any given object is to be called. As a simple example, these authors consider a world in which there are only three objects, *chairs*, *tables*, and *beds*, which are distinguishable on the basis of only two tests. The distinctions are expressed as:

Key:
(i) Does it have a *seat*? If *yes*, call it a chair; if not, go to (ii).
(ii) Does it have a *worktop*? If *yes*, call it a table; if not, call it a bed.

In every real world there will be many more tests and many more labelling possibilities, but the principle would be much the same. For situations where there are more tests with more outcomes and more labels, the decisions can be organized into convenient sets of decision tables which minimize redundancy.

Thus procedural semantics goes beyond feature theory by relating words to the basic perceptual and cognitive operations which underlie their use. The primitives used are the primitives of meaning, but rather than being just other words, they are real operations, and as such should satisfy the goal of being language-independent: they are non-linguistic processing operations applicable to the decomposition of words in any natural language.

3. Summary and conclusions

From this brief exposition of theoretical approaches to word semantics two central points have emerged. First, that it is useful to think of word meanings as consisting of sets of primitive components, and second, that the best way of characterizing the extension of a word is in terms of procedures which might embody tests for such components.

When it comes to evaluating such theories against what is known about actual human knowledge the task is not so easy, but the notion of semantic components does have certain implications for the way in which human knowledge might be organized. It is in terms of the relationships between concepts that the basis for knowledge organization lies, and this is what has been most extensively studied by experimental psychologists. Consequently, the next section of this chapter will be directed towards the mental organization of conceptual knowledge and the experimental investigation of such organization.

B. Structural Aspects of Knowledge Representation

1. Semantic networks and the distinction between implicit and explicit knowledge

It is a truism to say that concepts relate to other concepts. *Bird* relates to *animal*, *run* relates to *walk*, and so on. It is another matter to specify the exact nature of the relationships, and to find out how the relationships should best be represented. When workers in artificial intelligence (more strictly computer scientists) began to tackle the problem of representing large amounts of information about concepts, the idea of a semantic network was put forward as a suitable structure (Quillian, 1968).

The principle of the semantic network is really very simple: there are two elements in the network, the *node*, which represents some concept, and the labelled *arc*, which represents a relationship between the nodes. For instance, if we take the concepts Bird and Animal, they could be represented in a network as shown below:

ISA

Bird ⌒⟶ Animal

where 'Bird' and 'Animal' are nodes and 'ISA' is the label on the arc which links them. This graph could be translated into the statement 'A bird is an animal'. In any realistic network representation there would of course be many nodes which relate to Animal in this way, and it is the whole complex of nodes interconnected by relationships which constitutes the network.

To illustrate the use of such semantic networks, let us consider how they might incorporate both explicitly stated knowledge and implicit, or computed knowledge. Suppose a person is told two things:

(10) All policemen are friendly

and

(10′) All detectives are policemen.

From these two explicit facts, a third (implicit) fact emerges: all detectives are friendly. In effect, provided the person has the appropriate program to compute this third fact, there is a sense in which he *knows* it. However, until he has made the deduction, he only possesses explicit knowledge of the first two facts. However, in normal usage, computed knowledge and explicit knowledge are sometimes rolled into one idea of 'knowing'. One thing semantic network representations can do is to make the distinction between explicit and computable knowledge.

Semantic networks were introduced into early computer programs designed, in part, for the bulk storage of large quantities of knowledge. They provide a way of linking various concept names in an orderly way, and at the heart of this linkage is the idea of a *generalization hierarchy*. Such a hierarchy is shown in Figure 2.1(a); at each level there are a number of *nodes* (one at the top). The

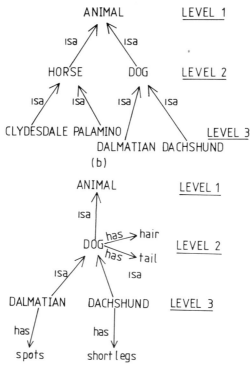

Figure 2.1   (a) Generalization hierarchy. (b) Hierarchy with some properties.

nodes are linked in an organized fashion by means of *labelled arcs* or pointers. In this case, the pointers are all labelled ISA, to denote class membership. The pointers point from the specific instance to the class name. In a generalization hierarchy, any property true of the concept at a given level is also true of every concept beneath it. What is true of animals is true of horses, dogs, etc. What is true of dogs is true of dalmatians and dachshunds, in the same way. Property relationships can be described in various ways, but one way is to use the labelled arcs IS (defining property relations for qualities) and HAS (defining property relations for objects). These two relations are used extensively by Norman, *et al.* (1975) in their description of their computer data-base. Figure 2.1(b) shows how various properties might be attributed to the labelled nodes of the skeleton generalization hierarchy shown in Figure 2.1(a).

Thus generalization hierarchies can be thought of as efficient ways of organizing concepts according to shared semantic components. Any concept below another concept in the hierarchy will share all the features of the higher concepts plus some additional distinctive feature. In fact, the organization of the hierarchy should ideally reflect the way in which semantic features are discovered in practice, since any two concepts adjacent in the hierarchy should be minimally distinguishable according to their set of features.

If knowledge of properties were stored in this way, given an appropriate procedure, other properties could be computed. For instance, in the hierarchy shown above, *dachshund* ISA *dog* is stored explicitly and *dog* ISA *animal* is stored explicitly. The fact that *dachshund* ISA *animal* is not stored directly, but it can be inferred from these two pieces of explicit knowledge. Similarly, there is no explicit statement to the effect that *dachshund* HAS *tail*, but this can be computed from the stored knowledge *dachshund* ISA *dog* and *dog* HAS *tail*.

What a generalization hierarchy does is to trade explicit knowledge for computation. If all instances of dogs have tails, then this fact requires only one proposition to be stored, but computation has to take place in order to verify that any given instance of a dog has a tail. On the other hand, if there are n instances of dogs, then to store the fact directly would require n HAS *tail* statements, and no computation would be required to verify the fact for any particular instance of the n. In this way, a generalization hierarchy provides an economy of storage at the expense of computation. This general tradeoff is extremely important in many practical computing situations: computation takes times, but direct storage takes up space. The principle of organization which minimizes direct storage has been called *cognitive economy* (Quillian, 1969).

There are a number of distinct issues surrounding the idea of a generalization hierarchy. Consider a child who learns for the first time that a chaffinch is a bird, but knows nothing else about it. In the absence of any other knowledge, that child will use the generalization hierarchy if asked whether a chaffinch has wings, since having wings is a property of all birds. The generalization hierarchy thus provides a basis for making new generalizations under these circumstances. Similarly, in a piece of discourse, one might encounter:

(11) The rinnet is a South American bird.
(11′) Its wings are extremely large.

The second sentence coheres with the first because wings are a property possessed by birds in general.

The question of whether storage of all information of this type is arranged according to a principle of cognitive economy is, however, a rather different one. Cognitive economy in humans sounds reasonable if it is assumed that each proposition stored in long-term memory takes up a significant storage space, given an expected lifetime of storing propositions (the 'space' argument) — but this might not be the case. Secondly, if cognitive economy is to be the rule, at what stage could HAS *wings* become attached only at the *bird* node? The answer may lie in the way generalization hierarchies evolve in the developing child. According to one theory (Rosch, 1977; Chapter 6 of the present book), things are labelled in accordance with a principle of maximal featural overlap, the so-called 'basic-level term hypothesis'. So a child may learn much about *birds* by having instances of them referred to as *bird* because *bird* is the label which maximizes feature overlap of its subordinates. Once this procedure is underway, it makes sense to suppose that much of the information about specific birds may be stored at the bird node, with only information peculiar to specific examples stored at the particular instance node. This, of course, is in the spirit of Quillian's argument (see especially Collins and Quillian, 1972b).

2. Cognitive economy in human beings

Collins and Quillian (1972a) set out to test the theory of the generalization hierarchy and cognitive economy as an analogy for how class membership and property information is stored in humans. Their procedure was to present subjects with sentences for verification (true/false decision) and measure the time taken to do this. The hypothesis was that those cases in which verification required computation would take longer than those cases where the knowledge was stored explicitly. They used materials of two types: class membership statements and property statements. Examples of class membership statements were:

> (S0) A maple is a maple.
> (S1) A cedar is a tree.
> (S2) An elm is a plant.

Property statements included:

> (P0) An oak has acorns.
> (P1) A spruce has branches.
> (P2) A birch has seeds.

Considering the property statements, it was hypothesized that HAS *acorns* is peculiar to oaks, and should be stored at the node for *oak*, so (P0) could be verified directly on the basis of explicitly stored knowledge. On the other hand, in (P2), HAS *seeds* is a property of plants in general, and should require a chain of inference to be verified, perhaps using a chain like: A *spruce* ISA *tree* ISA *plant* HAS *seeds*. (P1) requires a similar but shorter chain for verification.

Using materials like these, based on various intuitive hierarchies, Collins and Quillian produced results which appeared to support the generalization hierarchy and cognitive economy hypotheses, as shown in Figure 2.2. Verification times go up apparently linearly with the number of steps in the inference chain.

In later arguments it was questioned whether these results actually reflect true economy of storage, and in a discussion of various criticisms of this study, Collins and Loftus (1975) point out that the experiment only gives real support to a *weak economy* principle: some properties are stored

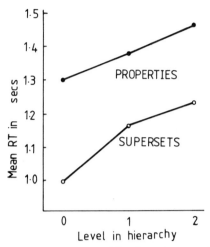

Figure 2.2 The relationship of mean verification time to level in an assumed generalization hierarchy (after Collins and Quillian, 1972a).

at the highest level possible in a hierarchy, others are not. Let us see two ways in which weak economy could operate.

In learning about the nature of objects, properties general to a class of which an object is a member could well be stored with the object itself, at least sometimes. Suppose a task is to verify the proposition:

(12) Chinese have skin.

There are two ways in which this might be verified. One is through an inferential chain, ending with *animal* HAS *skin*, for instance. The other way (probably more realistic) is to use directly stored knowledge that Chinese people have *yellow skin*. The point is that when any general property is further refined by being specified more for a particular instance, both the general property and the specific version of it will be directly stored at the node for the specific instance. It can be argued that this is not a rare phenomenon, but occurs in numerous cases. For instance,

(13) An oak has leaves

could be stored directly with oak for everyone who is familiar with the particular specifications of an oak's leaves. In general, this argument reduces to one in which the outcome of concentrating on the specific features (perceptual or otherwise) which characterize a named instance will result in those features being stored at the named node for that instance, thus making cognitive economy weak.

A second way in which direct storage may come about (according to Collins and Loftus) is through *assertion*. Suppose the network does not have *an oak has roots* stored directly, *roots* having been considered in, say, the *tree*-label context. Encountering the assertion that oaks have roots could cause this HAS *roots* knowledge to become attached directly to the oak node. This idea has experimental implications. Repeated exposure to sentences for verification should ultimately result in the demonstration of no cognitive economy for the storage of information which those sentences test. Indeed, Conrad (1972) used a multiple-presentation procedure and failed to replicate Collins and Quillian's economy results — and, Collins and Loftus suggested that this could well have resulted from the methodological flaw.

Rather than thinking in terms of strict cognitive economy, therefore, it seems more appropriate to consider the theory as having a bearing on the ability people have to make use of hierarchical information to verify relatively novel propositions. If our analysis is correct, inferences should be used when a proposition has never been encountered (either through assertion or through familiarity with the property in relation to the name node). For example:

(14) A great crested grebe has a beak. (Unless the reader is an ornithologist.)
(15) Ice-cream has protons.
(16) Richard Nixon has ligaments.

The picture which emerges, therefore, is one in which properties are stored directly at a node referring to the object (or some general set of that object) if the object and those properties are often encountered together, but in which novel combinations can only be verified by inference.

3. The advantages and limitations of hierarchies

Generalization hierarchies are ubiquitous in classification systems. Taxonomists in all fields of enquiry make use of them, and they are certainly an effective way of presenting information. But there are considerable problems with storing a great amount of knowledge in a single hierarchy. Consider the proposition:

(17) A man is an animal.

Although most people would agree with this statement, it seems a rather odd thing to say. As Lakoff (1972b) has pointed out, we would normally qualify such statements with a 'hedge' remark like: 'Strictly speaking a man is an animal', or 'Scientifically speaking . . .' etc. One explanation of the use of such hedging remarks is that for each category, such as animal, there is a set of 'typical' features, well represented in certain animals like 'dogs' but not in others like 'man'. So, for instance, Rosch (1973) has suggested that there is a low overlap between the typical features for 'animal' and those for 'man', although 'man' might have all the necessary features to be scientifically described by the term 'animal'. According to such an argument, 'man' is a poor example of the general category 'animal'.

There is, however, an alternative explanation for the use of such 'hedges' which seems more plausible. That we would not normally say 'A man is a typical animal' but would say 'Scientifically speaking, a man is an animal' might relate to the fact that we are really referring to two distinct generalization hierarchies: one a layman's hierarchy and the other a scientific hierarchy, with 'animal' in the lay hierarchy corresponding to something like 'mammal' in the scientific one (see Figure 2.3). It would seem plausible that two or more

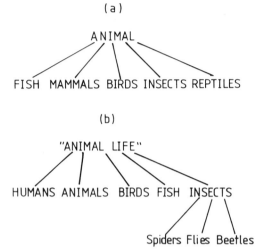

(a)

ANIMAL

FISH MAMMALS BIRDS INSECTS REPTILES

(b)

"ANIMAL LIFE"

HUMANS ANIMALS BIRDS FISH INSECTS

Spiders Flies Beetles

Figure 2.3   A schematic representation of two partial animal hierarchies, with (a) corresponding to a scientific hierarchy and (b) corresponding to a layman's hierarchy.

such hierarchies coexist and that they would be contextually labelled and represented independently.

The hierarchy representation poses an important question. Could all knowledge be represented as a single complex hierarchy, a sort of super-encyclopaedia? The answer to this is surely no. It is not always clear how a hierarchy should be organized for certain concepts. Indeed, linguists such as Chomsky (1965) have pointed out that many classificatory dimensions do not yield hierarchies unless arbitrary orderings are imposed upon them. For instance, there is no natural ordering of the solid/liquid contrast and the natural/man-made contrast. Hierarchies for many things can be constructed, some easily, some with difficulty, and if they are remembered by the person who constructed them, they become part of the knowledge-base and can be used as part of what the person understands by any term used in them. But the example of the two animal-world hierarchies indicates that they can be represented independently as ways of classifying animals from two different perspectives.

The idea that knowledge might be organized in terms of settings in which it is used takes us a long way from traditional concepts of semantics. And yet much of our knowledge *is* situational: what to do and what to expect in various situations. Hierarchies cannot provide an adequate basis for knowledge of this sort; how it might be represented is discussed in Section C. However, before leaving the hierarchy idea, one further point will be considered which relates to networks in general. Given that concepts are linked in various ways, even if the linkage is not within a strict hierarchy, can these links provide a simple means of moving in a search from one node to another?

4. Linking knowledge clusters

Throughout the recent history of associationism in psychology, researchers have been aware that the association between two ideas, A and B, need not be symmetrical. If subjects are presented with a stimulus word A, this may produce response B with a certain regularity. However, presentation of B as a stimulus may seldom if ever evoke A as a response. For example, in an analysis of a number of sets of word-association results, Miller (1969) noted two very interesting asymetries. Where the class membership relation held between any two items, an instance was more likely to produce a class name than a class name an instance. Thus *dog* produced *animal* more often than *animal* produced *dog*. Similarly, *part-of* names were more often produced by words denoting things possessing the part than were things by stimuli which denote parts of those things. So *tree* might produce *root* more often than *root* produces *tree*. Miller speculated that ISA and HAS might be more readily used as retrieval plans than the corresponding inverses. He noted that people easily say *A robin is a bird*, but that there is no ready construction for the inverse (which would have to be something syntactically complex like *A bird has as a member of its class the instance 'robin'*).

Suppose that part of a semantic network contains the explicit information *Alpaca* ISA *animal*. Does this mean that the inverse knowledge, *Animal* HAS EXAMPLE *alpaca*, is explicitly available too? If it were, then this would mean that the network actually contained *two* pointers:

One way of illustrating this problem is to suppose that a network search is going to begin at the *Alpaca* node. In the figure above there is only one pointer away from the node, labelled ISA, and this points to *Animal*. If the search began at the *Animal* node, and there was no ISA-INVERSE pointer, then there would be no pointer to *Alpaca*. Thus the knowledge *Alpaca* ISA *animal* would be present, but not *Animal* ISA-INVERSE *alpaca*.

This argument has a bearing on the execution of a very simple task — listing instances of a given category. Suppose a person can recognize *n* names of animals. On a simple network account, this will be because of *n* ISA pointers to the animal node. But a simple stored list of *n* animal names would consist of *n* ISA-INVERSE pointers. This is precisely what a directly stored list of category instances is. If a subject is set the task of listing all instances of a class which he knows — for instance *animal* or *states of the U.S.A.* — a set of ISA-INVERSE relations could be processed by simply reading off the nodes to which they point. If the processing system kept track of which nodes had been read off, the instances listed would cumulate linearly with time on the task. If the system could not keep track of which pointers had been used already, then the search process would be one of sampling 'with replacement', which is characterized by a curve that begins steeply and gradually flattens off (e.g. Bousfield and Sedgewick, 1944).

In practice, measures of the number of instances listed as a function of time show a function of the latter type; a typical set of data is shown in Figure 2.4.

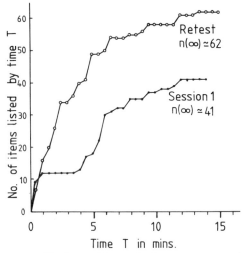

Figure 2.4 Response profile for subject asked to generate animal names on two different sessions, showing number of names generated by a given time (from Sanford, unpublished study). A good fit to such curves is given by the equation $n(t) = n(\infty)(1-\exp\lambda t)$, where $n(t)$ is the number of items listed by time t, and λ and $n(\infty)$ are constants. $n(\infty)$ describes the asymptote.

The fit of the curve to the data is usually reasonably good, and looks consistent with the idea of an ISA-INVERSE search. However, there are a number of other features of the data which militate against this interpretation. In the first place, the asymptote of the curve ($n(\infty)$) supposedly gives an estimate of the total pool of exemplars available to the class node. This should be constant from one time to another in a given person, unless he learns some new exemplars. And yet when a subject does this task more than once, estimates of $n(\infty)$ increase, as though they knew more and more exemplars each time. Obviously, the number of ISA links should not increase with practice. The observed increase is shown in Figure 2.4.

A second interesting feature is that individual subjects seldom produce smooth curves, although the general trend follows the negative exponential. Rather, they tend to produce *clusters* of items in spurts, and then have relatively long gaps before producing new clusters. This indicates that groups of exemplars are stored together in some way. Introspective data suggest a reason for this. Subjects frequently report using fairly complex mental processes while they carry out this task. For example, when listing animals, subjects develop strategies like thinking of situations in which they might find instances of animals (e.g. at the zoo, in children's books, on the farm). Occasionally, an animal thought of in one context might remind them of another context, as yet unthought of, in which they might find still other animals. (See Schank (1975) for a similar discussion.)

What this suggests is that just because a person has the explicit knowledge *Alpaca* ISA *animal* (which anyone has who can verify the statement appropriately) does not mean to say that he also has the knowledge *Animal* ISA-INVERSE *alpaca*, otherwise there should be no reason why all instances of a given category should not be listed, and certainly no reason why n (∞) should increase with practice. It seems inappropriate to think of category names as being connected by ISA-INVERSE links (thus forming a list) to each and every instance, but that instances are organized around situational packages, like *what is at the zoo*, or *what is found on farms*. The contrast is represented in Figure 2.5. It is proposed that Figure 2.5 (a) is inappropriate, and that Figure 2.5(b) is perhaps nearer to representing the way exemplars are

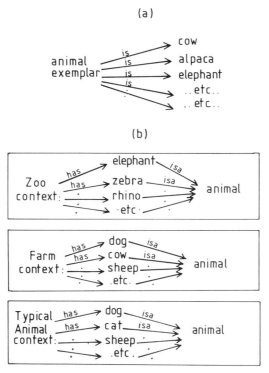

Figure 2.5 Two ways of storing animal instances. In (a) all animal exemplars are connected to one node for animal; in (b) they are stored in separate memory structures, where the lists may overlap but are embedded under different contexts of usage. In (b) there is no ISA-*inverse* as such, but it has a homologue in the storage of instances under the typical animal category.

stored. Thus, information about *alpaca* is more likely to be stored with other information about *sources of wool* rather than connected directly to *animal* through an ISA-INVERSE link. 'Alpaca' will only be produced as a response in this case if a subject happens to hit upon *sources of wool* during his memory search. Of course, some animals may very well be stored as examples of an animal, but all examples which have been encountered will not be stored as such. Indeed, even the relationship *Alpaca* ISA *animal* may not be stored as such, but it may be possible to infer this if the network contains the information that sources of wool are all animals. The argument again points to knowledge being stored in a largely situation-determined way, just as seemed to be the case in the discussion of hierarchies.

C. Situational Knowledge and Frames

1. Acting and expecting

In the discussion of listing instances of a prespecified category, it was suggested that instances are often retrieved along with information about the situations in which they are found. Once situational knowledge itself is considered, the face of the organization problem takes on a very different appearance. Consider the specification of knowledge of *what to do* in order to travel on a bus. Such knowledge cannot be considered in terms of features or semantic networks. It has to be thought of as a list of sequential actions:

Step 1: Stop the correct bus
2: Get on bus
3: Pay fare
4: Get up as destination approaches
5: Stop bus at destination
6: Get off bus.

Each one of these steps is capable of further, more detailed expansion. For instance, step 1 entails a subsequence of activities, such as:

Step 1 Step (i): Stand by kerb
(ii): Check for bus
(iii): Continue (ii) until bus comes
(iv): Raise arm in front of driver's visual field
(v): Maintain (iv) until bus stops by you
etc.

The list resembles a program or (Schank and Abelson, 1977) a script. Of course, the list is *not* a program; even the more detailed breakdown is only a description of further actions which can be broken down further. The ultimate primitives of an action sequence of this kind would have to be bodily movements and perceptual tests on the environment which enable a human or a robot to actually stop a bus. It is rather nearer the mark to consider such a list as an incomplete *description* of an action sequence. Provided the list can make contact with the underlying primitives, it would serve very well to tell a child steps 1 — 6, without much elaboration, and he could carry out the actions, even if he had never been on a bus before. Furthermore, sequences of this kind can be part of a person's knowledge *without* actually making contact with the appropriate actions, simply because they are not detailed enough. Most people could describe the actions of riding a bicycle in some sequential form, for example, even if they could not actually do it themselves. The point is that while the ability to perform certain actions may be present as part of our 'motor knowledge', descriptive sequential knowledge may be present even without this knowledge actually being part of a program for carrying out the actions themselves.

Action-sequence knowledge is quite different from the kind of property knowledge discussed earlier. It is descriptive of *what to do* in various situations. Closely related to knowledge of what to do is knowledge of what to *expect*. For example, the specification of a child's birthday party might include:

Dress:	Sunday Best
Present:	Must please host
	Must be gift-wrapped
Games:	E.g. hide and seek, pin tail on donkey
Decor:	Balloons, favours, crepe paper . . .
Party meal:	Cake, ice-cream, soft drinks, hot dogs . . .
Cake:	Has candles. Candles to be blown out at right point and then sing birthday song
Ice-cream:	Suitable flavours . . . .

(Adapted from Minsky, 1975)

This is a partial plan of *what to do* if one is organizing a child's birthday party, and *what to expect* and do if one is a child. Like the bus-ride example, the birthday party prescription is very specific and contains action elements as well as things which a party HAS or IS.

2. Minsky's concept of the frame

Such examples as these are instances of what Minsky (1975) calls *frames*. In his essay on the subject, Minsky puts forward the frame as a basic building-block of knowledge, and conceives of memory as comprising millions of frames. The properties of frames can be illustrated with the aid of the example given above.

Frames are described by Minsky as hierarchical data structures. The top levels of any frame consist of fixed, necessary features of the situation. Thus a *host* and *guests* constitute necessary features of the birthday party. Lower down the hierarchy are lists of features which become progressively less well defined and/or optional. For instance, the headings *present*, *games*, *decor*, etc., represent normal features of the party. That the presents must be gift-wrapped and please the host are usual features of the situation, but even if these expectations were violated, it would still be a child's birthday party, whereas no guests means no party as most people would understand it. In other words, some aspects of the situation are more important than others, although people have expectations about what would normally occur in the situation.

Let us consider another example. The concept of *room* has requirements like *walls, a floor, a ceiling, door(s), window(s)*. In Britain, there would commonly be *four* walls — this is what people would normally expect (more strictly, perhaps, the walls are usually arranged at right angles, even if the room is L-shaped). But a *circular* room is still a room, although it would be sufficiently unexpected to draw a comment from most people encountering such a case. The point should be clear: for a room to be called such, walls are essential, but the specification of their geometry is not, even if the frame contains 'typical' information about the geometry to expect.

These normal expectations are called *default* values. Typical defaults are, therefore, *candles* on a birthday cake; *walls meeting at right angles* in a room; and *eleven men* in a soccer team. Expectations also apply to sequences of events in much the same way. At a meal, most people in Great Britain would expect an ordering of dishes like:

(1) Starter

(2) Main course

(3) Dessert

(4) Cheese.

In France, on the other hand, (3) and (4) are almost always reversed.

Minsky's argument is that structuring knowledge into situational frames of this sort provides a means of implementing some of the complex processes of understanding, as well as providing a representation of our knowledge of situations. Later, we shall examine the application of the frame concept to understanding natural language by both man and machine. For the moment, let us consider how Minsky sees a frame working in perception.

What happens when someone is seated waiting to watch a football (soccer) match? One of the frames which is activated in this situation might be a soccer-match frame. Now such a frame has certain necessary features, the top levels of the frame: for instance, that there be two sides of players, a ball, and a football field marked out in accordance with the rule system. At the lower levels are optional characteristics — for instance, team colours and number of players. It would still be a football match if the teams did not wear their expected (default) colours, or even if they played in bizarre outfits (like wearing no shirts, or wearing pullovers). Concentrating on the sides, some of their characteristics may be specified as:

Sides *Two groups of players*

Players (1): Number (normally 11)

Shirt colour (normally red)

Players (2): Number (normally 11)

Shirt colour (normally green).

The brackets are called *slots*, and although in the case shown above they are instantiated with default expectations, the defaults can be overwritten with real values. So if, when the players actually come out, one team has only 10 players, and the teams are playing in different colours, then the subpart of the frame will read:

Sides: *Two groups of players*
Players (1): Number (11)
  Shirt colour (blue)
Players (2): Number (10)
  Shirt colour (green stripes).

The frame of a keen soccer fan may also contain specific defaults: personalities or names for players in particular positions, etc.

Our discussion up to now enables a number of interesting points to emerge. First, since frames are assumed to contain many default values, an unattended aspect of the situation can be 'filled in' mentally, by the default. Someone who did not check the number of players may thus 'remember' there being 11 in each team. Such distortions of memory towards the expected situation characterize much of human misremembering; this will be discussed in Chapter 4.

A second point is that the presence of default expectations enables deviations to be *noticed*. Events in a restaurant (e.g. dessert offered before cheese), or the configurations of a room (e.g. circular wall), can all be interpreted as unexpected, and such mismatch signals can provide a stimulus for making comments or seeking out reasons for the mismatch. Thus, by providing a structured system of important elements in a situation, and by providing a system of slots, frames for situations can serve to make specific instances of that situation intelligible, whether they fit the stereotype or deviate from it slightly.

When reading a piece of discourse, it is often the case that the reader encounters partial descriptions of situations, situations which are recognizable on the basis of the information the writer has provided. Frames could provide the information describing the fuller situation which the reader needs to understand, and the fuller situation to which the writer is referring when he produces his references to it.

3. Varieties of frames

Minsky's view is that frames form a family of data structures possessing more or less the same characteristics: they are hierarchical, and have defining or (more strictly) necessary characteristics at the top levels and more optional characteristics at the lower levels. Any structured situation could be described in frame terms. Some examples are:

(a) *Frames for objects*. Minsky discusses the recognition procedures for seeing a *cube* from all angles in frame terms. Since a cube cannot be seen from all angles at once, the value of default expectancies is immediately apparent. Kuipers (1975) discusses this issue in some detail.

(b) *Temporal or programmatic frames.* What to do and expect at a restaurant, on an airplane, at a lecture, etc., follows a programmatic sequence. Schank (Schank and Abelson, 1977) has implemented the programmatic frame idea, calling the information structures *scripts.* These are discussed at length in the next chapter.

(c) *Mixed frames for situations.* The birthday party is an example of this: it is partly descriptive of the things one expects to find at a birthday party, and partly descriptive of *event sequences* at a party.

(d) *Grammar frames.* Most cognitive scientists view verbs as frames, or information structures which allocate the other parts of speech in a sentence into a relationship with the verb. Consequently, a verb frame can be viewed as the centre of the action or state described by the sentence in which it appears.

(e) *Narrative or text frames.* Consider a fairy story. Linguists have recently noted that simple folk stories have a regular, predictable structure (e.g. Propp, 1968): they have heroes, villains, a setting, a plot, a series of episodes, and a resolution of the main problem, usually accompanied by a moral. Similarly, scientific papers usually have a fixed structure: introduction, method, results, discussion. A reader of a folk tale or a scientific paper may make use of such frames to organize the components of the discourse into a sensible structure. Rumelhart (1975), for example, has made this point, and in Chapter 4 his idea will be discussed.

(f) *Scientific paradigms.* Kuhn (1970) has argued that revolutionary insights in the progress of science result from the overthrow of old paradigms of thinking for new ones. Paradigms can be viewed as frames, indicating as they do the conceptual relationship between various observables and restricting the range of potential candidates (empirical observations) to fill the slots of the frame.

At first sight, such a list may suggest that frames are all things to all men, covering any aspect of knowledge. This is bound to be the impression any description of a broad theory might convey, and there is little doubt of Minsky's intention of breadth of applicability. However, Minsky's proposal is of a specific way of organizing knowledge, so that the rules and procedures pertinent to a particular situation are stored together as single, modular units, rather than having the information dispersed through memory in an arbitrary way, or according to a formal hierarchy.

4. The organization of frame systems

Minsky suggests that frames relate to one another in a variety of ways. One way is through embedding: part of a restaurant frame might include a reference to a general frame for paying bills, for instance. Another is through subframes: a room frame may have specific versions for lecture room, office, bedroom, bathroom, etc. Similarly, a soccer frame may have certain general rules associated with it, but could be related to a number of specific subframes. Such subframes may be *five-a-side soccer, informal soccer games, children's 'pretend' soccer games*, etc. If the processor is using the general soccer frame initially, it could move to a specific related subframe by a particular instantiation or by mismatches. So, for instance, if the soccer match turns out to be in a gym, and to have only 10 players, this would serve to call up the five-a-side subframe.

An important aspect of the subframe idea is the way in which entities which are bound to frames can play different roles. For example, a *waiter* in the subframes for restaurants would play different roles in the customer's subframe, the *waiter's* own subframe, and, say, the subframe from the point of view of a manager. Minsky's (1975) own example is of the alternator of a car, which could be looked at from a *mechanical* or *electrical* point of view. From the mechanical point of view, a support bracket would play an entirely different role from the one it would play viewed from the electrical subframe point of view. It is the incorporation of context in this way which makes the frame so compelling an idea for language-processing, where one of the major problems is that the significance of a piece of discourse is so dependent on the surrounding context. In the next chapter, and in Chapter 6, this point will be discussed in full.

A second way in which Minsky suggests frames might be linked is through *advice* and *similarity* networks. An example of this, used by Minsky, is in handling the 'family resemblance' problem with the concept *furniture*. The suggestion is that the object frames for *stool, chair*, etc., are connected to each other by 'difference' markers. Mismatches between what is said (or read) could then be used to find a pointer to a more appropriate frame. Part of such a network is shown in Figure 2.6.

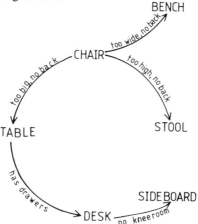

Figure 2.6   Advice network connecting furniture frames (From Minsky, 1975: *The Psychology of Computer Vision* (Ed. P. H. Winston). Copyright © 1975 McGraw-Hill Book Company. Used with the permission of McGraw-Hill Book Company).

This advice network should not appear entirely unfamiliar. Such networks are essentially the same as the 'decision tables' of Miller and Johnson-Laird (1976). The similarity results directly from the fact that frames are not merely descriptive of knowledge, but are procedural in the sense of posing a series of tests to be applied to the environment. When the outcomes of these tests 'mismatch' with what is expected, the mismatch itself is the pointer to the next frame.

D. An Appraisal of the Knowledge Problem

The issue of knowledge representation is fundamental to all branches of cognitive psychology, and the growth of interest in problems of knowledge organization can be traced directly to the recent developments in computer science and artificial intelligence. Those attempting to model human cognitive processes in computers have found that they need to implement 'knowledge' in all its varieties in order to come up with anything like a convincing simulation of normal human behaviour. In language, the classic problems have been seen at those of describing the rules of syntax and the meaning of words and sentences. So long as investigators concentrated on analysis at the level of the sentence, the problems encountered tended to be related to the *intensional* aspect of a word meaning, and how this might be represented. Thus the primary task was one of characterizing the various semantic components which might underlie a word's meaning. However, discourse never occurs in a vacuum. Even single sentences are uttered or written for a purpose, and so they relate to some knowledge domain in the head of the speaker/writer and (hopefully) listener/reader. Such extensional considerations, discussed informally in Chapter 1, lead inexorably into problems of how to represent knowledge of a broader aspect: relationships between terms and situational knowledge.

In addition to the question of the range of knowledge needed to understand a discourse, or even a single sentence or utterance, there is the computational problem of how best to arrange such knowledge in a program or a human mind so that it is optimally configured. This problem was touched upon in the discussion of generalization hierarchies and cognitive economy. In any given situation requiring a mapping to be made between a mental representation and an input of some kind, *either* the important aspects of the situation can be built into a structure in advance, *or* the important aspects of the situation have to be computed on the spot in some way. Kuipers (1975) describes frames in this context as follows:

> Briefly, the idea is that if there is too little computation time when a problem comes up, do some of the work in advance and keep the computed results available. (p. 152)

This is one of the attractive aspects of frames. Much of the computation required in familiar situations has already been done before encountering the situation again, and is stored as the frame itself. Of course, the discussion of frames is very much a current issue, and it is fair to say that most workers have their own views of how to implement the idea. From our point of view, part of the appeal is that they provide a good mechanism for the phenomenological experience of recognizing something as familiar. Furthermore, frames provide a way of handling the extensional as well as the intensional aspect of word meaning, simply because they are designed to carry out *operations* of various kinds, be they perceptual, conceptual, or prescriptions of action. Whatever the shortcomings of particular implementations, they provide a connection between knowledge and the procedures for using knowledge which is bound to lead to useful structural formulations, rather than scholastic descriptions.

In comprehending discourse, all of the issues raised in this chapter are directly implicated. Semantic knowledge, knowledge of relationships amongst concepts, and situational knowledge all play a key role. The connection of knowledge to comprehension is discussed in the next chapter.

Note

1. This is only an illustration. In later chapters the complexities of the resolution of pronoun reference will be discussed more fully.

CHAPTER 3

Relating Discourse to Knowledge: Background Considerations

The major objective of this chapter is to consider the kind of representation which a discourse produces in the mind of a reader. The early parts of it address the problem of how to represent the meaning of simple event descriptions, and in the later parts fuller and more complex pieces of text are considered.

The basic issue is this. On the page before the reader is a linguistic object, be it a single sentence or a larger piece of discourse; and in the mind of the reader reside knowledge structures of various kinds. By reading, the words and sentences somehow manipulate these knowledge structures in order to produce a unique configuration, which is the representation of the meaning of the discourse. The problems are: how the words relate to knowledge structures, which knowledge structures seem to be essential, and how the knowledge structures work to produce a final representation. Indeed, the entire book is concerned with this problem. In the present chapter, some of the important elements which enter into a more detailed formulation of the question are considered.

Although we are primarily interested in human processing and mental representations, much of this chapter is concerned with the work of researchers attempting to implement programs in computers which can take in a text, 'understand' it, and then produce a written summary, or paraphrase, or translation into a foreign language. The ability of a program to do this is an indication of whether it has 'understood' the text, of course. However, the details of how such programs are implemented will not be given. Rather, we adopt the view that the careful analysis of the comprehension problem which underlies even moderately successful programs is a rich source of analogies for the elements of human comprehension. Similarly, the earlier parts of the chapter contain descriptions of work deriving from linguists' efforts at the analysis of the 'meaning' problem. These efforts have also produced a large set of subtle ideas which enter into psychological theories.

The first main issue which arises when one considers representing the meaning of a sentence is how to characterize the semantics of verbs. Verbs, unlike the simple nominal concepts considered in the previous chapter, seem to have two functions in a sentence. First, they indicate some state or action, and second, they determine a set of contingent relationships between the other nominal concepts in the sentence. So, in a simple sentence like 'Bill hit Tom', the verb indicates that the action of 'hitting' occurred, but furthermore, it signals a contingent relationship between 'Bill' and 'Tom', with Bill being responsible for the act of hitting and Tom being its recipient. The first problem considered in this chapter is how best to characterize the verb-contingent relationships, and then we turn to the additional problem of representing the action or state portrayed by the verb.

A. Representing Simple Actions and Events

In any natural language there are two aspects to a simple sentence: there is a surface structure, the ordering of the words on the page, and there is the semantic structure of the sentence itself. Consider an example like:

(1) Sheena worries Tony.

In this sentence, Sheena is portrayed as acting in some way so as to have the effect of worrying Tony. Sheena can be called the *agent* in the situation and Tony the *recipient*. By expressing the same information in a passive form of sentence, the ordering of the words is changed but the basic meaning is the same:

(2) Tony is worried by Sheena.

In both cases, Tony is the recipient and Sheena is the agent. We can represent both (1) and (2) in the form of a network, as shown in Figure 3.1(a).

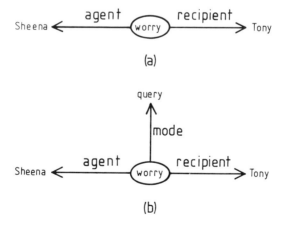

Figure 3.1 Network representation of the underlying meaning of (a) *Sheena worries Tony* or *Tony is worried by Sheena* and (b) *Does Sheena worry Tony?* or *Is Tony worried by Sheena?*

In fact, this simple representation is at the heart of all possible syntactic variants of the surface structure of (1). Table 3.1 lists these variants, while in Figure 3.1 (b) we have sketched out an underlying representation of two examples — the query and the passive query forms. In this case, another specification on the verb has been introduced called *mode*.

	Sentence Type	*Example*
1.	Active	Sheena worries Tony
2.	Passive	Tony is worried by Sheena
3.	Negative	Sheena doesn't worry Tony
4.	Query	Does Sheena worry Tony?
5.	Negative passive	Tony isn't worried by Sheena
6.	Negative query	Doesn't Sheena worry Tony?
7.	Passive query	Is Tony worried by Sheena?
8.	Negative passive query	Isn't Tony worried by Sheena?

It will be noticed that the representational format which is being used here portrays the verb as the centre of an event description; connected to the verb are a series of arrows to which labels have been assigned, like *agent, recipient*, etc., and assigning noun-phrases to the ends of these arrows crucially affects the meaning. Verbs can thus be thought of in much the same way as Minsky thinks of frames, that is as structures having *slots* for agent, recipient, etc., until we have enough slots to handle all possibilities in the language. Indeed, Minsky himself referred to verbs as 'case-frames'.

The form of analysis in which verbs are treated in this way has its origins in the case-grammars of Fillmore (1968; see also Anderson, 1971), with the basic idea of devising a small number of slots which would provide a basis for meaning representation. Fillmore has been concerned with the problem of elucidating such a set of slots (or cases), a venture which has only been partly successful. A typical listing is given in Table 3.2. Using these, a sentence like:

(3) Mary is knitting a sweater for her mother

breaks into:
Action: Knitting
Agent: Mary
Object: A sweater
Recipient: Her mother.
As a final example, take:

(4) Last week, at the river, I caught a huge trout with my new fishing rod.

This could be analysed as shown in Figure 3.2, based on the parse:

Table 3.2   The parts of an event.

Action	The event itself. In a sentence, the action is usually described by a *verb:* The man was *bitten* by the dog.
Agent	The actor who has caused the action to take place: The man was bitten by the *dog.*
Conditional	A logical condition that exists between two events: The trout can be caught *only if* it does not suspect.
Instrument	The thing or device that caused or implemented the event: The *bullet* hit the soldier.
Location	The place where the event takes place. Often two different locations are involved, one at the start of the event and one at the conclusion. These are identified as *from* and *to* locations: They travelled from *Rome* to *Paris.*
Object	The thing that is affected by the action: The fly attracted the *fish.*
Purpose	Identified the purpose of the event: Simon went to the river *to catch fish.*
Quality	A descriptor, one that modifies a concept: The budgerigar was *yellow.*
Recipient	The person who is the receiver of the effect of the action: Mary cooked dinner for *Simon.*
Time	When an event takes place: The salmon were jumping *yesterday.*
Truth	Used primarily for false statements: A canary is *not* a robin.

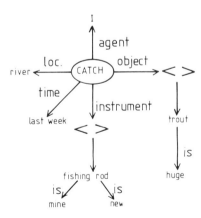

Figure 3.2   Graphical representation for the meaning of the sentence 'Last week, at the river, I caught a huge trout with my new fishing rod', using case assignments.

Action:	Catch
Agent:	I
Object:	A huge trout
Location:	River
Instrument:	My new fishing rod
Time:	Last week.

In the full graphical representation of this, shown in Figure 3.2, the instrument is analysed as a concept *(fishing rod)* having two properties, *is mine* and *is new*. Similarly, the object is analysed as a concept *(a trout)* with a property *(is huge)*.

Some new ideas are introduced in this figure. The primary one is that the entry for *instrument* and *object* is < > and not *fishing rod* and *trout*. It is essential to know this, since we can easily include the fact that the particular fishing rod *is a fishing rod*, and so it will have all of the properties normally associated with fishing rods in general, while on the other hand it is *my new* fishing rod, and this is not a property of fishing rods in general. The extra nodes < > keep general information and information specific to the objects and events in question appropriately separated.

Semantic network systems of this kind provide a way of representing basic information about events. From the network shown in Figure 3.2, we have all of the information to enable us to answer questions like 'Where did I catch a trout?', 'What did I catch at the river?', 'Was it my new fishing rod I used yesterday?', etc. Furthermore, it is clear that stored facts and sentences currently being read can make a connection with each other.

It may be asked why it should be thought necessary to have a meaning representation which is independent of surface structure. Are we any better off with structures like those given above than we are with the original sentence? That they are necessary can be illustrated easily by a sentence having more than one meaning. What is meant by:

(5) They are working students.

It could mean that *they* are agents, the actions is *making students work*, and *students* are the recipients. Or it could mean that *they* ISA example of students who are currently working. Or even that *they* ISA example of students who go out to work. Even sentences which are syntactically very different in their surface structures may contain elements playing the same role in a deep case-grammar analysis, for instance the *I* and *me* in (6) and (7):

(6) John strikes me as pompous.
(7) I regard John as pompous.

Case-grammars of this kind may very well capture something of the meaning of sentences, but are they any use as models of how humans understand text? There are two basic problems: one is that some machinery is necessary to enable the processing system to decide upon case allocations; the other is that vital aspects of meaning are still missed from this formulation.

This second question will be tackled in the next section. For the present the case-allocation problem will be discussed, because it is a general problem for other more elaborate schemes for representing meaning.

If the case analysis is to be of any value for sentence comprehension, it is obviously important that the processor be able to allocate noun-phrases to their appropriate cases. The starting point for any such analysis has been the idea that each case may have associated with it a defining set of semantic attributes or features. So, for instance, the agent or experiencer[1] cases need to be filled by living things, whereas the instrument or object cases require non-living things. If one could discriminate all cases according to such primitive semantic features it would be a relatively straightforward problem to make assignments to cases *via* a superficial semantic analysis of each noun-phrase in the sentence. There is in fact some evidence to suggest that cases can be represented in terms of semantic distinctions, but it is not clear to what extent the distinctions result from the assignments themselves as opposed to properties intrinsic in the elements. This problem is made clearer when one considers the psychological basis for case assignments.

For instance, Shafto (1973) used a modified concept learning task in order to discover the perceived semantic relationship between the agent, experiencer, instrument and object cases on the basis of the subject's pattern of confusion errors. The subject was given a set of sentences and asked to classify them into one of four predefined categories according to the relationship between the underlined word and the rest of the sentence. Examples of the various case categories are shown in Table 3.3. Multidimensional scaling of the confusion data yielded two dimensions of importance: active/passive and living/non-living. The agent, instrument, experiencer, and object cases fell neatly into the space defined by these dimensions, in the manner shown in Table 3.4. Whereas the living/non-living dimension is clearly a feature of any noun, the active/passive dimension seems to come about as a result of the noun's *perceived role* in the sentence rather than as a feature of the noun itself. This can be illustrated with the following example:

(8) The rock smashed the window

in which rock is in the case of instrument. That a rock is non-living is part of its semantic definition, but that it is active can only be determined by its role in this particular sentence.

In other words, there seems to be some correspondence between semantic features and case definitions but it is not sufficient to discriminate between all the cases. Consequently, the sort of assignment procedures that are needed will entail more general tests of the form: 'Could this noun be active in this sentence, and if so, given that it is non-living, may it thus fit into the instrument case?'. In order to determine whether the noun is 'active' in this case, one would need to know whether it was the underlying subject of the sentence, and this will of course depend upon a syntactic analysis. We would therefore expect case-assignment procedures to involve a mixture of semantic

44

Table 3.3   Examples of sentences for the case concepts (from Schafto, 1973).

Agent
　　The *lioness* snarled fiercely.
　　The *judge* freed the prisoners.
　　The ambush was planted by the *militia*.
　　The auditon was recommended by the *composer*.
Experiencer
　　The *editor* was shocked by the novel.
　　The speech was heard by the *diplomat*.
　　The *performer* was calm.
　　The noise frightened the *baby*.
Instrument
　　The rats dies from the *poison*.
　　The *movie* was sad.
　　The point was illustrated by several *facts*.
　　The *puppy* was lovable.
Object
　　The *trunk* was in the attic.
　　The *prelate* was condemned by the Church.
　　The *vegetables* thawed slowly.
　　The wind blew the *papers* away.

Table 3.4.

	Active	Passive
Living	Agent	Instrument
Non-living	Experiencer	Object

analysis of the nouns and syntactic analysis of the sentence in question. Although this is by no means impossible, it is clearly a more complicated process than might be imagined when one looks at the straightforward examples usually given in the linguistic literature, where the case is so often determined by the element itself, with 'hammers' being instruments, 'windows' objects, and so on.

B. Representing Events and Verbs More Fully

1. Aspects of verb meaning

Our second question was: To what extent does a simple case representation actually convey meaning? It is an easy matter to demonstrate that it does not take us very far to work with a representation which is an allocation of noun-phrases and other parts of speech to the slots as listed in Table 3.2. It does not tell us anything which is *peculiar* to the actual event being described. So in the case of a sentence like 'John broke the window', we may end up with John =

agent; window = object; event = broke. But it only makes sense to the reader because he knows what *broke* entails, and of course there is nothing in the simple case representations to show what this knowledge of meaning is. Once this is admitted, it is clearly necessary to specify the meaning in a fuller, more comprehensive way. The analysis of nominal concepts, described in the previous chapter, would suggest that a verb might also be broken down into more primitive components which convey its meaning. Such components would be action- or state-elements implied by the verb.

Let us illustrate two such decompositions. When something is *broken*, it is transformed from a *whole object* to a *not-whole object*, by some *agent* using some *method*. Furthermore, the object undergoing this transformation has to be breakable by the method applied. Similarly, the verb *to kick* has as one of its meaning packages that of moving a foot in a certain way towards the object being kicked. At first sight, this all seems very straightforward. All that is necessary is to specify the underlying structure in some way. However, in practice this is an extremely difficult task, and the underlying meanings appear to have numerous necessary components for their adequate description. The reader can get the feel of this by considering how difficult it would be to specify the dynamics and nature of the movements of the foot in *kick*, for example. If the reader started to make a list of the necessary and typical features of kicking, he would probably still be thinking of new things hours later. One way of considering the decomposition idea is to appreciate the complexities underlying the meaning of a verb in this way.

It is a simple matter to demonstrate the importance of decomposition by stepping beyond the boundaries of single events for a moment and considering what happens in the comprehension of a snippet of discourse consisting of a pair of sentences, such as (9):

(9) Alf kicked the football hard.
(9′) His foot got bruised.

How does (9′) relate to the antecedent sentence? An understanding of these sentences as a coherent whole implies that *kicking* has as part of its underlying meaning *moving a foot*. Unless the connection between *kick* and *foot* is made, there is no way of even starting to achieve a coherent understanding. Another example emerges with the resolution of the following problem in pronoun assignment:

(10) Mary gave a clock to Jacqueline.
(10′) She said that she would keep the clock in her office.

Who is the *she* in (10′)? Although strictly speaking *she* is ambiguous with regard to a choice of referent, people have no obvious difficulty in assigning *she* to Jacqueline. In order to do this, it is necessary to decompose the meaning of *gave* in such a way that the clock was *transferred* from being in the possession of Mary to being in the possession of Jacqueline, hence Jacqueline can dictate where it is to be kept. The point is that some kind of decomposition of *gave* in (10) is necessary in order to interpret (10′).

Investigators concerned with producing programs capable of language comprehension have attempted to solve this problem by devising sets of primitive underlying descriptions in order to capture at least some of the meaning of some verbs. We shall illustrate two similar approaches to this problem in the two sections which follow. Although they come from different laboratories with slightly different objectives, both purport to capture meaning in a working computer system capable of understanding natural language to at least a limited extent. Let us begin by describing their ways of representing verbs (and events) before continuing a discussion of the problems of decomposition.

2. The Norman, Rumelhart, and LNR system

Norman *et al.* (1975; see also Rumelhart and Ortony, 1976) use the term 'active structural network' to describe their fuller conception of the representation of meaning. A verb in their dictionary points to a description in terms of an underlying *schema*, or network of primitive components, which is purported to capture the meaning of that verb. Thus the schema pointed to by the verb *to break* is called the BREAK schema. These writers use the network notation with which the reader is already familiar, and its interpretation should cause little problem.

Figure 3.3 shows the 'simplified' schema for BREAK. There are three slots for variables, an agent slot (X), a method slot (M), and an object slot (Y). Starting at the key lexical item, BREAK, this points to when break happens by an arrow labelled ISWHEN. Thus, BREAK ISWHEN some agent causes a change from a whole state to a not-whole state in an object Y. CAUSE is a primitive for the verb break, as it is with many other verbs in the descriptions of Norman *et al.* This primitive has two arguments (slots): something which was done (the DO primitive) and something which was the result (the CHANGE primitive). The entries X, Y, and M are variables which are normally instantiated when the BREAK schema is used. There are restrictions operating on the values these variables can take. For example, the line connecting BREAK to Y carries the label *brittle object* — this is a restriction on the value the variable Y can take. X is connected to BREAK by an arrow labelled *agent*, indicating that the value X can take must be agentive. (Agentive restrictions are difficult to deal with, as we have indicated, but the agentive property roughly corresponds to the concept 'animate'.) The diagram of the schema in Figure 3.3, then, tells what 'to break' *expects* (X, Y, and M) and something of what the restrictions are on these variables.

In a situation where the BREAK schema is used, the task is basically to test the noun-phrases in the sentence evoking its use for their applicability as values for X, Y, and M. In discussing this matter, Rumelhart and Ortony consider the sentence 'John broke the window'. The BREAK schema is evoked by the word *'broke'*. The other linguistic entities are assigned to X, Y, and M following a

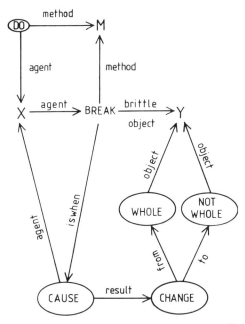

Figure 3.3 Simplified BREAK schema (Adapted from Rumelhart and Ortony, 'The representation of knowledge in memory', in *Schooling and the Acquisition of Knowledge* (Eds. R. J. Spiro and W. E. Montague). Lawrence Erlbaum Associates, 1977).

series of tests. In searching for a brittle object, *window* is found to fit (Y) since its breakable quality is part of the information we have stored at the node for window. *John* is a person and persons are agentive forces, so John becomes assigned to X. We do not have any entries for M, and so cannot instantiate M, although we may ask 'How was it broken?' as a request for information to fill a vacant slot.

A connected graph of this sort is one way of representing something of the underlying meaning of the verb. Other primitives come into play in the description of other verbs. For example, *give, take, buy*, and *sell* all require the primitive concepts of POSSESSION, CHANGE, and CAUSE; to give or to take something both mean doing something which causes a change of the person who possesses the object. With *buy* and *sell* things are slightly more complicated still, since they require some description of a change in possession of money as well as a change in possession of goods.

The basic objective in this type of analysis is to represent the meaning of a verb using as few primitives as possible, so as to keep the representation relatively simple. One thing that becomes clear is that large numbers of verbs in any language bear a family resemblance to each other (for instance, verbs of motion — cf. Miller and Johnson-Laird, 1976), and that many verbs are elaborations of other verbs. So, 'buy' and 'sell' can be thought of as elaborations of 'give' and 'take', the latter requiring the addition of a few primitives to be derived from the former, as we indicated earlier.

An approach of a similar kind is seen in the analysis carried out by Roger Schank (1973; also Schank and Abelson, 1977). The reader will see that in many ways his primitives have much in common with those described above, although his notation is somewhat different.

3. Conceptual dependency primitives (Schank, 1973)

Just as with the first system, Schank's objective was to produce case-frames for verbs, although the cases produced differ somewhat from the linguistically derived categories of Fillmore. Nevertheless, he was concerned to produce meaning-representations such that there was only one representation for sentences which mean the same thing, and to capture the 'fuller' meaning of a sentence in the same way as active structural networks. Norman *et al.* (1975) point out that Schank's analyses have influenced their own work in various ways.

Schank and Abelson (1977) tabulate 11 primitive ACTs underlying nonstative verbs, and claim that these (together with some varieties of CAUSE primitive) capture a good deal of the meaning of most verbs. They use stative and action formulations for verb-forms which describe states and actions respectively. *Stative* formulations are the case-frame:

An object is in *some state* (with *some value*).
>   Examples of statives are:
>   John is depressed
>   John is at the cinema
>   John is dead
>   Etc.

ACTs imply actions of some sort, and all of the primitives have a basically simple case-form:

Actor, action, object, direction, and instrument.

The 'human' orientation of Schank's choice of primitives is quite clear from the simplified listing given in Table 3.5. The present writers include this table to give the reader a feel for some of the details of how primitives might be analysed. Only the general idea is important for understanding our discussions of the subject.

Just as in Norman *et al.*'s case, verbs in Schank's system are entered as descriptions in terms of these ACTs. Let us examine one such entry, the verb-ACT dictionary representation of *throw at*. The graphical notation used by Schank is idiosyncratic, differing in many ways from the labelled graphs used up to now.

Throw at is represented as shown in Figure 3.4; the figure has more familiar features than may first meet the eye. Y $\Longleftrightarrow$ PTRANS means that Y is the actor executing the PTRANS. Note that Y has the selection restricting *human*.

$\underline{O}$ XY means that X (a physical object) is the object of the PTRANS. On the right of the diagram $\longrightarrow \begin{array}{l} \longrightarrow \text{somewhere} \\ \longleftarrow \text{Y} \end{array}$ represents the direction of the

Table 3.5   Simplified listing of primitive ACTs (reduced from Schank and Abelson, 1977, p. 12).

ATRANS   The transfer of an abstract relationship such as possession, ownership or control. Thus, one sense of 'give' is: **ATRANS** something to someone else; a sense of 'take' is: **ATRANS** something to oneself. 'Buy' is made up of two conceptualizations that cause each other, one an **ATRANS** of money, the other an **ATRANS** of the object being bought.

PTRANS   The transfer of the physical location of an object. Thus, 'go' is **PTRANS** oneself to a place; 'put' is **PTRANS** of an object to a place.

PROPEL   The application of a physical force to an object. **PROPEL** is used whenever any force is applied, regardless of whether a movement (**PTRANS**) took place. In English, 'push', 'pull', 'throw', 'kick' have **PROPEL** as part of them. 'John pushed the table to the wall' is a **PROPEL** that causes a **PTRANS**.

MOVE   The movement of a body part of an animal by that animal. **MOVE** is nearly always the ACT in an instrumental conceptualization for other ACTs. That is, in order to throw, it is necessary to **MOVE** one's arm.

GRASP   The grasping of an object by an actor. The verbs 'hold', 'grab', 'let go', and 'throw' involve **GRASP** or the ending of a **GRASP**.

INGEST   The taking in of an object by an animal to the inside of that animal.

EXPEL   The expulsion of an object from the body of an animal into the physical world. Whatever is **EXPEL**led is very likely to have been previously **INGEST**ed. Words for excretion and secretion are described by **EXPEL**, among them, 'sweat', 'spit', and 'cry'.

MTRANS   The transfer of mental information between animals or within an animal. We partition memory into two pieces: the CP (conscious processor where something is thought of) and the LTM (long-term memory where things are stored). The various sense organs can also serve as the originators of an **MTRANS**. Thus, 'tell' is **MTRANS** between people, 'see' is **MTRANS** from eyes to CP, 'remember' is **MTRANS** from LTM to CP, 'forget' is the inability to do that, 'learn' is the **MTRANS**ing of new information to LTM.

MBUILD   The construction by an animal of new information from old information. Thus, 'decide', 'conclude', 'image', 'consider' are common examples of **MBUILD**.

SPEAK   The actions of producing sounds. Many objects can **SPEAK**, but human ones usually are **SPEAK**ing as an instrument of **MTRANS**ing. The words 'say', 'play music', 'purr', 'scream' involve **SPEAK**.

ATTEND   The action of attending or focusing a sense organ towards a stimulus. **ATTEND** ear is 'listen', **ATTEND** eye is 'see', and so on. **ATTEND** is nearly always referred to in English as the instrument of **MTRANS**. Thus, in conceptual dependency, 'see' is treated as **MTRANS** to CP from eye by instrument of **ATTEND** eye to object.

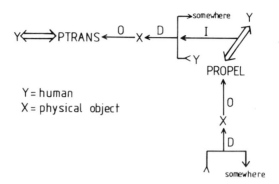

Figure 3.4   A graphical representation of the verb-ACT dictionary representation for the verb *'throw at'* (from Schank, 1973).

movement of the object away from Y towards somewhere: that is, away from the actor. The remainder of the figure describes the instrumental means by which this PTRANS is executed. Thus:

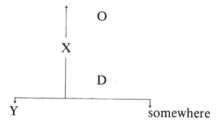

means that the instrument (I) of the PTRANS is Y (the actor) PROPELling. Finally:

$$\begin{array}{c} \uparrow \quad O \\ X \\ \uparrow \quad D \\ Y \qquad\qquad \text{somewhere} \end{array}$$

means that the object (O) of PROPEL is X moved in a direction (D) away from Y and towards somewhere. In passing, it is perhaps worth mentioning that by representing instrumentals in this way, Schank has clarified much of the assignment issue raised earlier in the context of Fillmore's case analysis in the sense that the *instrument* is a whole actor-action-object complex, rather than just the instrument itself.

Despite differences in case-form and notation, both Schank's system and that of Rumelhart *et al.* are designed to capture the meaning underlying verbs, and to provide slots with specified selection restrictions so that an input sentence can be properly parsed into a meaning structure. Although both have restrictions in applicability, they exemplify working systems which are actual implementations of verb decomposition.

4. Questions of 'how much' and 'when'

Given that some kind of decomposition is necessary to translate short pieces of discourse into a cohesive structure, two practical questions become apparent. How much decomposition is necessary, and when does it become necessary in the comprehension process? Let us consider the 'how much' question first.

The sentence:

(11) John punched Mary

has been analysed by Schank (1973, p. 226) in the following way (we shall use a language description rather than a network diagram):

John PROPELS John's fist from John to Mary.
The instrument of the process is John MOVEing his fist to Mary.
The outcome is that the fist and Mary come into physical contact.

Although this captures some important things (using fist; making contact) it does not describe the dynamics of the motion involved, which is really rather important. Indeed, 'friendly' or 'playful' punches are normally quite different in their dynamics of motion from the aggressive kind. The point is that MOVE could have as part of its specification not only *fist* in this verb, but also some description of force, momentum or acceleration specified on some sort of scale. Such a description would have to be a range of possible values, rather in the way that Minsky conceives frames as having slots which specify a range of values for possible instantiations. Other aspects of *John punched Mary* are more complex still. For instance, *punching* is undesirable except in self-defence, is aggressive, and predicts the likely behaviour or state of the recipient (for example, pain, aggression, fear, anger, etc.).

Another illustration of how much should be included in a verb representation is shown in (12) and (12'):

(12) John drove to San Francisco.
(12') The car broke down halfway.

Driving (in this sense) could be based on primitives having *car* as part of the specification, just as *punch* had *fist*. So when (12') is encountered, *the car* is treated as a given entity in the situation. For this reason, (12) and (12') cohere. However, if (12') had been:

(13) The Porsche broke down halfway

there would still be no noticeable difficulty in understanding the message. But does it make sense to suppose that part of the *drive* representation contains a list of exemplars of the category *car*, or even all *vehicles*? This seems far-fetched. It seems much more likely that the processor tries to make a connection with a representation having *car* (or perhaps even *vehicle*) in it, and on encountering (13), extracts the information that *the Porsche* ISA *example of a Porsche* ISA *car*. The point is that while it is possible to speculate about the limits of verb representation, it is not possible to decide precisely what they might be. All we can say at this stage is that in some situations all of the kinds of knowledge discussed become necessary for understanding.

Let us turn to the 'when' question. Are sentences decomposed into meaning structures when they are encountered, or are they only decomposed when a new sentence seems to demand it for integration? Schank and Abelson (1977) argue that it is necessary to decompose verbs almost immediately in almost all discourse, and in their computer implementations such decompositions are done at the time each sentence is encountered. Some of the advantages of this will be discussed a little later. However, an important aspect of the 'when' question relates to the 'how much' question discussed earlier. In the case of an example like (12) and (12'), sentence (12) should produce a representation having a *car* or *vehicle* default as part of it. If it does not have *Porsche* (and the authors guess it would not), then extra inferential processing should have to occur at the time (13) is encountered. In other words, more processing at the time of encountering the second sentence should be required if it is (13) rather than (12').

5. From sentences to fuller discourse

In the discussions above the argument has been made that in order to understand simple event descriptions, an underlying meaning structure has to be accessed, whether the understanding is by man or machine. We concentrated on verbs especially. Sentences can be thought of as being parsed into these meaning structures, which form some of the building blocks of understanding. The meaning structures of the verbs themselves, be they called schemata or conceptual dependencies, are based on the idea that they are capable of being described in terms of primitives, which enter into case-like frames. There is considerable argument over the number of primitives necessary for an adequate model, and the argument can be extended to the question of how much pragmatic information should also be included in a usable description of a verb.

It is easier to think about the scope of the representation which might be needed for a sentence if it is considered as an antecedent for other sentences. When this is done, it becomes clear that a considerable depth of meaning often has to be reached before two sentences can form a cohesive structure and seem sensible. Whether a particular depth of meaning is extracted at the time of reading the sentence or later as needed, it is still necessary to be able to access the meaning at some point to effect an integration. This is equivalent to saying that the words on the page serve the function of activating knowledge structures in the brain (or computer program), and that it is the overlap between *these* structures which constitutes cohesion. It would be wrong to try to find the overlaps on a page of writing itself, because they will not be discovered there.

In the sections which follow, consideration will be given to what must be involved in understanding pieces of discourse that are longer than have been examined up to now. When this is done, it becomes even more clear that much human understanding of discourse is not intrinsic in the semantics of words, but depends upon pragmatic knowledge, or knowledge of how things normally work, rather than how they necessarily work.

C. Using Knowledge to Understand Episodes

(14) Mary was on her way to school.
She got off the bus two stops early.
Then she went into a cafe and had a coffee.
She browsed through records in a stationer's, and later went to the cinema.
At four in the afternoon, she walked home.

A simple tale of this kind illustrates how much knowledge is brought to bear when comprehension beyond the single sentence is required. True, it is possible to represent each sentence in (14) as event representations like those discussed above. In this particular example, the temporal sequencing is quite straightforward; each representation at the sentence level could simply be connected to the previous one by the link 'then'. If the passage were stored in this way, questions could be asked like 'What did Mary do after going to the cinema?' and the answer would be the last line of the passage. But the passage seems to convey much more than this. Most people would think that Mary is a schoolgirl; that she is probably playing truant; that she is probably a teenager; and so on. Such interpretations are not necessary in the logical sense, but form an important aspect of how people normally interpret text.

In this section it is proposed to examine the connection between a given text and the ideas that it seems to evoke. The arguments revolve around the notion that the behaviour of characters in texts is generally goal-directed, and that many situations described are ones with which readers have some familiarity, either through their own interactions in the world or through knowledge acquired from others. Furthermore, we shall be building on the idea that what is presented in a text is a *fragmentary* description of situations of which we have knowledge.

1. Predictable sequences of behaviour

A number of workers in artificial intelligence have made use of some variant of Minsky's frame hypothesis (*vide* Chapter 2) to model the discourse comprehension process (e.g. Charniak, 1972; Schank and Abelson, 1977). The basic principle is that some pieces of text can be understood if they can be related to a situational stereotype. This can be illustrated with a simple example:

(15) John was in court since Mary had filed a divorce petition.
(15′) He was worried about the alimony she might get.

In order to integrate these two sentences, it is necessary to invoke a representation of the sequence of events in a divorce case. Only by relating (15′) to such a representation is it possible to interpret the appearance of *alimony* and to interpret why he should be worried.

Schank (Schank and Abelson, 1977) has developed a representation of predictable situational sequences — a subclass of Minsky's frame — which he calls a *script*. A script is a detailed list of events, in sequence, which characterize a given 'standard' situation. It is complete with a list of roles played by the characters in the script, why it might be used (for instance the *goals* which a person might have to bring him into that situation), and what to do when things go wrong in the situation.

Table 3.6 (from Schank and Abelson, 1977) shows the structure of the script for what happens in a restaurant from the point of view of a customer. At the top of the script there is a list of roles and props, followed by the sequence itself, complete with options. The sequence is written in terms of the primitive ACTs of Schank's conceptual dependency system described earlier. Of course, the idea of a script does not depend upon using the ACT formulation: any action descriptions could be used, in theory. We have left his table as it was in order to show the continuity of representation in his particular theory. Scriptal knowledge is exemplified by Table 3.6; humans must possess knowledge of this type for many situations.

Once a script is accessed by a language processor, it provides a set of expectations about what will happen next, or, more generally, what the order of events should be. It also provides a set of expectations about which entities are likely to be involved. Let us suppose that sentence (16) calls up a restaurant script:

(16) Feeling hungry, John went into a restaurant.
(16′) The waiter brought him the menu.

How does sentence (16′) come to be connected to its antecedent? Neither the action itself, nor *the waiter*, nor *the menu* as individual items are mentioned in (16). If the reader has a script, there is no problem. Not only can the processor refer to the words mentioned explicitly in (16), but it can also refer to those roles, props, and actions in the activated script. And in the restaurant script we find *the waiter*, *the menu*, and the complete conceptualization underlying the action described by (16′). In other words, the script expands the domain of reference in a limited, context-dependent way.

A more complex example of the use of scripts is seen in one of Schank's own examples (Schank, 1975):

(17) John wanted to go to Hawaii.
(17′) He called his travel agent.
(17″) He said they took cheques.

Assuming (17) and (17′) invoke a travel-agent script, Schank claims that (17″) is immediately intelligible. Who is the *he* referring to in (17″)? Schank claims

Table 3.6   A fragment of the restaurant script (from Schank and Abelson, 1977).

Script: RESTAURANT
Track: Coffee shop

Props: Tables
Menu
F—Food
Check
Money

Roles: S—Customer
W—Waiter
C—Cook
M—Cashier
O—Owner

Entry conditions: S is hungry
S has money

Results: S has less money
O has more money
S is not hungry
S is pleased (optional)

Scene 1: Entering
S **PTRANS** S into restaurant
S **ATTEND** eyes TO tables
S **MBUILD** where to sit
S **PTRANS** S TO table
S **MOVE** S TO sitting position

Scene 2: Ordering
(menu on table)   (W brings menu)   (S asks for menu)
S **PTRANS** menu TO S   S **MTRANS** signal TO W
                                                   W **PTRANS** W TO table
                                                   S **MTRANS** 'need menu'
                                                     TO W
                                                   W **PTRANS** W TO menu

W **PTRANS** W TO table
W **ATRANS** menu TO S

S **MTRANS** food list TO CP (S)
*S **MBUILD** choice of F
S **MTRANS** signal TO W
W **PTRANS** W TO table
S **MTRANS** 'I want F' TO W

W **PTRANS** W TO C
W **MTRANS** (**ATRANS** F) TO C

C **MTRANS** 'no F' TO W   C **DO** (prepare F script)
W **PTRANS** W TO S   to Scene 3
W **MTRANS** 'no F' TO S
(go back to *) or
(go to Scene 4 at no pay path)

Scene 3: Eating
C **ATRANS** F TO W
W **ATRANS** F TO S
S **INGEST** F

(optionally return to Scene 2 to order more;
otherwise go to Scene 4)

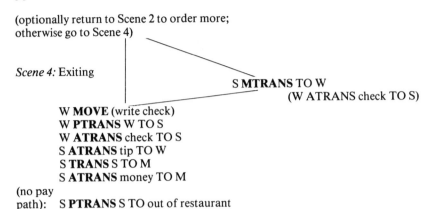

Scene 4: Exiting

S **MTRANS** TO W
                 (W ATRANS check TO S)

W **MOVE** (write check)
W **PTRANS** W TO S
W **ATRANS** check TO S
S **ATRANS** tip TO W
S **TRANS** S TO M
S **ATRANS** money TO M

(no pay
path):   S **PTRANS** S TO out of restaurant

---

that this is easily handled because we know that payment is something travel agents expect — it is part of the script for dealing with travel agents. Furthermore, using a script means that *took* is interpreted as *accepted* and not as *stolen* or *cheated* or *removed*, as it would be in (18'):

(18) The police interviewed John about the break-in at his house.
(18') He said they took cheques.

In other words, the script can serve to make sense selection at the lexical level immediate, and can help to resolve pronominal assignment problems.

The entities and actions in a script are the *default expectations* which we described when discussing Minsky's frames. Similarly, a script can be instantiated: when *John* is eating in a restaurant, *John* is the value which instantiates the customer role slot. If the waiter has a limp, this fact instantiates the waiter slot.

Thus far the illustrations have dealt only with discourse which follows a script. When a piece of discourse does not follow the script, Schank and Abelson claim that the divergence can still be interpreted in terms of the script. For example:

(19) John went for a meal in the restaurant.
(19') He spent 10 minutes trying to catch the waiter's eye.

Sentence (19') is intelligible in terms of the restaurant script—catching the waiter's eye is an aspect of the ordering scene. However, it tells us that for 10 minutes this scene was not completed, and that the other stages in the script could not be completed in the meantime. It makes linguistic sense to say:

(20) John could not get a waiter to take his soup order. So he contented himself with eating his sweet course.

On the other hand, it does not make *pragmatic* sense. Any comprehension system resembling that used by a human would have to see (20) as anomalous, whether it is linguistically acceptable or not. Of course, the script would provide an easy way of spotting the anomaly — if progress through the script is held up at an early stage, it does not make sense to move on to later stages, unless a means of bypassing the block is explicitly stated in the text.

Schank's claim is that understanding should rely on script knowledge to interpret a new input as much as possible. Of course, understanding does not cease when this cannot be done, but the processing has to be different. The contrast can be seen in Schank's own examples:

(21) John wanted to go to Hawaii. He phoned his travel agent.

Phoning a travel agent is (claims Schank) predicted by the travel-methods script. Now compare:

(22) John wanted to go to Hawaii. He phoned his mother.

In no way is phoning *his mother* predicted by the first sentence. To make a connection, a travel script could not be used: some other form of problem-solving has to take place — to seek out a reason for this behaviour. Depending on the particular text involved, a small number of alternatives may be produced — perhaps John's mother is rich and he is poor, or perhaps he wishes her to come with him. Alternatively, *no* immediate interpretation may be made. It could be 'held off' until sufficient extra information to explain it is presented in the text. After all, the writer usually intends the sentences of his writing to 'follow on' in a commonsense way, and not merely in a linguistically acceptable way.

It is possible to sit down and draw up a long list of scripts for familiar situations. They could be simple instrumental scripts, like *how to make beef stroganoff*, or role scripts, like *being a spy*, or situational scripts, like *eating at a restaurant*. But even if the use of scripts is one way for a human to understand, understanding is still possible in situations where it would be far-fetched to assume possession of a script. Some illustrations are given in the next section.

2. Understanding beyond scripts and without scripts

In this section we propose to examine two questions: first, what else is required for understanding apart from scripts, and second, are scripts necessary for understanding anyway? After all, if understanding can occur in the absence of a script, why should they *ever* be used.

The following example is quite intelligible, but it seems doubtful that it forms part of a script in the elaborate sense of the stylized restaurant example given above:

(23) Joan didn't want Freda to be so angry.
(23') They had been arguing all evening.
(23") Around midnight, Joan managed to mollify her.

In (23), the sentence can be represented as a *goal* which Joan has, the goal to reduce the anger level in Freda. Verbs like wish, want, desire, and feel (state) can all be considered as overt textual indicators of goal states. In (23″), Joan realizes her goal. The goal states of characters in a text predict that they will attempt to realize their goals, and often a story will consist of the plans they bring into use to do this. The ability to hold these goals open in a representation of a text is an important feature of how understanding works. For instance, in a story where the hero wishes to rescue a heroine who is in captivity, many things might happen between the goal being specified and it being realized. Some of these may be quite unrelated to the main plot of realizing the goal, while others may be subgoals to enable conditions to be made ready for the realization of the main goal. Yet the complete goalstructure has to be represented if the story is to make any sense. Consider the following short episode in this way:

> (24) The spy wanted to get hold of the microfilm in the Ruritanian Embassy.
> (24a) He went to a theatrical agent's and bought a Ruritanian soldier's outfit.
> (24b) Then he went to the Embassy and pretended to be a guard.
> (24c) He made his way to the record room.
> (24d) On the way he was stopped by a real guard.
> (24e) He hit him over the head.
> (24f) Then he got the microfilm and bolted.

In this story, the main goal for the spy is to get his hands on the microfilm. This does not happen until line (f). The goal is held while various methods of realizing it are enacted. Each of these methods could be described as a subgoal plus ways of realizing it. Getting an outfit satisfies a subgoal of pretending to be a guard, and so on. A story such as this would not be based on script-like information: it is a goal, and plan-based.

Representing goal-directed behaviour is clearly an essential part of human understanding. So far as machine understanding is concerned, Schank and Abelson (1977) discuss goal- and plan-based comprehension fairly thoroughly, and describe some of the mechanics of extracting goal structure from a text. Just as goal states can be considered as part of the description of many statives, so in their system goal states point to general strategies for their resolution. Some of these strategies use stereotyped, scriptal, behaviour sequences. So, being hungry (= goal: to be fed) points to the restaurant script, eating at home, etc. Others use simple preestablished strings of subgoals in order to realize the main goal. For instance, being hungry is associated with the subgoal of getting near some food. The point is that goalstates can be connected both to lexical input and to descriptions of procedures for satisfying the goal. The behaviour being described in a text is thus already represented in some form or other in the computer program.

Goal-based behaviour therefore may invoke the use of scripts, but need not necessarily do so. In any case, the representation of meaning in stories like (24) must consist of a goal-list in part.

Obviously, script-based understanding cannot occur in situations where no suitable script exists, or where there are insufficient cues in the text to call up a script.[2] Yorick Wilks (1976) has pointed out that, nevertheless, understanding occurs, which the examples above clearly show to be the case. He considers an example of a puberty rite. For most people he claims, there could be no script for anything as unfamiliar as a story about a puberty rite. His specific example is:

(25) At the puberty rite, little Kamathi's mother dropped her shoga.
(25') The crowd drew back in horror.

The point he makes is that this can be understood on the basis of an *inference rule*; he suggests:

| Humans show horrified reaction | $\rightarrow$ | Other humans did wrong thing |

There is, of course, no doubt about it. The reader must possess such inference rules, and it would also make sense to have them in computer programs aimed at comprehension. The question he poses is that if such rules are available, is it necessary to have script-like structures to facilitate comprehension?

Certainly, any understanding system would need to have various general inferential rules as in Wilks' example as part of its long-term memory. Theoretically, it might indeed be possible to implement computer understanding without scripts describing step-by-step events expected in stereotyped situations. Schank and Abelson (1977) themselves say that scripts are really only situation-specific lists of fragments of planned behaviour, which it is convenient to organize as a script because they always occur together in the situation which the scripts are supposed to describe. Wilks concludes that whether or not scripts are the best way of organizing the database of a computer program for understanding is not yet decidable. However, Wilks' arguments are made in the context of information-processing in computers — 'pure' artificial intelligence. But the present work is concerned with *human* comprehension: does the script concept carry any utility for that?

This is a question which can only be answered by recourse to empirical studies with human readers. In the next chapter, experiments will be reported which have been put forward as supporting the idea that human understanding is at least partly script-based. We shall set the stage for the empirical argument in the next section. A rather more general point relates to *levels of understanding*. Is the understanding a reader has of (25) and (25') the same as his understanding of a two-line story which could be related to a script? It seems to the authors that with the more familiar script examples, readers are not simply displaying minimal comprehension based on the application of single inference rules but have a feeling of familiarity *because* they can relate the sentences to a complex redundant structure which is likely to be script-like in nature.

D. Summary, and Problems in Producing Mental Representations of Discourse

1. Summary

Verbs serve to put the other parts of sentences into specific roles which are dictated by the underlying structure of the verbs themselves. The underlying structures rely upon certain primitive operations; while there is no agreement on precisely which primitives are necessary, there is some agreement as to the main types of primitives which seem to be required (*causes, changes, transfers* or *movements*, etc.), and moderately successful computer programs have been implemented on the basis of some sets of primitives. It may be possible to determine the primitives: underlying human comprehension by psychological analyses (cf. Miller and Johnson-Laird, 1976), but the problem is difficult to solve. However, regardless of the exact nature of the schemata underlying verbs, it is still possible to ask sensible questions about decomposition in human comprehension: how much decomposition is required, and when it takes place, for instance.

Beyond simple events, frames provide an interesting analogy for human comprehension. The script implementation of Schank is a particular example of a frame application. Although script-based understanding is useful up to a point, some sort of understanding is possible even when scripts could not be invoked. The authors doubt whether goal-based understanding or the use of simple inference rules could replace script-based understanding entirely, because of subjective differences in the degree of understanding which these methods produce.

Having explored some of the considerable problems which are encountered when attempts are made to represent meaning in discourse as a structure, we are now in a position to begin thinking about some of the knottier problems of how simple stories are actually represented in human memory. The purpose of the sections below is rather a general one — to elucidate the main classes of problem and to set the scene for the remainder of the book.

2. Gist and detail

Suppose that by application of a computer comprehension system a story can be represented as a complete chain of events, connected by representations based on suitable meaning decompositions and a suitable goal structure. The program written by Schank and his colleagues (cf. Schank and Abelson, 1977) is capable of doing this, at least with a handful of stories. Would this match up to what humans remember of the story? It seems plausible that it would match to some extent, in that humans can remember stories in a meaningful way. But the most obvious thing about human remembering is that it is incomplete. Without laborious learning people are seldom able to recite a complete story, but nevertheless usually manage to put over the gist of what it contained. In the next chapter the notion of gist will be explored in relation to data on precisely what it is that humans do remember. There are two basic problems.

The first is the question of whether every representation (every decomposition, every script, inference, goal, and so on) forms the complete representation of a story in the human mind, or whether only certain aspects of these representations are retained — those which are divined to be important to the story in some as yet unspecified way. There are many psychological experiments which show that subjects can often *recognize* more of the material which they have seen before than they can *recall* (e.g. Kintsch, 1977). The second problem is that, whether or not the mental representation contains all of the *working* representations used in comprehension, some rule for incomplete recall must be established. At one extreme, forgetting may be random, of course; but it is everyone's experience that forgetting appears not to be random: gist is usually retained, and the details forgotten. What can the basis of this effect be? What are the rules by which selection of gist takes place?

A closely related problem is that of paraphrase or summary production for a previously read story. People can paraphrase and produce summaries easily, at least for simple stories. So far as understanding by computer programs is concerned, some investigators have been concerned to emulate these processes. Thus, Schank and his colleagues (cf. Schank and Abelson, 1977) have tried to produce a package of programs which can take in a text, analyse it by means of conceptual dependencies, scripts, and goal structures, and end up with a representation which can print out summaries and paraphrases and also answer questions which require inferences to be made. Some of his programs will also produce translations, including summaries and paraphrases. The production of summary and paraphrase relates closely to the normal pattern of recall, and it is important to establish the rules which govern this process, since it is an integral part of what we normally call understanding.

3. The nature of on-line processing in human comprehension

No matter how well a computer program fares at approximating human performance, this does not mean to say that its mechanics resemble human processing. Similarly, no matter how well a linguistic description seems to capture the meaning of an utterance or the structure of a discourse, it does not describe the way in which people understand. Of course, it is true to say that the results of such enquiries may be formulated as theories of human understanding, and they undoubtedly give rise to indispensable concepts which should be part of one's armoury in any investigation of understanding from whatever standpoint. But in order to develop adequate theories of understanding which relate directly to human performance, empirical investigations using people have to be carried out. Earlier in this chapter, aspects of decomposition were considered. The burden of the argument was that some decomposition is necessary in order that comprehension can take place. The 'how much' and 'when' questions were posed as issues which could be approached in an empirical way with human subjects. Similarly, the idea of the script as a possible component of human understanding can also be examined empirically. Indeed, most of the ideas encountered in this review will recur in various ways in the empirical investigations to be described from this point onwards.

Note

1. *Experiencer* is a case alternative for *recipient* in some classifications.
2. We shall discuss script entry conditions in Chapter 6.

CHAPTER 4

The Nature of Text Representation in Human Memory

In the preceding chapters we have attempted to show some of the ways in which knowledge is used in comprehending pieces of discourse. The comprehension of even the simplest examples required considerable interpretation in terms of the reader's knowledge-base, and a number of ways of realizing these interpretive processes were discussed. One of the outcomes of our discussion was that the final memory representation of a text which a reader has encountered will be a product of comprehension itself. Of course, it is possible to 'read' a piece of text and learn it by heart, without anything other than very shallow or patchy understanding. Schoolchildren learning Shakespeare by heart often seem to do this. But such rote learning is not characteristic of normal 'memory for text'. As we suggested earlier, people typically remember the gist of what they have read, rather in the fashion of a summary, perhaps embellished with a few verbatim phrases of particular interest. This immediately raises the question of what has happened to bring about the representation of 'gist'.

Another point is that if memory is the product of the comprehension process, then memory experiments may provide clues about the nature of comprehension itself. This claim is considered in the present chapter. Not all of the investigators have been directly concerned with the process of comprehension: memory for text is in itself an important and interesting issue. However, what is of primary concern here is what there is to be gleaned about comprehension from our knowledge of text memory, and how useful memory techniques may be as a tool for investigating understanding.

A. Some Phenomena of Text Memory

1. Meaning and surface structure

Some acts of verbal learning require that the original materials be reproduced verbatim. Such learning is almost always achieved by slow and difficult rote methods, using rhythmical or pause-bounded groupings of the material. This is the way people seem to learn pieces of Shakespeare, the Lord's Prayer, the alphabet, the multiplication tables, etc. What is learned is analogous to a procedure or programme for producing the text verbatim, probably based on vocal or subvocal speech production (cf. Rubin, 1977, for a full discussion). However, it is usually a much quicker and easier process to extract and retain the gist or 'logical points' of what was said (e.g. Cofer, 1941), and this is the way we normally remember things.

Formal experiments lend support to the further claim that although the surface structure (wording of sentences in passages) may be available initially in memory, much of this surface structure is rapidly forgotten. For example, Sachs (1967) had people listen to tape-recorded passages taken from factual articles. From time to time the subjects were interrupted and shown a test sentence. They were required to judge whether the test sentence was identical to or changed from one they had heard before. 'Different' sentences produced by changes of word order or changes from active to passive voice were easily confused with the original sentences, but sentences changed in meaning were clearly recognized as different. This effect was greatest after some delay (80 syllables of intervening material) between the original and the test sentences, and was almost negligible when there was no delay. Such experiments demonstrate how gist endures and surface structures fades.

As we said, the final memory representation of a discourse is seldom verbatim. One of the earliest and best-known pieces of research into the recall of narrative stories was carried out by Frederick Bartlett (1932), and this illustrated some of the 'distortions' which occur in memory and recall. He read his subjects a North American Indian folk story, and then had them recall it at various later points in time. Bartlett noted first that recall was extremely inaccurate: often only the outline of a story was remembered, the details being forgotten, or at least not present at recall. Secondly, various systematic distortions crept in: things which fitted the story but were not actually present in it appeared in the protocols. Finally, when their memory of a story was so bad that only isolated fragments could be remembered, subjects sometimes invented plausible stories around these details. Furthermore, many of these errors showed an adherence to stereotyped situations with which the subjects were familiar. Thus, in one instance Bartlett quotes, the rather curious Indian folk-tale took on the character of a standard Wild West story in the recall protocol.

Bartlett's observations illustrate some of the complexities of recall protocols and their interpretation. Since the accurate part of recall is not random, but relates to the gist of a story, comprehension processes are implicated in the way the story is stored in memory. Furthermore, although the systematic nature of the errors reinforces this view, some of the protocol errors clearly resulted from constructive processes at the time of recall, rather than from operations at the time of listening to the story. When less exotic materials are used, recall appears to be less reconstructive, and fairly accurate, in the sense of capturing gist (Gomulicki, 1956; Zangwill, 1972; Cofer, 1973). Intrusion errors resulting from inferences seem to be more related to what was necessary for comprehension than to 'unnecessary' elaborations (Gomulicki, 1956). As Kintsch (1977) points out, whether recall is primarily reproductive or reconstructive depends upon the subject's familiarity with the materials, how standardized the story format is, and other factors unrelated to the nature of the materials, such as the delay between encountering the story and being asked to recall it. Reconstruction errors seem to be prominent only after long delays (e.g. Sulin and Dooling, 1974; Dooling and Christiaansen, 1977).

In part at least, what is remembered is allegedly a product of the comprehension process. If this is indeed the case, then inferential processes operating during comprehension should have a predictable effect on the kinds of distortions appearing in recall. Various lines of evidence have been put forward to support this viewpoint. For instance, Thorndyke (1975b, 1977) carried out a recognition memory experiment to see whether or not people confuse inferences which are necessary to comprehension with what was actually presented in the text. Consider the following example:

(1) The hamburger chain owner was afraid his love for french fries would ruin his marriage.

Thorndyke suggests that in order to understand this, one might draw on the following inferences:

(1a) The hamburger chain owner got his french fries free.
(1b) The hamburger chain owner's wife didn't like french fries.
(1c) The hamburger chain owner was very fat.

Later in the text the sentence below occurs:

(2) The hamburger chain owner decided to join weight-watchers in order to save his marriage.

In order to understand (2), the reader would need an inference chain back to (1c), and the probable validity of inference (1c) would be reinforced. On the other hand, encountering a sentence other than (2) might not reinforce the validity of (1c) since it says nothing which relates to it; for example:

(3) The hamburger chain owner decided to see a marriage counsellor in order to save his marriage.

Thorndyke carried out an experiment using materials like these, embedded in longer passages about various topics. Subjects had to read through the passages, and were later given a recognition memory test. The recognition test-items included some sentences which were in fact *plausible inferences* rather than materials which were actually presented on the page. When a plausible inference had been reinforced by a later sentence, it was more likely to be falsely recognized as having been presented than was the case if the inference had not been reinforced. This implies that the memory representation for a text contains both what was stated and the inferences needed to understand this, with the two being essentially indistinguishable. Memory is largely for the product of comprehension itself.

A somewhat different approach to the problem of inferences was taken by Kingsch (1974). He argued that if an inference is made during comprehension, and is incorporated in the memory representation, then it should be accepted as being true relative to that text as rapidly as if it actually had been presented. His results tended to bear this out. Subjects accepted an inferential statement as true just as rapidly as the same statement when it had really been made. However, this was only the case with delays of 20 minutes or more between the paragraph and the test-item. With short delays, explicitly presented information was processed faster than implicit information, but Kintsch suggests that this is due to the retention of some surface structure over brief periods, providing an extra source of information for the memory-match process. Of course, it is remotely possibly that inferences *develop* sometime after reading, but this is a very unlikely explanation. Kintsch's result seems to support the idea that some inferences at least are made at the time of reading and become part of the memory representation for the text.

There are many other studies supporting the view that text memory is not verbatim but is largely the product of deeper comprehension. For instance, Bransford *et al.* (1972) had subjects listen to one or other of the following sentences:

(4) Three turtles rested beside a floating log, and a fish swam beneath them.
(5) Three turtles rested on a floating log, and a fish swam beneath them.

After a series of sentences, a recognition test was administered, which included test items like:

(6) Three turtles rested beside a floating log, and a fish swam beneath it.
(7) Three turtles rested on a floating log, and a fish swam beneath it.

Subjects who heard sentence (4) realized (6) and (7) had not been presented before; however, those who heard (5) rejected (6) but not (7). The explanation is that (7) is a correct inference, which could be derived from sentence (5) (but not (4)); on the other hand, neither (6) nor (7) follows from (4). If turtles are on a log, then largish things passing under them will also pass under the log.

As a final example, let us consider an experiment by Garnham (1979), which used the somewhat different procedure of *cued recall*. Suppose a subject read a sentence like:

(8) The housewife cooked the chips.

How are chips (french fries) cooked? Most people would infer that they are fried. Using materials of this type, Garnham showed that the recall cue *cooked* was less effective in helping subjects to remember the original sentence than was the cue *fried*. Garnham suggested that what happens is that a sentence such as (8) is understood by producing a knowledge-based *model* of the situation, which is essentially non-linguistic in nature. The word *fried* maps into this model better than *cooked* in the present case.

In fact, the situation is fairly complex. Other evidence presented by Garnham suggests that *cooked* is not simply translated into *fried* and stored in that lexical form and no other. Surface information too is retained, since recognition memory tests show that the sentence is also recalled in its original form. Similar observations were made by R. C. Anderson *et al.* (1976), using noun-phrases as cues instead of verbs; indeed, their study is a direct precursor of Garnham's investigation. At a general level, such studies support the claim that what is retained of a sentence is, in part, a knowledge-based model of the situation is describes rather than some propositional analogue of the text itself.

Finally, a whole series of somewhat less sophisticated experiments demonstrate that memory is poor if the discourse structure is such that it is difficult to understand. In Chapter 1 we described a passage about 'Christopher Columbus' used in a study by Dooling and Lachman (1971). In this study, the passage could only be remembered at all well if the title was presented first. Performance was equally poor either in the absence of a title or if it was presented after the passage (Dooling and Mullet 1973). The Columbus passage is almost entirely unintelligible in the absence of an orienting title, largely because it is rich in metaphor and it is difficult to identify referents for the individuals mentioned in it. With texts which are a little more intelligible in the absence of a title, titles help somewhat even if they are given after the text (e.g. Bransford and Johnson, 1973). Using rather more simple materials, Kieras (1978; see also Chapter 9) showed that memory was considerably impaired by paragraph structures in which entities were mentioned as though they had been previously introduced but in fact had not been. He argued that in the absence of integrating 'given' material, the sentences have to be held for too long in short-term memory to be effectively integrated with a later sentence which explain the 'point' of the paragraph. This effect leads on to the problem of what 'the point' or 'the gist' of something might be.

2. Memory, gist, and representation

One of the most noticeable features of many recall protocols is the way in which they are not simply random samples of the original discourse, but somehow seem to capture the gist of the passage. Gist is a most elusive thing to define, although with simple passages at least, people seem to have little difficulty in agreeing upon whether a protocol has captured it. Dictionary definitions, such as 'real ground or point, substance or pith of a matter' (*Concise Oxford English Dictionary*, 1956), do not help at all. It was against this background of intuition that Bartlett (1932), amongst others, observed that much of memory seemed to be for gist.

Since gist itself is so difficult to define, the claim that memory tends to be for gist might appear to stand on shaky ground. However, the claim is far from being valueless, either empirically or theoretically. One way of obtaining an independent estimate of what is contained in the gist of a passage is to ask a group of people to write a summary statement or precis of it: a summary being the equivalent of gist in terms of everyday human performance. van Dijk (1975) and his collaborators compared the protocols from summary production and recall. They found that summaries were somewhat shorter than the contents of recall, but that most of what appeared in the summaries also appeared in the recall protocols. The additional contents of recall tended to be details of various descriptions. These, however, were omitted from the recall protocols when testing was delayed. Furthermore, the material included in the summaries was much the same for many of the subjects, indicating a fair degree of consensus for the gist of the passage used. This was also true for the recall protocols. The strong correlation between summary contents and recall contents offered clear support for the view that memory is for gist, and led van Dijk to conclude that summarizing rules and strategies are based on the same principles as those determining storage and retrieval.

Van Dijk's study supports the view held by many psychologists that what is recalled is basically a summary plus some detail. But the most interesting question is what it is about certain aspects of a discourse which cause those parts to be identified as the gist. There have been a number of approaches to this question, each of which have common elements, even if the solutions vary somewhat. The first step is to discover a way of segmenting or breaking up the text into atoms of some kind. Here we have spoken rather loosely of 'the content of summaries' or 'certain aspects of a discourse', but what is required is some specific theoretically motivated way of breaking up the discourse.

With this in view, Kintsch (1974) devised a scheme in which simple texts were broken down into a network of propositions which he argued reflected the content of the text. He then attempted to relate the role a given proposition played in the network to its memorability. Rumelhart (1975) and Thorndyke (1975b) looked beyond this local level of analysis towards the general pattern of organization to be found in a discourse — in this case simple stories — and used a set of general rules to segment the stories. The segments were then used, as atoms of discourse, in trying to track down the roots of gist and recall pattern. A similar approach was taken by van Dijk (1975; also Kintsch and van Dijk, 1978), although the aim in this case was to unravel complex stories containing several different episodes.

Although these two approaches provide a means of segmenting discourse, they are really quite different. Whereas Kintsch's (1974) account makes little reference to prior knowledge, the other accounts assume specialized frame-like knowledge structures (story-frames) which would enable a reader to recognize and parse a story when he encountered one. An even more subtle and complex use of background knowledge is found in yet another approach, that of Schank and Abelson (1977). It will be recalled that these authors believe understanding to be aided by access to scripts. On this view, the kind of memory structure built up during comprehension is not merely what is on the page, but also incorporates considerable general knowledge of situations.

These different theories vary widely in sophistication, plausibility, and breadth of attack. At one extreme, the theory of Kintsch (1974) makes very little reference to the mechanics of on-line comprehension, being concerned almost solely with the expression of a text in terms of propositional structures. The others do make such references (especially the theory of Schank and Abelson), and derive from the view that comprehension does not produce a representation in the mind of the reader which is simply a translation of the text itself: they explicitly acknowledge the rather complex process of reading between the lines which seems to characterize comprehension. In the next sections we shall examine each of the theories outlined above with respect to the following criteria:

(a) How well do the theories handle the problem of 'gist' memory?

(b) How well do they handle the kind of errors made in remembering?

(c) Do they make any contact with the process of understanding while reading?

B. Texts as Hierarchies of Propositions

1. Kintsch's (1974) theory

Kintsch (1974) put forward the view that the meaning of a text (that is, the final memory representation of it) can be captured by its underlying propositional content. He suggests that the propositions underlying a passage can be concatenated into a structure in the mind of the reader — a structure which he calls a text-base. For any given text-base, different surface structures, or texts, can be produced, but they would all have the same meaning. This idea is analogous to the relation of surface structure to meaning as exemplified by the case-grammar approach described in the preceding chapter.

A proposition is a predicator followed by one or more arguments:

(Predicator, Argument$_1$, Argument$_2$, . . . Argument$_n$).

This representational format was introduced earlier, in Chapter 2, as (for example):

(ISA, DOG, ANIMAL).

So, for example, 'John sleeps' could be represented as

(SLEEPS, JOHN)

or 'A bird has feathers' as

(HAVE, BIRD, FEATHERS).

The hierarchical tree structure used to represent a complete text-base results in part from the embedding of simple propositions within higher-level ones. For instance, the sentence 'If Mary trusts John then she is a fool' consists of two simple propositions embedded in a more complex one:

Prop. 1 (TRUST, MARY, JOHN)

Prop. 2 (FOOL, MARY)

Prop. 3 (IF Prop. 1, Prop. 2).

Proposition 3 is a shorthand way of writing the combination 1 and 2, embedded in a new proposition:

(If (TRUST, MARY, JOHN), & (FOOL, MARY)).

This may also be represented diagrammatically as a tree structure, as in Figure 4.1.

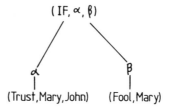

Figure 4.1   Propositional tree resulting from 'If Mary trusts John then she is a fool'.

There is another way in which a proposition may be subsumed under another proposition, and that is when initial propositions denominate subsequent ones. For instance, 'The snow melts slowly' is analysed by Kintsch as two propositions:

(MELT, SNOW), & (SLOW, MELT).

'Melt' in the first proposition is the same 'melt' as 'melt' in the second proposition. An example of a text and its text-base, taken from Kintsch *et al.* (1975), is given in Figure 4.2. The hierarchical structure has levels which result from the subordination of initial propositions to subsequent ones. The lines indicate repetitions between arguments of the numbered propositions.

In his (1974) book, Kintsch argued that entire texts can be represented in this way, and attempted to use such a description of the 'stimulus-object' to account for what is remembered of relatively simple materials. His arguments was that the uppermost (dominating) propositions of a text will be recalled more readily than lower-level (dependent) propositions. This suggestion has been confirmed by Kintsch and Keenan (1973) using very brief passages, and by Kintsch *et al.* (1975) for 70-word paragraphs about history and science. With delayed recall, the results are even more conclusive than with immediate recall, suggesting that superordinate propositions are not only processed preferentially, but are also better retained or retrieved.

In Kintsch and Keenan (1973), the investigators also noted that for passages containing the same number of words, the time subjects took to read the materials increased in a roughly linear fashion with the number of propositions in the sentences. These two lines of evidence led the investigators to suppose that the propositional analysis of a text is a good description of it, that the process of comprehension is one of constructing propositional text-bases from stimulus texts, and that the hierarchical structure of a text-base is a good predictor of what will be recalled of a text.

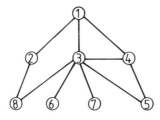

Text: The Greeks loved beautiful art. When the Romans conquered the Greeks, they copied them, and, thus, learned to create beautiful art.

Text-base: 1. (Love, Greek, Art)
2. (Beautiful, Art)
3. (Conquer, Roman, Greek)
4. (Copy, Roman, Greek)
5. (When, 3, 4)
6. (Learn, Roman, 8)
7. (Consequence, 3, 6)
8. (Create, Roman, 2)

Figure 4.2   Hierarchical structure and associated text and text-base (after Kintsch *et al.*, 1975).

2. *Limitations of Kintsch's theory*

There are a number of deficiencies in the Kintsch theory, and these will provide a basis for the next part of our discussion.

First, as it stands, the correlation between ease of recall and position in the hierarchy provides no explanation of *why* dependent propositions are more poorly remembered. That is, the account given is not a model of memory, although it might be construed as propaedeutic to one. Kintsch and his co-workers have gone some way in exploring this problem, however. For example, McKoon (1977) presented subjects with statements, some of which were from a previously read text, and measured the time it took the subjects to decide whether or not each statement was in fact part of the presented text. She found that statements based on propositions high up in the text-base hierarchy were verified faster than statements low down in it. The fact that people had good recognition memory rules out any simple theory that dependent propositions are simply represented less often (in an all-or-none fashion) in the final memory structure. Rather, the difference in latency suggests that the lower-level propositions came to be represented in a way which is somehow weaker, or more difficult to access. This is only one small step in the direction of a model of memory for text, but further elaborations by Kintsch and van Dijk (1978), to be described later, offer a more theoretically motivated closure of this particular gap. Thorndyke (1975b) has pointed out other difficulties in Kintsch's empirical work. For example, in some of the studies (e.g. Kintsch and Keenan, 1973), reading times and memory for sentences containing equal numbers of words but different numbers of propositions were compared.

An example is:

(9) Romulus, the legendary founder of Rome, took the women of the Sabine by force
(16 words, including commas, and 4 propositions)

versus

(10) Cleopatra's downfall lay in her foolish trust in the fickle political figures of the Roman world
(16 words, 9 propositions).

As Thorndyke points out, these sentences differ not only in the number of propositions they contain, but also in syntactic complexity. So, any claim about memory differences or reading-time differences confounds effects due to the number of propositions and their dependencies with syntactic complexity.

If these problems do not invalidate Kintsch's claims, then his view seems to provide a way of characterizing 'gist' in the simple situations which he considers. Consider what would happen in recall based only on levels 1 and 2 of the hierarchy produced by sentence (10), as shown in Figure 4.3. The result

Propositions

1. (Because, α, β)
2. (Fell down, Cleopatra) = α
3. (Trust, Cleopatra, Figures) = β
4. (Foolish, Trust)
5. (Fickle, Figures)
6. (Political, Figures)
7. (Part of, Figures, World)
8. (Roman, World)

Tree structure

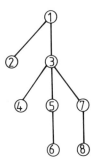

Figure 4.3   Propositional breakdown and tree structure for 'Cleopatra's downfall lay in her foolish trust in the fickle political figures of the Roman world' (after Kintsch and Keenan, 1973).

would be something like 'Cleopatra's downfall lay in her trust of some people'. Including lower levels would further specify Cleopatra's trust and the figures in whom she had trust. Although anecdotal, this example gives the impression of conveying 'gist', and fits the rule that gist and memory are closely related. Other examples produce similar intuitively plausible results.

When we turn to the kinds of errors occurring in memory, the theory does not fare so well. A major deficiency is the inability to handle the observations of Garnham (1979; also Anderson *et al.*, 1976). It will be recalled that Garnham showed the verb *fried* to be a better recall cue than *cooked* for the

memory of the sentence 'The housewife cooked the chips'. In Kintsch's system, this sentence would presumably be represented as something like:
(COOK, HOUSEWIFE, CHIPS).

Without a great deal of supplementary theorizing about the processes operating on such a representation at the retrieval stage, it is difficult to see how Kintsch could account for Garnham's results. Garnham's experiment is an interesting one, suggesting as it does that what is remembered is a *model* of the situation described by the sentence, rather than the sentence itself or some propositional analogue of it. Kintsch makes the propositional analysis of text the very heart of his theory, claiming that it forms the basis of all text representation. Our view is that Kintsch's claim is probably wrong in that his propositional structures are essentially text-based. Garnham's examples illustrate this well. Of course, at one level it is true that *any* coherent representation (capable of being implemented and used in processing) can be framed in a propositional format — including a situational model. But this has little to do with Kintsch's text-based propositional analysis.

The theory also gives no explicit answer to the question of what happens during reading — indeed, Kintsch (1974) clearly states that he is not concerned about these processes, in particular about how 'propositional' parsing takes place, but more with the issue of representation. The theory merely assumes that, during reading, propositions are extracted from the text (with additional 'inferential' propositions, if necessary), and Kintsch cites his findings on the relation of the number of propositions in the text-base to reading time as evidence in support of this. However, complexity in terms of propositional content could correlate with other forms of complexity, as discussed earlier. Another problem is that there is no algorism for partitioning a text up into propositions. However, even if a system for doing this could be designed, it would still be pointless if the final representation should be a model and not a text-based propositional system, as Garnham's results suggests.

Kintsch's account was initially tested using rather short passages — sometimes only single sentences. When more complex materials are considered, such as stories with characters displaying goal-directed behaviour, his account seems even less adequate. For instance, in a standard fairy story, a knight hearing that a maiden has been captured by a dragon may be expected to carry out goal-directed behaviour to rescue her. Expectations cannot be handled by Kintsch's (1974) system. In the theory which follows, some attempts to get around these problems are introduced.

C. Story- and Text-Grammars

Linguists and anthropologists have noted that various cultures seem to have conventions about what is expected to appear in a story, and these conventions comprise formulae for the composition of folk-tales (e.g. Colby, 1972; Lakoff, 1972a; Propp, 1968). Psychologists have recently shown some interest in such structures. Rumelhart (1975) has argued that the conventions

74

of story construction can be formalized as a phrase-structure grammar, just as phrase-structure grammars can be written for sentences. Thorndyke (1975b; 1976) has used a set of grammar rules based on Rumelhart's to parse stories, and he has related the results of parsing to memory, with some apparent degree of success.

1. A sample story-grammar

The grammar consists of a set of re-write rules defining various components, the first one being:

Rule 1. Story → Setting + Theme + Plot + Resolution.

This can be interpreted as 'A story is a setting, a theme, a plot, and a resolution'. These components themselves are defined by the other rules of the grammar; Thorndyke's 10 rules are given in Table 4.1.

Table 4.1   A set of grammar rules for simple stories (from Thorndyke, 1977b).

Rule No.	Rule
1	Story → Setting + Theme + Plot + Resolution
2	Setting → Characters + Location + Time
3	Theme → (Event)* + Goal
4	Plot → Episode*
5	Episode → Subgoal + Attempts* + Outcome
6	Attempts → $\begin{cases} \text{Event*} \\ \text{Episode} \end{cases}$
7	Outcome → $\begin{cases} \text{Event*} \\ \text{State} \end{cases}$
8	Resolution → $\begin{cases} \text{Event} \\ \text{State} \end{cases}$
9	$\left.\begin{matrix} \text{Subgoal} \\ \text{Goal} \end{matrix}\right\}$ → Desired state
10	$\left.\begin{matrix} \text{Characters} \\ \text{Location} \\ \text{Time} \end{matrix}\right\}$ → Statives

→   Can be rewritten as.
( )   Content optional rather than necessary.
*   Could be more than one of these.

$\left.\begin{matrix} \\ \\ \end{matrix}\right\}$ Alternatives.

Rule 2 defines what is meant by a setting — it is the introduction of the characters, the location, and when the story is anchored in time. Rule 3 defines the theme, which is an optional series of events leading up to a goal. Rule 4 defines the plot as a series of episodes each of which is a cluster of actions

(Rule 5) representing a subgoal plus a series of attempts to satisfy the subgoal plus an outcome. The definition of episodes in terms of subgoals and attempts is important because it captures the goal-directed nature of many folk-stories. An attempt at realizing a subgoal may be direct, or may involve other subgoals, as in Rule 6. So, to rescue a damsel (main goal), a knight may need to find a way of doing this (another subgoal subsidiary to the first). The grammar rules allow for this kind of nested structure.

The outcome of any episode (Rule 7) is either a resulting state or another event. If the outcome is a failure to realize the goal, an additional attempt may occur within the episode. If it is a success, the episode is terminated and the result utilized. The resolution (Rule 8) is the statement of the final result of a story with respect to the theme. Rules 9 and 10 speak for themselves.

From this description it is clear that the grammar is largely a way of expressing a particular configuration of goal states together with attempts to realize the goals. It therefore appears to be a good description of many real-life situations. The application of the story-grammar produces a hierarchical structuring around the goals and subgoals in a given story. As an illustration, Figure 4.4 shows the result of applying story-grammar rules to the 'Circle Island' passage shown in Table 4.2.

Table 4.2.

Circle Island

(1) Circle Island is located in the middle of the Atlantic Ocean, (2) north of Ronald Island. (3) The main occupations on the island are farming and ranching. (4) Circle Island has good soil, (5) but few rivers and (6) hence a shortage of water. (7) The island is run democratically. (8) All issues are decided by a majority vote of the islanders. (9) The governing body is a senate, (10) whose job is to carry out the will of the majority. (11) Recently, an island scientist discovered a cheap method (12) of converting salt water into fresh water. (13) As a result, the island farmers wanted (14) to build a canal across the island, (15) so that they could use water from the canal (16) to cultivate the island's central region. (17) Therefore, the farmers formed a pro-canal association (18) and persuaded a few senators (19) to join. (20) The pro-canal association brought the construction idea to a vote. (21) All the islanders voted. (22) The majority voted in favour of construction. (23) The senate, however, decided that (24) the farmers' proposed canal was ecologically unsound. (25) The senators agreed (26) to build a smaller canal (27) that was 2 feet wide and 1 foot deep. (28) After starting construction on the smaller canal, (29) the islanders discovered that (30) no water would flow into it. (31) Thus the project was abandoned. (32) The farmers were angry (33) because of the failure of the canal project. (34) Civil war appeared inevitable.

The numbered 'propositions' in the table correspond to the numbers in the hierarchy in the figure. The *horizontal* lines connecting propositions designate a single event or state expressed by two or more mutually dependent propositions. At the third line of the hierarchy the main goal is expressed (propositions 13 and 14, 15 and 16). Subgoals to *convince senate* and *pass vote* are subsidiary and appear at lower levels in the hierarchy. The hierarchy can be

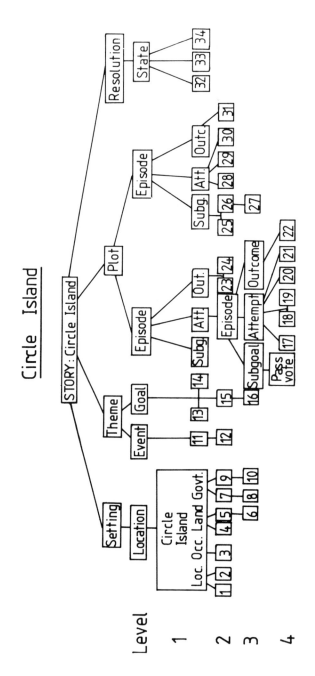

Figure 4.4 Hierarchical structure for the Circle Island story resulting from a story grammar analysis (after Thorndyke, 1977b).

seen to result both from grammar-rule dependencies *and* from semantic dependencies of the kind suggested by Kintsch (1974). Thus the main goal appears in 13, 14, 15, and 16:

Prop. 13. As a result, the farmers wanted
Prop. 14. to build a canal across the island
Prop. 15. so that they could use water from the canal
Prop. 16. to cultivate the island's central region.

The rationale is that (13) and (14) are part of one 'idea' and appear at the same level in the hierarchy, but (15) is dependent on (13) and (14), and (16) is dependent on (15), so this is reflected in their levels in the hierarchy.

Now this formulation seems to capture 'gist' in some ways. The numbers on the left-hand side of the figure show hierarchy levels where segments of the text itself are present. Thorndyke's contention was that the higher levels should be most readily remembered, and portray something closer to the gist than the lower levels. So a recall based only on level 1 might be:

'An island scientist discovered a cheap method of converting salt water into fresh water. As a result the farmers wanted to build a canal across the island. The project failed and the farmers were angry. Civil war appeared inevitable.'

This summary captures the main goal, its enabling condition, the outcome, and the consequence.

Thorndyke explored the relationship of memory for the Circle Island story (and another, called 'The Old Farmer') with levels of their components within the hierarchy. For both stories his basic hypothesis was confirmed: recall was indeed better for parts of the stories higher up in the hierarchies. In another phase of the experiment, subjects were asked to produce *summaries* from memory, emphasizing only the important parts of the passages which were high up in the grammar hierarchies. Such summaries were shorter than the recall protocols, and as with van Dijk (1975), the conclusion was that recall consists of a summary plus some additional detail.

From these data it would appear that the grammar provides a basis for describing gist, and that memory is for gist plus detail. The use of goal hierarchies in the description of these stories goes beyond the simple view of gist as the top levels of text-based propositional trees.

Up to this point we have found two rules which seem to work to establish gist. The first, based on Kintsch, would say that, in descriptions, dependent propositions are less important than those on which they depend. The second, exemplified by the goal-based results of the story-grammar, suggests that main goals are more important than subgoals. Rules of this type have been described by Rumelhart (1975) in the form of a set of summarization principles, although the details have not yet been worked out and tested adequately on human subjects.

A similar line of research is due to van Dijk (1975; Kintsch and van Dijk, 1978). van Dijk refers to the process of using summarization principles as the application of *macro-operators*. He sees a text as having a microstructure, in which all the propositions are represented as a network, and a macrostructure, based on generalization and deletion rules. The macrostructure represents gist, and is used in summary production and recall. Like Rumelhart, van Dijk lists several such macro-operators, and provides analyses of memory results based on his own text-grammar which are broadly consistent with the claims the rules make. The problem with both approaches is that they are essentially of a preliminary nature, and have not been examined sufficiently closely at the empirical level for any distinguishing aspects to be appraised.

2. Story-frames and the comprehension process

Certainly, some pieces of discourse can be characterized by story-grammars or (more generally) hierarchies of goals, although it is not clear to what extent any particular formulation would have advantages over any other: the story-grammar presented here can be seen either as a complete parsing system or as a convenient way of expressing goal-based relationships. What is clear is that Rumelhart (1975), and more explicitly Thorndyke (1975b, 1976), see it as a parsing system. The idea is that when people read a story they parse it into the syntactically defined categories of the grammar. Let us examine this claim more closely, since it carries with it obvious implications about the process of comprehension itself.

Thorndyke (1975b, 1976) suggests that the grammar rules can be looked at as a frame structure in Minsky's sense. Since people are familiar with the situation *read a simple story*, they are alleged to have a frame to represent this situation. The terminals of the frame have *slots* like any other frame, and these slots are said to be the syntactic categories of the story. So, once a reader knows that he is in the *read a simple story* situation, the story-frame is called up, and demands its slots for *time, place*, and *characters*. Each one of these slots would have selection rules for possible values — for instance, the *character* would have to pass the *animacy* test. Similar arguments might be made for the other components of the story.

Thorndyke argues that if structural information in stories is used to construct plot frameworks into which particular events of a story are mapped, then the extent to which this information can be used should influence comprehension and memory. He manipulated the availability of structural information in a number of ways, and examined the effect the manipulations had on ratings of comprehensibility and on recall. In the *story* conditions, subjects read the story as it would be normally presented, and they were asked to recall as much of it as possible at some later point. The other conditions were aimed at steadily reducing the amount of story-like structure in the text. Thus, in the *narrative-after theme* condition, the main statements of theme were removed from their natural place in the text and (after slight modification) replaced near the end of the text — so that subjects could only get the point of the story at the end. In the third condition, he simply left out the theme altogether *(narrative-no theme)*. As a further condition, Thorndyke altered the orderings of the various sentences making up the passage, preserving only clarity of nominal and pronominal reference — the *description* condition.

In the recall test, he found a regular decrease in the amount of the text subjects could recall as the restructuring conditions progressed from story to description, as shown in Figure 4.5.

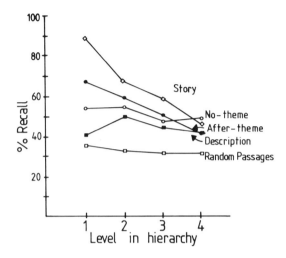

Figure 4.5   Recall probabilities for propositions of the Circle Island passages as a function of location in the organizational hierarchy (after Thorndyke, 1977b).

Furthermore, the relationship of recall to level in the hierarchy deteriorates. These results are taken by Thorndyke to mean that there is something about the standard story format which aids recall, making it superior to other layouts. It also appears that at least some of these effects are due to processes occurring at the time of reading, since providing the theme at the end *(narrative-after theme)* resulted in performance which was inferior to that obtained by providing theme information in its natural place. Consistent with this interpretation, Thorndyke found that the rated comprehensibility of the poorly structured passages was poorer than that of the story-format passage.

On the basis of these observations, Thorndyke makes the claim that when the *story* versions are presented to subjects, they activate a general frame for 'stories', and instantiate the slots in the frame with incoming propositions from the text. In the case of the *narrative* passages, no global story-frame can be used, and the reader has to rely upon local 'causal' links or simple temporal ordering. Comprehensibility suffers as a result. From the memory point of view, the story-frame is seen as a better retrieval structure than local links, because the frame holds everything together in a way which relies upon pre-established rather than arbitrary connections.

To the extent that human beings seem to produce gist representations that are based on goal structures, and can separate settings from the action, and one episode from the next, it would appear that the story-frame idea is capturing something which is important. The frame is a knowledge structure in the mind of the reader, and not in the text itself, and the reader uses the structure to interpret the text. However, no-one has yet related the operations of a story-frame to the way text is processed, sentence by sentence, in enough detail to enable any particular theory to be verified.

Story-grammars are portrayed as parsing the text into propositional structures. As such, they do not explain results which seem to imply that what is remembered is a *model* of the situation (as in the work of Anderson *et al.* (1976), Garnham (1979), and Bransford *et al.* (1972)). In this way, they do not capture the nature of the final representation properly. This a serious deficiency, although it does not detract from the analytic work on summarization which is part and parcel of the general approach. So, while the text-grammar approach does not provide a solution to the problem of how text is represented in memory, it provides an interesting analysis of certain aspects of the gist problem.

D. Schema-Based Theories of Comprehension and Memory

The story-grammar was called by Rumelhart (1975) 'a schema for simple stories'. The word schema is used in the same sense as Minsky's expression 'frame', and has a considerable history in cognitive psychology. We shall use the word schema to describe the variants of the frame hypothesis.

Schema-based theories of comprehension and memory are based on the assumption that the world is understood by being interpreted in terms of schemata. Thus, our examples of football-match frames, room frames, and story-frames are all variants on this basic principle. Schemata, as knowledge structures, are supposed to be used at various stages during reading and recalling. The ideas on the page are supposed to call up schemata which relate the ideas to one another; Schank and Abelson's (1977) script examples, described in the previous chapter, being one instance of such a process. Theorists invoking schemata as explanatory devices therefore assume that the final (meaning) representation in memory is in terms of the interactions of the words on the page with the schemata used in interpretation. Furthermore, the ideas in a person's mind during the act of recall, perhaps fragments of text, can serve to call up schemata at this point. Consequently, under some conditions, recall may include schema-based information not actually present in the discourse itself but nevertheless compatible with the discourse. Such errors were observed by Bartlett (1932), and were explained by him (albeit somewhat loosely) in terms of schemata acting at retrieval. At the time of writing, the most explicit schema-based account of memory is that of Schank and Abelson.

The memory representation of a story can be considered at both a microscopic and macroscopic level. So, at the microscopic level, for Schank (1975) a story would be represented as a causal chain connecting each conceptual dependency representation of the events and states making it up. Schank and Abelson introduce more macroscopic ways of looking at the representation. They suggest that when scripts are invoked, the script in full is not incorporated into the story representation. Instead, elements of the story which match the script are simply represented as a tag indicating which main scene of the script was used as the basis of understanding. In this way, the details of a description of a 'normal' ordering scene in a restaurant script would be represented as 'ordering' together with a tag indicating the script to which the ordering belongs. In this case, the act of ordering is only one of the various events which make up the complete ordering scene, but it is the *main* event, or MAINCON (main conceptualization) as Schank and Abelson call it. This form of representation provides a ready-made account of how details may be forgotten, and gist remembered, in a script-based comprehension system. At recall, all that would be found would be the MAINCON pointer to the script, so memory would either be for the gist or would be reconstructed as the basis of the stereotyped element of the script. This reconstructive aspect is exactly the same as the argument made by Bartlett (1932) when he noted how people tended to produce stereotyped errors in remembering, especially after long delays.

It can be argued that the MAINCON formulation is not at all arbitrary. The actions of a script can be thought of as goal structures, and the MAINCON the action which is the topmost goal of the hierarchy. So, in the *ordering* scene, all actions other than ordering itself are subsidiary subgoals enabling the act of ordering to be carried out — calling a waiter, for example. In this way, Schank and Abelson's formulation is a specific version of the idea that main goals are closer to the 'gist' of goal-based discourse than are the subgoals enabling the main goal to be realized. The psychological reality of this was illustrated in the previous section.

A second aspect of this theory deals with events and actions which do not fit the script in the predicted way. Since such deviations cannot be matched directly to the script, they are assumed to be tagged as a 'weird list', and are especially to be remembered by being put explicitly and completely in the final representation.

Bower *et al.* (1979) carried out an investigation having a bearing on the psychological validity of the Schank and Abelson claims. To begin with, they required subjects to produce written descriptions of what goes on in detail during familiar activities. Subjects agreed on the nature of the characters, props, and actions, and the order of the actions, and on how to segment the activities into scenes. Such agreements are, of course, primary requisites of any theory of understanding which is going to use 'stereotyped' scripts. A further series of experiments was concerned with the claims about memory. Texts were produced which narrated actions from various scripts, and subjects were asked to recall these texts. Subjects tended to confuse actions which were stated with unstated actions from the script. A further study was aimed at memory for deviations from scripts — the 'weird list'. For example, a story based on the familiar restaurant script may contain a statement that 'the man at the next table had an epileptic seizure'. In free recall of such passages, subjects showed a higher likelihood of recall for the unusual event than the commonplace script-based events themselves.

These findings are quite compatible with a schema-based theory, and offer particular support for the Schank and Abelson version. Indeed, this particular theory matches up to our initial criteria fairly well. It handles gist and recall patterns (for this type of material) quite well; it is consistent with some known patterns of error in remembering. Furthermore, the account makes obvious contact with a theory of comprehension. Whatever its shortcomings, the fact that the computer implementation of an understanding and summarizing system based on these principles has been carried out indicates that it is a coherent model.

It may be objected that in our discussion we have not considered Garnham's (1979) finding which was so damaging to text-based views of representation. With the present system, the answer should lie in the script itself. A script for cooking chips should have 'frying' as one of its MAINCONS, so 'fried' should be a good retrieval cue for the sentence 'The housewife cooked the chips'. If anything, the problem should be how to explain the fact that it is a cue for the retrieval of the *original* sentence incorporating the original verb ('cooked'). It is difficult to know how a script-based system can handle this, unless the claim is made that some surface retention remains.

A further issue is that not all understanding is script-based, as Schank and Abelson have argued themselves at length in their book. However, even with stories that are goal-based, it can be argued that many will invoke scriptal knowledge at various points. Furthermore, since scripts can be viewed in terms of goals, it would appear that the main summarization rule being invoked is one in which principal goals are remembered over subsidiary goals.

Numerous others have put forward arguments similar to those described above, but without providing so much explicit detail. It is implied in Bartlett (1932); Minsky (1975) argues that memory representations should be thought of as instantiated frames, and Norman and Bobrow (1975) argue along similar lines. What is required are details of how the process works in human beings in some example situations.

E. Kintsch and van Dijk's Model

An account by Kintsch and van Dijk (1978) has recently appeared which represents an attempt to link text-processing to memory in a broad way. Their account contains many interesting ideas, and a description of it is worth considering in some detail because it outlines a number of issues which are important in text-processing.

The argument they put forward presumes that text-processing begins with the abstraction of propositional information from the text itself. Superficially, this sounds very much like the system outlined in Section B — rather than writing *The students complained*, Kintsch and van Dijk would write (COMPLAIN, STUDENTS). However, it would appear that Kintsch and van

Dijk intend the capitalized 'predicates' and 'arguments' to denote rather more than mere word concepts — a view which, as we demonstrated earlier, is inadequate. To quote, 'For example, COMPLAIN is merely the name of a knowledge complex that specifies the normal use of this concept, including antecedents and consequences'. Beyond this they do not go, but at least they open up the possibility of the 'proposition'[1] going beyond word concepts alone. We shall return to this later.

Secondly, they assume that all propositions so abstracted from the text are processed, and end up in the final memory representation. They conjecture that the processor works by reading a limited number of propositions into a memory buffer of limited capacity. These become connected to the propositions still residing in the memory buffer after the previous sample was taken — connection occurring through argument repetition. If argument repetition fails, then the processor is assumed to search through long-term memory for a representation containing an argument of the same kind: that is, a referential search takes place. With continued cycles, the buffer becomes full, and earlier propositions are lost from it, although they have a certain probability of being retained in long-term memory. The result of this cyclical process is that the propositions of the discourse become linked as a coherent, connected structure.

At each cycle, the assumption is that a number of propositions are selected to be held over for the next cycle. The selection depends upon which are important — also, the more times propositions are selected for inclusion in the buffer, the greater the strength with which they are supposed to be stored in long-term memory. Obviously, the selection should depend on 'gist', since gist propositions are more likely to be of use in providing arguments for integration with subsequent inputs. One selection principle which Kintsch and van Dijk suggest is that propositions which connect to many others are likely to be important; another is to select propositions which occurred recently, since much of reference is to recently presented things in good discourse. Regardless of how it comes about, Kintsch and van Dijk argue that it is the number of cycles a proposition is in the buffer that is a determinant of its probability of being recalled.

Clearly, Kintsch and van Dijk have not produced a process model, but what they have done is to bring out some of the issues involved in developing one. However, there are problems with many of the suggestions they make. Consider, for instance, the idea that the 'propositions' are possibly made up of knowledge structures other than words. If this is the case, then it is difficult to see why they should be called propositions at all. If the elements of the 'propositions' are frames of some sort (which Kintsch and van Dijk suggest they might be), then the pseudo-propositional format could be potentially misleading. Thus, if 'The housewife cooked the chips' is to be considered as having a model-based representation in which the main action is *frying*, it is difficult to see how this could be encapsulated in an expanded version of (COOK, HOUSEWIFE, CHIPS). Such a model could not be embodied in the separate frames for COOK and CHIPS (should such exist), but is a composite of the two which has no obvious representation in the propositional format. Until the issue of what the fundamental building-blocks might be is resolved, the pseudo-propositions could denote practically anything. This is clearly at the heart of the problem of the comprehension process.

Beyond this, Kintsch and van Dijk have made an intuitively plausible account of the operations of a limited-capacity memory buffer, although if the 'items' in it are pseudo-propositions, it is difficult to appreciate what kind of limited capacity it might have. We shall return to this issue in a later chapter, since a limited-capacity buffer does seem to be an important characteristic of cognitive information-processing in general, and can explain a variety of linguistic phenomena.

F. Summary: The Relationship of Memory and Comprehension

It is clear that memory studies have a strong bearing on language comprehension. They indicate something of the nature of the final representation which is the result of the process of understanding. It has long been recognised that memory is for 'gist', and throughout the bulk of this chapter we have attempted to describe systems which have something to say about what gist might be in terms of information-processing. Arguments about the details of method notwithstanding, it may be possible to characterize a number of processes entering into the summarization:

(1) Main propositions in descriptions are nearer to the idea of gist than their dependents.

This, of course, raises the problem of ways of determining what 'main propositions' are. If comprehension proceeds by mapping text input into situational models, then main propositions may be given *a priori* by the situational model itself. This is discussed in more detail in Chapter 8.

(2) Main goals are nearer to the gist than are subgoals which form part of the instrument used to realize main goals.

The general problem here is to determine what is a main goal. In a simple story like 'Circle Island', this does not appear to be much of a problem. Principal goal information is generally given at the start of simple stories. If it is not, comprehension and memory are both known to suffer (Thorndyke, 1975b, 1976). Accordingly, it might be argued that for any particular story, the convention is that main-goal information is introduced early. The important thing about this idea is that such a convention would enable subsequent information to be *interpreted* in terms of a schema called up by the principal goal statement. In terms of a limited workspace account of integration (e.g. Kintsch and van Dijk, 1978), such a process could very well reduce the amount of material which had to be held in working memory before being integrated into a schema-based structure.

(3) Main actions in stereotyped situations are nearer the gist than the details of the actions.

This can be interpreted as a specific version of (2), since the actions in stereotyped situations are after all carried out in the service of resolving goals.

How these three principles operate together in complex texts remains to be seen. For instance, the story-grammar analysis combines principles (1) and (2), and so should enable tests of the relative importance of them to be established. At present, no analysis at this level of detail has been carried out to the authors' knowledge.

Doubtless other principles enter into summaries, be they more basic or more specific. More specific and detailed analyses are given by Rumelhart (1975) and van Dijk (1975), but the details have not been explored in any thorough experimental way in their work.

Whether or not 'gist' is extracted at the time of reading, or later, probably cannot be answered simply. In reading anything other than the shortest piece of discourse, many separate episodes may be encountered. It may therefore be surmised that memory for earlier episodes will have a 'gist' representation and memory for very recent material a fuller representation. Kintsch and van Dijk (1978) imply that this is the view they would take. However, few of the models give a blow-by-blow account of how the gist memory representation is actually built up. Schank and Abelson's account does go through the processing involved in some detail, but has very little in the way of psychological experimentation to back up its details. Kintsch and van Dijk's account has the appearance of a process model, but the conditions under which the macro-operators actually function are unclear. It seems unlikely that these problems will ever be solved by memory studies alone; a more direct approach to the moment-by-moment process of comprehension is called for. Perhaps a convergence between the results of such an analysis and the results of experiments on memory for text would then be possible.

The other set of results which emerges from the memory studies to which we would like to draw the reader's attention concerns the basic *form* of a memory representation. Several of the studies described suggest that the representation is not text-based at all, but is some sort of model of a world to which the text is referring. Various demonstrations of this are quite convincing (Kintsch (1974); Thorndyke's (1977) work on inferences; Bransford *et al.*'s (1972) work on recognition memory errors; the work on cued recall by Anderson *et al.* (1976) and by Garnham (1979)). The value of this point of view is well illustrated by the studies to be reported in the next part of the book, in which on-line aspects of comprehension are examined more closely using empirical procedures.

Note

1. In this section all references to propositions should be considered as being in inverted commas.

Part 2

Introduction

In the first section our aim was to review some of what is known about semantic representation as it relates to human knowledge. It began with some rather general considerations of the sort of information that has to be incorporated in a semantic representation; this led to more specific suggestions about the organization of semantic knowledge in the context of discourse comprehension. The review was in the main theoretical; the only empirical basis for the majority of claims was from simulation of natural language comprehension in computer systems. While the outcome of exercises in simulation cannot of course be ignored by psychologists, their main value is to set the general limits on theories of *human* comprehension rather than to pick out any specific theory.

In Chapter 4 a more experimental approach was taken with the review of work on memory for discourse. However, as we were at pains to point out, there is a wide gap between the process of understanding something and the process of subsequently recalling it, and to this extent at least, the memory studies lack any real precision when it comes to differentiating theories of comprehension. Thus, the first section of the book can be seen as defining the prerequisites of a psychological account; giving the ingredients without a recipe.

In Section 2 a somewhat different approach is taken. This is to confront the reading process directly by giving a very detailed experimental analysis of one particular part of it, that of resolving reference in text. While this may at first seem rather limited in scope, we will argue that reference resolution in all its forms constitutes the cornerstone of successful comprehension in terms of the reader's task of building an appropriate mental model of what is being said. If one can understand how reference is resolved, then an understanding of other parts of the general comprehension process will follow automatically.

In Chapter 5 a framework is set up for looking at simple anaphoric reference, and we consider some of the approaches to the problem which are already available in the literature. Chapters 6 and 7 constitute an extension of this preliminary analysis with a detailed investigation of reference to things previously implied (Chapter 6) and reference to things explicitly mentioned in the prior context (Chapter 7). This will include a detailed analysis of the processes called for in the interpretation of pronominal reference. Although these chapters are primarily directed towards the reference issue, there will be many occasions when other more general issues like those discussed in the first section will be considered. In fact, in many respects the second section of the book presents a reanalysis of what has already been discussed but in the context of a circumscribed problem — reference — and with the aid of experimental procedures which monitor the moment-to-moment processing decisions made by human readers.

In Chapter 8 an attempt is made to pull together all the observations on reference resolution into one general processing framework for text. It is then possible to reconsider the varied claims discussed in Section 1 in the context of a unified account of comprehension and at the same time suggest a variety of predictions which seem to follow from this account.

CHAPTER 5

Reference Resolution and On-Line Processing

In the first part of the book the emphasis has been on the mental representation of knowledge and how this relates to a reader's memory for the gist of a text. Little has been said about what happens in the mind of the reader during comprehension. The time has come to turn our attention directly to this problem.

Those who investigate the structure of text are in a position to consider the text as a whole and derive the suprasentential relationships in terms of the total product. From a reader's viewpoint the situation is somewhat different. He can only encounter the text sequentially sentence by sentence, yet each sentence encountered will be related in some way to the previous material. Much of the reader's task in comprehension beyond the sentence is therefore in trying to determine these relationships between what is currently under interpretation and what has been interpreted already. But before one can look at the nature of this process, it is first necessary to characterize the types of intersentential relationship that seem to be important.

In any text, there are a wide variety of relationships between the sentences which correspond to different levels of complexity in interpretation. At the lowest level is the explicit repetition of noun-phrases between one sentence and the next. For example:

(1) Mary went shopping yesterday.
(1′) Mary bought a coat.

Possibly the most complex are relationships which depend upon the reader's knowledge of the situation described, for instance:

(2) Harry felt terribly ill.
(2′) Jill called for the doctor.

Here there is no repetition, yet the two sentences are clearly related through the events which they describe. When people feel ill they commonly consult a doctor. Between these two extremes there is a spectrum of relationships of intermediate complexity, but the vast majority of them come about through some form of referential repetition, or so-called anaphora. It is this latter type of cohesive relationship which will be the basis for discussion in this chapter. Relationships dependent solely on the events described will be considered in the next chapter.

Cohesive relationships in text have received considerable attention from certain linguists (notably Halliday, 1967a,b; and Grimes, 1975), with perhaps the most influential discussion coming from Halliday, with his distinction between Given information and New information. We will therefore begin by summarizing Halliday's conclusions.

A. Given and New information

Halliday starts off his analysis by drawing a distinction between two types of information conveyed within any sentence of a text. One type he refers to as 'Given' information, in that it seems to relate in a direct way to what has come before, and the other as 'New', in that it is being introduced in the text for the first time. He goes on to suggest that the 'Given — New' partition can apply to any sentence in a discourse and is signalled both in its syntax and intonation. To take a simple example, the sentence 'It was Mary who left' seems to break down into Given: 'Someone left'; and New: 'The someone who left was Mary'. So one would expect to encounter such a sentence in a context where one already knew someone had left, but did not know that it was Mary. In other words, it would serve as a natural answer to the question 'Who was it that left?'.

The way in which the partition is signalled is unfortunately rather complicated. However, the general rule appears to be that anything receiving primary stress is treated as 'New' information, the rest of the sentence being treated as 'Given' (Halliday, 1967a; Grimes, 1975). It may seem odd that one could then say that the written sentence 'It was Mary who left' makes *Mary* New information, since assigning primary stress is an option available to the speaker. However, a brief look at the rules of stress assignment should make the situation clearer.

When someone utters a sentence he has to assign some intonation contour to it, and it is necessary that each contour (point between pauses for breath) carries with it at least one primary stress point which normally comes at the end. This means that if one wants to stress something, one usually arranges to have a contour ending over the point to be stressed. Thus, if a speaker wants to stress every word in a sentence he makes a pause between each word, whereas if he only wishes to stress the final noun he makes a pause at the end of the sentence, and so on. But this still does not explain how *Mary* in our example comes to be stressed. In order to do this we have to consider how one normally makes pauses when reading aloud.

To grossly oversimplify, we can take it as a rule of thumb that one pauses between clause boundaries when reading aloud, so assigning primary stress to the final component of each clause. Now if we go back to our example, we see that this is naturally read as 'It was **MARY**// who **LEFT**//, meaning that **MARY** and **LEFT** are given stress, and so treated as New information, whereas 'It was' and 'who' are not given stress, and so treated as Given. The 'someone' underlying 'It was' and 'who' is known, but that 'Mary left' is not known. Note that one could alternatively say 'The person who **LEFT**// was **MARY**//' and still have the same effect, but not produce it with the simpler sentence 'Mary **LEFT**'. So, one way in which text cohesion comes about is through this system, which seems to point to the part of a sentence which should relate to prior context and the part which should not.

Stress assignment, however, is only part of the story. In written text we also rely on syntactic signals to indicate Given and New, perhaps the most prominent example being the use of the signals for anaphora. Anaphora, which comes from a Greek root meaning 'carrying back', occurs whenever a pronoun or pronoun-like element is used to identify the reference to something which has been previously introduced into the text. To take a simple example, in sentences (3) and (3') below the phrase *the bus* in (3') is anaphoric on the phrase *a bus* in sentence (3).

(3) A bus came trundling down the hill.
(3') The bus nearly flattened a pedestrian.

Clearly, any such anaphoric reference will have to fall within the Given information in the sentence. This means that the variety of anaphoric elements in text, such as pronouns or definite noun-phrases, can also serve as cues for the partition into Given and New.

We are now able to summarize Halliday's conclusions and see how they relate to cohesion. He is suggesting that part of the structure of discourse has the function of indicating what should be recoverable from context as opposed to what is being freshly introduced. Furthermore, he argues that this structure is derivable from both the stress assignments and the syntax of the sentences in question. This conclusion leads to the attractive idea that a reader or listener is able, simply on the basis of an initial syntactic analysis of any sentence he encounters, to know what it is in the sentence which relates it to the prior material. In fact, this idea has been formalized by Clark and Haviland (1977) into an explicit model of cohesion processes.

B. Clark and Haviland's Theory of Bridging

The core of Clark and Haviland's account is the idea, most clearly stated by Grice (1975), that a speaker and listener have an implicit communication contract which depends upon the Given-New structure of the language. Clark (1975) argues that the speaker and listener utilize this distinction in the following way. The speaker must agree to try to construct his utterances so that the Given information contains things that he believes the listener already knows and so the New information is in fact new to the listener; the listener for his part tacitly agrees to interpret the sentences as if the speaker were trying to do this.

This means that in interpreting any sentence, the listener first identifies the Given and the New, realizes that he is expected to know about the Given already, and so searches back in his memory for something to match it. When he finds the matching information, this is then set up as antecedent to the particular piece of Given information in the current sentence.

Such a strategy will, of course, handle the simple cases of anaphora, since the presence of the definite noun-phrase indicates to the reader or listener that he is dealing with Given information, and so should search for an appropriate antecedent.[1] The interesting case arises when in discovering an antecedent the reader has to make a bridging inference or implicature. To illustrate this, consider the following pair of sentences:

(4) Mary unpacked the picnic things.
(4') The beer was warm.

On encountering the second sentence the reader will discover that *the beer* is Given information, and so set out to find some antecedent. There is, however, no direct mention of beer in the preceding sentence, so the reader will have to make a bridging inference of the following sort: beer is an example of picnic things, therefore the antecedent for beer is one of the picnic things mentioned in sentence (4). Such a bridging inference would not, of course, be necessary with the matching pair of sentences:

(5) Mary unpacked *the beer*.
(5') *The beer* was warm.

This suggested to Haviland and Clark (1974) a way of empirically testing their ideas about bridging inferences. If their account were correct, one would expect that it would take longer to comprehend a sentence such as (4') in the context of the sentence containing only an indirect antecedent than to comprehend the identical sentence (5') in the context of a direct antecedent. To test this prediction they presented the two sentences in succession, and required the subject to press a key when he had understood the second sentence. By measuring the time from presentation of the second sentence to the time that the subject pressed the key, they were then able to obtain an estimate of comprehension time. The results were in line with the prediction. When the subjects had to make a bridging inference, comprehension time was reliably increased by about 200 msec.

However, as they pointed out, the results are open to a much simpler alternative interpretation. Whenever there was a direct antecedent present, the critical phrase in the following sentence contained a repetition of the noun, whereas with the indirect antecedent this was not the case. Perhaps it was simply the repetition which accounted for the reading-time advantage. To rule this out they carried out a similar experiment but with slightly different materials, an example of which is illustrated below:

(6) Tom wanted an *alligator* for Christmas.
(6') The *alligator* was his favourite present.

(7) Tom got an *alligator* for Christmas.

(7') The *alligator* was his favourite present.

As has been pointed out by Chafe (1972), verbs like *want* in sentence (6) have the unusual feature of not presupposing the existence of their objects. You can want something which does not exist. As a result of this, the phrase *an alligator* in sentence (6) does not necessarily set up a direct antecedent for subsequent anaphoric reference. So in interpreting sentence (6') in the context of (6) one needs to make a bridging inference to the effect that the alligator, which was Tom's favourite present, was in fact the one which he had wanted, and presumably received as a present. This sort of inference is not necessary in the case of sentence (7'). Haviland and Clark therefore argued that such materials should show the same comprehension time difference as those used in their earlier experiment, even though the critical noun is repeated in both cases. Yet again, they found a comprehension-time advantage for the condition with the direct antecedent.

This is good evidence that making referential bridging inferences takes up processing time, and that they are handled at the time of encountering the critical sentence. But how do readers go about making such inferences? We have already seen how the Given - New distinction could be used to tell us that some sort of inference is called for, but it tells us nothing about how we make the correct one. Perhaps the most straightforward type of inference is found in the case of noun-phrase anaphora. Consider, for instance, sentences (8) and (8'):

(8) *A bus* came trundling down the hill.

(8') *The vehicle* nearly flattened a pedestrian.

The noun-phrase *the vehicle* in (8') maps onto the earlier mention of *bus* in (8). In order for it to do so, it has to bear an appropriate semantic relation to the antecedent. In this case, we can note that the term 'vehicle' denotes a set of entities of which the antecedent 'bus' is a member. However, we could also have (9) and (9'), in which the antecedent is 'vehicle' and the anaphor 'bus':

(9) *A vehicle* came trundling down the hill.

(9') *The bus* almost flattened a pedestrian.

Although such an arrangement is slightly less common, it still maintains the anaphoric relation.[2] It would seem therefore that the relationship between anaphor and antecedent is one where *either* the antecedent or anaphoric noun-phrase denotes a member of the set of entities denoted by the other. In other words, the two should be semantically coextensive (see Stenning, 1975, 1977 for a fuller discussion). This means that for a reader to process a sentence such as (8') or (9') he must presumably retrieve the information that 'a bus is a vehicle'. The fact that the reader has to do this affords us a way of empirically checking the 'bridging inference' hypothesis.

As we have seen in Chapter 2, psychologists have for some years been interested in the way in which class membership information of this sort is stored and retrieved from memory, and in the process of their investigations they have found that the time it takes to retrieve such information is quite variable. It seems to depend critically upon the relationship between the instance of a class and the class itself. Instances that are readily thought of as being members of their class are retrieved more rapidly than those which are not. Battig and Montague (1969) derived a set of norms by giving subjects a list of categories such as vehicles, toys, etc., and requiring them to list exemplars of the categories which came to mind. Some exemplars were frequently listed, whereas others were only put down rarely. So, for instance, for 'bird' a common exemplar would be 'sparrow' and a rare one 'goose'. Following Wilkins (1971), we will refer to the common instances as sharing a high conjoint frequency (HCF) with the category and rare ones as having a low conjoint frequency (LCF).[3] When a subject is asked to retrieve class membership information in a verification task, conjoint frequency turns out to be a very good predictor of how long it will take. Thus, if someone is required to say 'true' or 'false' to a statement such as 'A sparrow is a bird', it takes considerably less time than for a statement such as 'A goose is a bird' (Wilkins, 1971; Rosch, 1973). The difference in verification time depends upon retrieval operations (Sanford and Garrod, 1975; Sanford and Seymour, 1974). In other words, it takes less time to retrieve information about the relation between an HCF exemplar and its category than an LCF exemplar and its category.

The present authors were able to capitalize on this fact to examine accounts of the kind described by Clark. If one needs to retrieve class membership information in making a bridging inference, then presumably having to retrieve information about an LCF pair should slow down the bridging process. Consider the following sentences:

(10) *A goose* would sometimes wander into the house.
(10′) *A robin* would sometimes wander into the house.
(11) The bird was attracted by the larder.

Sentence (11) should take longer to read following on from (10) than from (10′).

It was argued that if a conjoint frequency effect emerged in the reading time for such sentences, then this would support the idea that bridging inferences of this sort were made at the time of reading (Garrod and Sanford, 1977, 1978). In order to get an estimate of reading time, 16 sets of sentence pairs were produced with high or low conjoint frequency exemplars serving as antecedents for anaphoric reference, and for each pair an appropriate question was made up. The subjects were then presented with the materials one sentence at a time, using a computer-driven display device which allowed the subject control over the presentation time. Every time he pressed a key the next sentence would appear. When both sentences had been presented in this fashion the question would appear. At this point the subject would press one key for an affirmative response and another for a negative. (See Figure 5.1 for a diagrammatic description of the time course of any trial.)

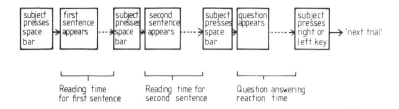

Figure 5.1   A schematic representation of the time course of any trial in the self-paced reading-time experiment.

By using this procedure, the authors were able to obtain an estimate of the reading time associated with the critical anaphoric sentence in the context of either a high or low conjoint frequency antecedent. The reading times from a number of such experiments were in line with the prediction. Reading a sentence which identified an HCF antecedent was faster by about 90 msec than reading one which identified an LCF one. This was true whether the anaphoric phrase contained the superordinate term or the instance. Furthermore, the magnitude of the conjoint frequency effect was not affected when the antecedent and anaphor were separated by two sentences in the text. For the details of these and other related studies we refer the reader to Garrod and Sanford (1977), and to Kennedy (1979) for replication and expansion of this work.

These results are quite consistent with Clark's suggestion that at the time of reading the reader creates referential bridges to connect information marked as Given with that already available from the context. But will Clark's account really handle the majority of cases where the reader makes such inferences?

The problem is that even though syntactic signals in a sentence do force one to look for antecedents to Given information, the reader often seems to infer connections in the *absence* of appropriate Given - New cues. To illustrate this, consider a case where an indirect reference by association is made (Clark, 1975). Take the following sentence pair:

(12) Tom entered the room.
(12') He walked over to the window.

The reader will identify *the window* as Given, and so set up a search for an antecedent. The outcome of this search is to create the bridge:

(12″) The room mentioned has a window.
This is the antecedent for the window.

However, even if (12') had read 'He walked over to *a window*' we would have made exactly the same inference: that is, we would still assume that the window was in the room mentioned earlier. In other words, even in cases where the syntactic signals do not indicate that the information is Given, the reader often makes the same sort of inference. This observation suggests that Clark's Given-New account is not telling the whole story. There could well be other mechanisms responsible for instigating the referential bridging inferences which give a text its cohesion.

C. Alternatives to Clark's System

Creating a referential bridge must always be a function of both the available contextual information and the form of particular sentence which is being processed. At one extreme, the syntactic form of the sentence may be critical for initiating a backward search for antecedents that are not immediately apparent, but in many cases this need not be so. In the examples which Clark has highlighted, the reader or listener is seen as looking back through the memory representation of the text in order to try and make sense of what he is currently interpreting. The immediate sentence has posed problems while the context holds the solution. However, it is equally appropriate to look at some cases of referential bridging from a different standpoint. In much the same way as a sentence may presuppose some antecedent, it is often the case that a text puts limits on the interpretation of what is to follow. This is most clearly seen in conversation, where what follows a question is usually to be interpreted as serving as an answer (see Schegloff, 1972). However, there are many less extreme cases where context constrains the interpretation of subsequent material. For instance, if we go back to the example of the room and the window (Sentences (12) and (12′)), the fact that the room has just been mentioned automatically constrains the interpretation of *window* to be a window in that room, whatever its syntactic environment, unless it is *explicitly* stated otherwise.

This suggests that in league with the operation of Clark's 'Given-New' strategy there may be a semantically controlled bridging process driven by the context in which the reference occurs. Before going into more details of how such a process could operate, we will consider some experimental evidence suggesting that a reader goes through the steps of testing for bridges even in the absence of the appropriate syntactic cues for 'Given' information.

As was pointed out above, one of the initial steps in making anaphoric bridges is to check that the potential antecedent bears the right class membership relation to the anaphoric reference. The conjoint frequency effect revealed by reading time gave empirical support for this step in the process. Now, if it is true that the bridging processes may be initiated independently of a syntactic analysis of the sentence, then we would expect to see conjoint frequency effects even in cases where the reference is not syntactically marked as anaphoric, since the class membership check will be carried out nevertheless. To test this prediction, Garrod and Sanford (1977) carried out a further pair of reading-time experiments with a modified set of the materials based on those used in the earlier experiment. In the first experiment there were two conditions, both using the same set of context sentences. The first condition was designed to replicate the earlier experiment, and so would consist of sentence pairs like (13) and (13′) below:

(13) A $\left\{ \begin{matrix} \text{bus} \\ \text{tank} \end{matrix} \right\}$ came trundling down the hill.

(13′) A pedestrian was killed by *the vehicle*.

However, in the second condition, the critical sentence contained a mention of the superordinate term but it was not syntactically marked as anaphoric, as in the example pair (14) and (14′):

(14) A $\left\{ \begin{matrix} \text{bus} \\ \text{tank} \end{matrix} \right\}$ came trundling down the hill.

(14′) It nearly smashed into *a vehicle*.

According to the Given-New account, we would not expect a check for class membership with tank or bus and vehicle in this case, since the syntax would not be such as to initiate it. However, if the mention of a vehicle in the context is sufficient to make us predict some subsequent mention, we might well expect to find evidence for semantic checking in sentence (14′). In other words, if the syntax rules out searches for referential bridges one would expect to see a conjoint frequency effect only for the first condition, whereas if it is not sufficient to rule out the search one would expect it in *both* conditions. The results from a variety of such experiments indicated that one does get a conjoint frequency effect in *both* conditions, suggesting that the syntax is *not* sufficient to block context-driven checks for semantic relationships between what is currently being interpreted and what has just been read. (See Table 5.1 for a summary of the results.)

Table 5.1 Reading times for the second sentences containing a potential anaphoric reference for high or low conjoint frequency antecedents, either in the syntactically favourable environment or without syntactic cues.

	Hi	Lo	Differences (msec)
With syntactic cues	1.383	1.480	97*
Without syntactic cues	1.348	1.394	46§

*$p < 0.025$.
§$p < 0.05$.

However, an alternative explanation of the results can be considered in terms of a different mechanism. It could be argued that the conjoint frequency effect does not result from an inference-making procedure at all, but is due in at least some degree to a 'priming' effect at the word level. There is now ample evidence that it is easier to read a single word if it has been preceded by an associate (e.g. Jacobson, 1973; Meyer *et al.*, 1975), and that preceding sentences make it easier to read words related to the concepts which they introduced (Kennedy, 1975). Since high conjoint frequency exemplars may prime their categories more than low conjoint frequency ones (which may be thought of as weaker associates), the conjoint frequency effect might conceivably emerge from differential priming (Sanford and Garrod, 1975; see also Sanford *et al.*, 1977 for complications, however).

Two results run against this argument. First, there is evidence that with a delay between two associates, or with an intervening activity, the resultant priming effect diminishes (Meyer *et al.*, 1975). However, Garrod and Sanford (1977) carried out a repeat of the basic antecedent-anaphor experiment but with an interpolated sentence, like the triple indicated below:

(15) A vehicle came trundling down the hill.

(15′) It had had a brake failure.

(15″) The $\left\{ \begin{array}{l} \text{bus} \\ \text{tank} \end{array} \right\}$ nearly flattened a pedestrian.

The conjoint frequency effect was not diminished by this procedure ruling out a simple priming explanation. It could, of course, be argued that when a concept is currently being used (e.g. being referred to by the *it* in sentence (15′)), other associated concepts have representations of words relating to them maintained in a primed state ready for use (e.g. *bus* or *tank* in sentence (15″)). However, this argument can be ruled out by a final experiment. The stimulus materials were non-coreferential, but each category in the second sentence was qualified by an adjective in such a way that the noun-phrase no longer served as superordinate to either of the instances in the context sentence — for example:

(16) A $\left\{ \begin{array}{l} \text{tank} \\ \text{bus} \end{array} \right\}$ came roaring round the corner.

(16′) It nearly hit a horse-drawn vehicle.

In this case no reliable conjoint frequency effect was observed. Now it can be argued that the word 'vehicle' should be just as well primed in this condition as in any other, and that the absence of a conjoint frequency effect rules out a word-priming explanation of the results.

To reiterate the conclusions to date. Clark's account of integration requires a processor to parse the sentence of current interest into its Given-New components and search back through the text representation for an antecedent to the given components. In the present authors' anaphora experiments, the evidence suggested that in a case where syntactic devices clearly indicated a noun-phrase to be *New* information, a check was still made to see whether it matched a semantically related noun-phrase antecedent. This shows that a syntactic parsing into Given-New is not the whole story where anaphora is concerned. That semantic relations are implicated is suggested by the fact that only when the non-coreferential noun-phrase is *unrelated* to an antecedent (e.g. *tank* and *horse-drawn vehicle*) does the conjoint frequency effect disappear.

D. Context-Motivated Bridging Processes

In the previous section it was argued that Clark's Given-New model could not in itself account for how and when the reader builds inferential bridges between information mentioned at different points in the text. It was suggested that such a system would need to be augmented with a context-driven process. However, there was no discussion of how such a process might operate.

The essential difference between an account such as Clark's and the one which is being entertained here may be expressed in terms of a contrast between data-driven and concept-driven processes. With an interpreter working in the data-driven mode, any decisions about how events mentioned in the current sentence can be related to previous material only arise as a result of the local analysis of the sentence in question. When interpretation is concept-driven, however, decisions, and sometimes potential inferences which could relate to the event, may be made even before the critical sentence is encountered.

The utility of either way of processing is very much a function of the payoff between computation and stored structure, similar to that mentioned in Chapter 2 in the context of cognitive economy. This can be illustrated with reference to the example given earlier of someone 'entering a room and going over to the window'. It may be more economical on computation for a processing system to represent the concept 'room' as some sort of decomposition which actually contains information about windows directly, so in a sense 'predicting' any reference to window (c.f. Minsky's frames, Chapters 2 and 3). In this way the processor would have made the bridge already, on encountering the initial sentence in this example. Of course, the extent to which the reader's mental representation of such concepts does embody this kind of direct decomposition of meaning is an empirical question.

A number of investigators have been interested in whether decomposition is an automatic process (as entailed by a conceptually driven processor), or whether it only occurs when necessary. A popular testing-ground for such investigations has been the study of sentence memory and reading time. Compare the following pair of sentences:

(17) John is accused of stealing.
(18) John is guilty of stealing.

Kintsch (1974) argued that (17) is more complex than (18), since (17) would be decomposed into something like:

(17') Someone says that John is guilty of stealing.

Because (17) is more complex ('propositionally') than (18), Kintsch argued that it should be more difficult to read, taking longer, and should be more poorly remembered. However, sentences like (17) and (18) did not show any differences either in reading time or in memorability. From this, Kintsch (1974; 1977) concluded that the representations of single sentences are not in the form of decompositions, but are rather stored as undecomposed 'propositions' literally reflecting the sentences themselves.

Such an argument is bedevilled with problems. It is based on the assumptions firstly that decomposition of any kind takes time, and secondly that more complex structures are harder to retain in memory than simpler structures. We shall refer to these assumptions as the 'complexity' theory of decomposition, following the nomenclature of Gentner (in press).

Gentner has paid particular attention to the first assumption. She contrasts the complexity theory with an alternative *connectedness* theory. While the first equates ease of remembering with the structured simplicity of the representation, the second equates it with how well connected in the representation are the various entities mentioned in the sentence. Let us take the following illustrative sentences:

(19) Ida *gave* her tenants a clock.
(20) Ida *mailed* her tenants a clock.
(21) Ida *sold* her tenants a clock.

The verb *gave* in (19) is simpler than either *mailed* or *sold* in terms of decomposition. Thus *gave* entails a change in possession of the clock (*from* Ida *to* tenants). *Mailed* entails not only a change in possession, but also a further specification of mailing (apply mail routine with source: Ida, object: clock, goal: tenants). *Sold* is more complex too, entailing not merely a change in possession of the clock (*from* Ida *to* tenants), but also a change in possession of money (*from* tenants *to* Ida). Thus *gave* is the simplest verb; but there are other differences between *mailed* and *sold*. According to Gentner, with *mailing*, Ida is the agent: with *selling*, Ida is the principal agent of the whole act, but is also the agent of transferring possession of the clock. However, it is the tenants who are the agents in transferring possession of the money. So, while *mailed* and *sold* are both more complex than *gave*, the *sold* representation has many more connections between Ida and tenants than does the *mailed* representation. Gentner refers to the three types of verb as 'general' (e.g. *gave*), 'specific with few connecting paths' (e.g. *mailed*), and 'specific with many connecting paths' (e.g. *sold*).

Gentner carried out a cued-recall experiment using materials of this type. Subjects read lists of sentences containing the three sentence types, and were later presented with the subject noun of each sentence. Their task was to recall the remainder of the sentence. According to Kintsch's (complexity) theory, if decomposition occurs, then sentences containing simpler 'general' verbs should be remembered better than sentences containing the more complex specific verbs. If decomposition does *not* occur, then there should be no differences as a function of verb type. According to the *connectivity* theory, the predictions are quite different. Recall is assumed to depend upon the number of connections between the various parts of the sentence (Ida and the tenants in our example). So *if* decomposition occurs, the simpler 'general' verb sentences should be *less well* remembered than specific highly connected verb sentences. Also, sentences containing specific but poorly connected verbs should be poorly remembered, but no more poorly than general verb sentences. Again, if decomposition does not occur, there should be no differences.

Gentner's results produced a pattern indicating that decomposition *did* occur, but also provided support for the connectivity theory. It is not complexity which determines ease or difficulty of recall, it is connectedness. Of course, Kintsch did not make this distinction when he constructed his materials, which almost certainly explains why he did not find evidence for decomposition. All in all, the refinements of argument and technique introduced by Gentner lead to the view that even when single sentences are read, decomposition occurs.

In what way could a contextually driven processor utilize decomposition in resolving problems of reference? In order to clarify how a contextually driven interpreter might work, we need a theory about the kind of text representation system which could incorporate decompositions of this kind. In Chapter 3 we have already seen examples of decomposed representations in discussing the theories of both Roger Schank and Rumelhart and Norman. It is in the very nature of Schank's conceptualization that on the basis of an ACT as stored in the verb-ACT dictionary there is a decomposition of word meaning. For instance, if one looks at the formulation of the conceptualization underlying the sentence 'Mary dressed the baby', it would contain the following:

1. Mary transfers *clothes* to baby
2. Baby changes from *not-clothed* to *clothed*
3. . . . .

Although clothes have never been mentioned, the conceptualization would have incorporated into it a slot which predicts that clothes were involved. So, if one were to take a similar sentence 'Mary put the baby's clothes on', it would only differ in its underlying conceptualization by replacing the implicit presence of clothes with the explicit presence of clothes.

We shall return to distinctions between explicit and implicit information shortly. For the present, however, note that in bridging terms, this means that the bridge between (22) and (22′) below could have been made *before* even encountering (22′), since it is already built into the conceptualization underlying (22).

(22) Mary dressed the baby.
(22′) *The clothes* were made of pink wool.

Using the reading-time procedure it is an easy matter to convert this speculation into an experimental prediction. Since we already have evidence that bridge-building operations can be detected in the reading time of the critical sentence, we can see whether or not they can be detected in these instances.

The critical test of the conceptually driven inferencing arises with a comparison of the reading time for sentences like (22′) either in the context of the *stated* antecedent or with only the *implied* antecedent. This is as shown in Table 5.2.

Table 5.2.

Stated Antecedent
Mary put the baby's clothes on.
The clothes were made of pink wool.

Implied antecedent
Mary dressed the baby.
The clothes were made of pink wool.

If, as we have been suggesting, the antecedent entity 'clothes' is already represented as part of the decomposition in the implied antecedent condition, we would expect *no* difference in the reading time for the critical sentences in both conditions, since no extra bridging operations would be necessary. However, if there are only data-driven bridging processes operating, this condition should lead to substantially longer reading times. (N.B. In Clark's earlier experiments, effects of 200 msec were reported.) An experimental test with a wide variety of such materials revealed no evidence for any such reading-time effects. Only a 7 msec difference was detected (with a standard error of 18 msec); this is clearly nowhere near what was to be expected if extra bridging operations had been involved. So here we have evidence for the operation of context-driven bridging in the case of antecedents implied by verbs.

Now this result raises a further interesting problem. Is it really the case that it makes no difference whether a writer states the antecedent explicitly or merely opts to leave it implied? At the level of text representation, there are two ways in which clothes may be implied. The representation could contain a default value for 'clothes', or it could contain an empty slot indicating where they would fit into the whole conceptualization if mentioned, but no more than this. The slot can be thought of as embodying a series of tests which examine the new text for concepts which could act as slot instantiations; clothing-like entities will all fit the bill, probably with 'clothing' itself being the first thing checked for, but other things, such as specific instances of clothing, being equally acceptable.

The use of 'slot' *versus* 'default' devices really reflects a difference in philosophy about processing. If one assumes that the role of the mental representation is both to augment the explicitly mentioned information by incorporating unmentioned but highly likely entities in events and at the same time to further specify the explicitly mentioned entities, then defaults are clearly called for. This conception of processing leads, among other things, to the instantiation hypothesis described by Anderson *et al.* (1976) for example. A person who is outstanding in the theatre is by default an actor, for instance. Alternatively, it is possible to think of the mental representation purely in terms of its interpretative or model function. In this case, the processor uses the model to specify the role of entities or events, but only when they are actually encountered in the text. In other words, it indicates where explicitly mentioned things fit into the whole conception of the text rather than further specifying their nature. For the reasons given in the preceding chapters and taken up in Chapter 8, we tend to favour the latter alternative.

It might be helpful to think of the 'slot' alternative as analagous to a situation where one can refer to entities in the immediate perceptual environment during conversation. If, say, two people are conversing about a room in which they are sitting which contains a table, it is possible for them to refer to 'the table' directly. The perceptual environment contains a slot 'table'. However, if there is no mention of the table, no information about it will be registered in either participant's representation of the conversation. In much the same way, if one encounters 'dressing' in the text, this will enable direct interpretation of 'the clothes' when subsequently mentioned without otherwise requiring them to be represented in the mind of the reader. In other words, it is suggested that the *domain of reference* can be extended to include certain entities implied by the verb, since there is now an interpretative framework available for these entities in the representation it evokes.

If, on the other hand, one takes a sentence like 'Mary put the baby's clothes on', the representation is going to be somewhat different. In this case, it will contain information *about* clothes; they will be represented explicitly since they are part of what is being talked about. Further discussion of the theoretical distinction between implied entities in an extended domain of reference and explicitly introduced entities will be left for Chapter 8. However, let us now consider one of the empirical outcomes of such a distinction.

If, after explicit reference to clothes, there is a subsequent reference to 'the material', it is now possible directly to make 'the material' dependent on the instantiated clothes, with a relation something like 'belonging to'. However, if no explicit mention has been made of the clothes, but they have merely been represented implicitly through a slot in the frame for the verb *dressed*, then the reader cannot make 'the material' dependent upon anything; there are no concepts there for it to depend on. Therefore, if one encountered the two sentences:

(23) Mary dressed the baby
(23′) The material was made of pink wool

one would have to make the bridge:

(23″) The baby was dressed with specific clothes, the antecedent for material is the clothes put on the baby, the clothes are made of the material.

Of course, the first part of the bridge would not be needed if the clothes had been explicitly mentioned. Again, this idea is amenable to experimental test through reading time. All we need do is compare the implied-*versus*-stated antecedent differences under conditions where there is a subsequent reference to a possible dependent concept, for instance with materials of the sort shown in Table 5.3.

Table 5.3.

Stated context
[Mary put the baby's clothes on.]

Implied context
Mary dressed the baby.

Target
  A The clothes were made of pink wool.

  B The material was made of pink wool.

We have already seen that there is no measurable reading-time difference for the target A under the two contexts; however, with targets like B we might well expect to find a difference associated with the extra step involved in forming bridge (23 "). In fact, such a reading-time effect is observed with materials of the second sort, producing a highly reliable advantage for the stated antecedent of the order of 70 msec.

Recently, Carpenter and Just (1977) reported a study on verbs which is similar to this, but which they interpreted somewhat differently. They presented subjects with a set of sentences containing critical pairs of interest. Subjects had to judge whether each successive sentence fitted in with the sentences immediately preceding it. They were interested in the idea that a verb like *murdered* entails an agent (a killer or a murderer) while a verb like *died* does not necessarily entail a killer. They argued that the time to judge (25) would be faster if it followed on from (24') than if it followed on from (24):

(24) It was dark and stormy the night the millionaire died.

(24') It was dark and stormy the night the millionaire was murdered.

(25) The killer left no clues for the police to trace.

The predicted result was obtained. Obviously, the finding is compatible with the general argument we are making: since *murdered* sets up a slot for 'killer', there is no need to construct a backward inference between (25) and (24'). However, in the case of (24), *died* does not have any such slot as part of its representation, and so a backward inference has to be made. In other words, the verb *murder* extends the domain of reference to include a murderer while *died* does not. But Carpenter and Just do not draw this conclusion from their results. They noted that the reading times for (24) and (24') did not differ. From this they went on to argue that a representation of *murdered* with more slots than *died* should take longer to set up at the time it is read, employing a version of the complexity argument: more complex decomposition should take longer. They therefore conclude that decomposition had not taken place but that backward inferencing occurred in both situations, that it was easier following on from (24′) because a slot for *killer* could be set up more directly from *murdered* than from *died*. With *died*, for example, we may suppose that the reader has to infer a method slot, which is instantiated by killer. Only the last stage is required with the verb *murdered*.

This argument is rather weak and unacceptable. In the first place, it is not at all clear why a verb representation rich in slots (e.g. murdered) should be any slower to retrieve from memory and use in understanding than a representation 'poorer' in slots (e.g. died). For instance, if verbs are thought of as simply calling up their schemata when they are encountered, there is no reason to suppose that the complexity of the schemata will influence retrieval time. Indeed, Thorndyke (1975b) found that verb imagery value rather than conceptual complexity correlated with reading time for sentences containing them. For this reason, we suggest that on the basis of Carpenter and Just's data, deciding on concept-driven predictive comprehension *versus* data-driven inferencing is inappropriate. Perhaps more convincing is our own evidence, described earlier, which cannot possibly be explained in terms of a data-driven inferencing process.

E. Summary and Conclusions

We started this chapter by pointing out that a well-written text gives the impression of cohesion, with each part fitting in with what had come before. This cohesion was attributed in the main to the fact that the writer makes repeated references to information recoverable from the prior text. In some cases, the references are to things which have been explicitly introduced; in others, to things which may only have been implied.

In the remainder of the chapter we attempted to build up a psychological account of how the reader is able to map these subsequent references onto his representation of the prior text. The experiments cited initially demonstrated that the mapping process occurs at the time of comprehending the sentence, and is a function of the semantic relatedness of an anaphor and its antecedent. If the anaphor and antecedent bear a low conjoint frequency relation to one another, the reading time is longer than with a high conjoint frequency relation. This conjoint frequency effect proved a useful index of when mapping operations take place, and was used to investigate various accounts of the process.

The most explicit extant model of the process is that of Clark and Haviland, which derives from the idea of a 'Given-New' strategy. They propose that the mapping is instigated through a syntactic analysis of the sentence in question, which partitions it into Given information, recoverable from context, and New information being introduced for the first time. While their account is capable of handling most of the types of anaphora that were considered, it could not explain how the reader seems to infer relations between information not marked as Given and that from prior context. More importantly, it cannot explain why one can detect conjoint frequency effects in a situation where the Given-New analysis should have ruled out attempts to establish co-reference.

We were therefore forced to entertain the alternative idea that the semantic relatedness of information in the representation and that being currently analysed is checked for in the course of interpreting the sentence. This idea can be best understood in terms of the concept-driven processing systems already discussed in Chapter 3. In these accounts, the representation is seen not only as a repository for information from the prior text, but also as a means of controlling subsequent sentential analysis. It was suggested that the control comes about through the reader's ability to utilize substantial frame-like structures as a basis for direct interpretation of the current material. So, for instance, when a verb like 'dress' is encountered this will evoke from memory a representation which contains slots for a variety of entities implied in the meaning of the verb, such as 'clothing'. The effect of having such a representation is to extend the domain of reference available to the reader to include the implied entities.

In the next chapter this line of argument is extended to include much more substantial types of interpretative structure, such as those which might characterize our knowledge of stereotyped situations, and it is suggested that the reader utilizes these structures in order to build up a general background scenario. It is through such a structure that the majority of entities and events mentioned in a text can be interpreted directly.

Notes

1. This is really an oversimplification, since there are certain cases where a definite noun-phrase can be used *de novo*. As, for instance, in generic statements such as 'The elephant is a wise animal'.
2. This kind of anaphora is sometimes referred to as 'cataphora' and is commonly used to introduce something without fully specifying it.
3. It should be pointed out that the conjoint frequency is in no way the same as the word frequency. It is a joint function of the *category* and the *exemplar*.

CHAPTER 6

Scenarios and the Domain of Reference

By now it will be apparent to the reader that there are two quite distinct views of how knowledge might be used in interpreting a text. The first derives from theories in which a text is seen as a sort of supersentence. One such theory, as advocated by Kintsch (1974), and described in Chapter 4, assumes that the mental representation of a text consists of a concatenation of propositions derived directly from its constituent sentences. According to this view, the reader has two tasks: he has to parse the text into propositional units, and he has to connect the resultant propositions in same way. In order to explain how the propositions might be related to an appropriate superstructure, a number of specific proposals have been suggested. For instance, in the case of simple stories, the story-grammar was put forward as a framework for integrating the various elements in the text. Nevertheless, the dominant characteristic of this type of theory can be found in the limited role that knowledge plays in the construction of the mental representation. Since the major problem for the reader is seen as one of linking together text-based propositions, the predominant mechanism is one of using propositional argument repetition as a means of cohesion. It is only when argument repetition fails that background knowledge is invoked. The most explicit formulation of this aspect of text-based propositional theories was given by Clark (1975) in his account of 'bridging' as a means of linking successive sentences.

The alternative view is that the reader uses the linguistic input to address knowledge directly, in an attempt to find a recognizable episode or setting corresponding in some way to the input itself. This viewpoint has its origin in artificial intelligence and is illustrated in some computer-based understanding systems (e.g. Schank and Abelson, 1977). According to this second view, the reader has two rather different problems. First, he must use the text to identify an appropriate domain of reference, loosely corresponding to what the text is about, and second, he must use the identified domain of reference to interpret the subsequent text as far as this is possible.

Use of such an extended domain of reference has already been demonstrated in the previous chapter. Thus, when a reader encounters the verb 'dress', there was evidence that a reference domain is set up which includes 'transfer of clothes'. So, subsequent mentions of 'clothes' may be mapped directly into this extended reference domain. The supportive empirical evidence was that such a mapping does not lead to any extra processing time over that taken for a mapping onto an explicit antecedent. Of course, extra time would be expected if bridging had to be carried out at the time of encountering the sentence in which 'clothes' were mentioned.

Verb decomposition of this kind serves to exemplify the idea of reference domain. The first (text-based propositional) view of comprehension would hold that the individuals available for direct reference comprise only those which have been explicitly mentioned. On the other hand, the second view would hold that the reference domain consists of those individuals made explicit plus those retrieved from long-term memory as part of the setting for the text, although the latter are only implicit. The argument can be extended readily from a consideration of verb semantics to one of more substantial situational knowledge. Consider frames and scripts. These can be looked upon as extended domains of reference. For instance, if in a program a restaurant script has been invoked, it is used as a basis for mapping entities which are 'new' in the text but predicted by the script (e.g. 'waiter', 'bill', 'tip', etc.).

From now on we shall refer to the account based on extended domains of reference as the *scenario* account, since one can think of knowledge of settings and situations as constituting the interpretative scenario behind a text. Our concern, in this chapter, is to establish the validity of the scenario account as a psychological theory, and subsequently to explore the details of scenario structure and utilization. Before considering the empirical evidence, let us examine the distinction between the two approaches in a little more detail.

So far we have only discussed differences in the way the two approaches handle references to implied entities. On the scenario view, such entities may be represented as slots in a scenario structure, and consequently, if they are subsequently mentioned in the text, they can be mapped directly into the representation. According to the inferential bridging account, no such direct mapping could occur since there is no prior representation of entities not explicitly mentioned; in order to interpret the reference, inferential bridges would have to be built. But this argument can be extended even further. If scenarios derive from knowledge, then they must consist of more than just a list of entities pertinent to the situation which they model. They must also capture the particular relationships which normally hold between these entities in this context. For instance, in some settings, entities are commonly linked through a predictable sequence of actions. Thus, in a restaurant, the 'waiters', 'customers', 'food', 'bills', 'money', etc., interact in well-known ways. This must be represented as the *programmatic component* of any scenario which corresponds to the setting 'restaurant'. The utility of such a component was made clear when describing Schank's scripts in Chapter 3. Having a script enables Schank's program to interpret actions in the text introduced for the first time but predicted in the script. Furthermore, if events were encountered which did not fit in with these predictions, then the nature of the mismatch between prediction and actual mention could serve to initiate meaningful searches of knowledge in order to relate these events to the remainder of the text (see Schank and Abelson, 1977). In other words, when a scenario fails to account for an input, the nature of this failure may be used to restrict the possible bridging inferences.

As in explanation of simple reference resolution, the difference between the scenario account and the bridging account lies in when knowledge of actions is called upon. As far as the scenario account is concerned, a certain amount of action knowledge will be represented in any invoked scenario (that is, it will be 'given'). As for the bridging account, appropriate knowledge will be sought only when it is needed, i.e. when the action is encountered. Indeed, a very extreme version of the text-based propositional theory need not have to deal with the coherence of actions at all. Provided the propositions could be connected by argument repetition, quite contradictory actions could still be concatenated in a connected structure. In contrast, the scenario-based theory would identify contradictory actions as incompatible with the current scenario.

A third difference between the two accounts is somewhat more subtle. If entities mentioned are identified with representations of them in scenarios, then those entities will be effectively acting in a role. For instance, if it is made clear that the appropriate scenario is of 'an operating theatre', and the reader encounters 'John made an incision with a scalpel', then *John* should be assigned to the 'surgeon' role, not the 'patient' role or the 'anaesthetist' role. If this does indeed happen, it should cause comprehension problems when the reader later encounters sentences portraying *John* either as someone other than a surgeon, or as doing something which is incompatible with being a surgeon. A text-based propositional theory would not have this apparent limitation. *John* would not be cast in a scenario-based role because there would be no scenario in which to do this.

These three issues form the basis of the first part of this chapter. In it we shall examine the empirical predictions which follow from the general claims made above. Later we shall consider some of the special problems associated with a scenario-based view of comprehension.

A. Scenarios: Implications for Human Comprehension

1. Scenarios and the domain of reference

It has been shown that verbs seem to invoke mini-scenarios (decompositions) with their consequent predictive properties. However, these alone will not go far in explaining the general problem of inference and use of background knowledge which has been alluded to throughout the book. As those working on computer simulation soon found, much more extensive background knowledge has to be utilized than that springing from the semantics of complex verbs. To illustrate this, we can imagine what might happen when one reads a newspaper article reporting a court case.

In much the same way that the verb *dress* evokes a slot for 'clothing' as part of its structure, so a *court-case* article might evoke a wide variety of entities such as *lawyers, a judge, a jury*, and so on, which need not be explicitly mentioned. We might think of all these as part of our background knowledge constituting the scenario behind a court case. After all, if a sufficient number of these entities were absent, one would not think of it as a court case at all. Furthermore, just as predictions can be made about the ease of referential mapping for information in the structure of a verb scenario, so it is possible to do the same sort of thing here. One would expect that introducing some entity such as 'the lawyer' for the first time in a text about a court case would not instigate time-consuming bridging processes. One should be able to carry out the mapping directly.

To test this prediction, the present authors performed a further reading-time experiment (Garrod and Sanford, 1980) designed along similar lines to the verb experiment reported earlier. The rationale was straightforward. If one could present passages which evoke a well-defined scenario such as a court case, then there should be no measurable increase in reading time when an entity implied by the scenario is introduced. If, on the other hand, a different scenario has been evoked, one should record a slower reading time for the same sentence due to the extra bridging processes. The predictions are best illustrated with reference to the materials shown in Table 6.1.

Table 6.1.

Appropriate scenario
Title: *In court*
    Fred was being questioned *(by a lawyer)*.
    He had been accused of murder.
Target: *The lawyer* was trying to prove his innocence.

Inappropriate scenario
Title: *Telling a lie*
    Fred was being questioned *(by a lawyer)*.
    He couldn't tell the truth.
Target: *The lawyer* was trying to prove his innocence.

At the top are shown materials for the appropriate scenario condition. The particular scenario is evoked by the title *In court* and reinforced in the second sentence. As part of the structure of the 'court' scenario one would expect there to be a slot for 'lawyer', so the mention of *lawyers* in the first and target sentences would be predicted through the supposed scenario. This, of course, would not be the case in the inappropriate scenario condition. While it is possible to have a lawyer involved in telling a lie, a slot for 'lawyer' is in no way required by a scenario for the situation of telling a lie.

In both conditions there is an option in the first sentence whereby the phrase *by a lawyer* can either be present or absent; we might call this the contrast between an implied and a stated antecedent (following Haviland and Clark's terminology). In line with the arguments given above, one would expect that under the appropriate scenario conditions no differential reading-time effects would emerge for the final sentence, whether the antecedent is implied or stated. However, under the inappropriate scenario conditions there should be a substantial reading-time effect.

Materials of this sort were constructed and the choice of appropriate or inappropriate title checked by giving a group of judges the titles along with the implied entities. The judges were asked to rate how likely it was for this entity to be found in a situation of the sort described by the title. For the appropriate titles the ratings were 90 per cent, and for the inappropriate 34 per cent.

The critical final sentence reading times are shown in Figure 6.1. It will be noticed immediately that the reading-time differences follow the prediction

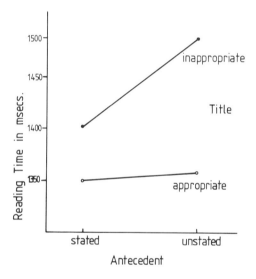

Figure 6.1　Reading times for target sentences which refer to either a stated or unstated antecedent, following appropriate or inappropriate titles.

made by the scenario model. When the title is inappropriate there is a substantial difference between the implied and the stated condition, whereas with the appropriate title a very much smaller, insignificant difference emerges.

The explanation is similar to that which we made for the verb study cited earlier, in that it shows that much information is retrieved by a title and supporting sentences. We suggest that they serve to bring in a scenario. A little later we shall present data which are consistent with the view that such scenarios can be called upon and changed with great swiftness and facility by appropriate linguistic cues. For the present, the thing to note is that the scenario enables references to individuals to be made in the first instance by a definite noun-phrase, because they are already *given* in the representation. Because they are given, they cause neither comment nor difficulty, and rapid pseudo-anaphoric mapping is possible. This is one way in which the scenario representation provides more information than is present in the propositional structure of the text input.

2. Entities and relationships

Insofar as a scenario contains representations of entities relevant to the situation being modelled, it might be thought of simply as a list of those entities. So, a list for a 'court-case' scenario might contain slots for 'lawyers', 'judge', 'jury', and so on. But knowledge of court cases goes beyond this, and certainly includes such very basic relationships as 'Lawyers probe witnesses and the defendants for evidence' and 'The jury evaluates the evidence and gives a verdict', etc. Each entity in the situation plays a specific role. Therefore, it seems a plausible hypothesis that scenarios might be representations not only of entities, but also of the role those entities play in the situation which the scenario represents.

This hypothesis carries important implications. When a piece of discourse calls up a scenario, the entities mentioned in that discourse should be mapped into the appropriate slots of the scenario by an identity relationship. If this happens, any entity will then be understood as playing a particular role. If, subsequently, the mapping is shown to be inappropriate, comprehension difficulties should result.

Consider the following example, introduced in Chapter 1:

(1) John was on his way to school.
(1′) He was terribly worried about the maths lesson.

When asked to say what they know about the key individual John, most people say that he is a schoolboy, yet there is nothing in the text that states this. That this assumption is made while reading these sentences is suggested from the following simple demonstration. If people read these two sentences, they usually find (1″) surprising:

(1″) He thought he might not be able to control the class again today.

If not, following this with (1′′′) is invariably surprising:

(1′′′) It was not a normal part of a janitor's duties.

What seems to be happening in these cases in that the reader has to fit *John* into the most likely slot available in the school scenario, which in this case is 'schoolboy'. Sentence (1″) causes trouble because it indicates that he should be a 'schoolmaster' and (1′′′) because it states that he is *a janitor* after all. None of these problems would emerge if the reader did not initially set up the school scenario, with all its associated roles.

Of course, it could be argued that carrying out conscious-meaning analysis of this type may induce evaluations about the nature of John which are not part of the normal working representation used in rapid reading. However, this question was tackled empirically (Sanford and Garrod, 1980) by using the reading-time technique with materials similar to those shown above. The critical time measure taken was how long the subjects spent on a target sentence in which a role shift was either present or absent, with the object of determining whether such shifts do require time-consuming mental reorganization before a satisfactory interpretation can be achieved.

As a preliminary, an assessment was made of the dominance of a particular role of an individual in a sentence by using a *continuation procedure*. This was carried out by presenting subjects with the sentence of interest and then asking them to write down a further sentence which fitted into the theme of the first one. By analysing the continuations of a number of subjects it was possible to assess the extent to which specific roles were chosen. For example, given sentence (1), all continuations yielding role information about John indicated that he was being thought of as a schoolboy. In the second phase, materials were produced containing a role shift (as in (1″)) or having an antecedent such that the target did not contain a role shift. An example is given in Table 6.2.

Table 6.2   Materials and target reading-time results from the role shift study.

	Reading time (sec)
Condition 1. No role change	
John was not looking forward to teaching maths.	
The bus trundled slowly along the road.	
He hoped he could control the class today (TARGET).	1723
Condition 2. Role change on target	
John was on his way to school.	
The bus trundled slowly along the road.	
He hoped he could control the class today (TARGET).	1893

The results show a distinct advantage in terms of reading time when no role shift occurs. This implies that we are interpreting *John* in our example as playing a *role* in a situation. The important points are that this role is not explicit in the text and that the interpretation must take place quite quickly, since the materials used are so brief.

How is it that such role-assignment takes place? One compelling answer is along the lines of our argument that we use a linguistic input to call up *representations of situations or events from long-term memory* as soon as we have enough information to do so. In other words, a scenario is invoked. Implicit background information would be incorporated within the structure of the initial scenario as part of its definition, while new information from the text would be used to fill partially defined slots available in the skeleton structure, or to otherwise modify it. It will be recalled that one of the features of an event description is that it contains slots for entities such as *agents*, *recipients*, *instruments*, etc. What we are suggesting is that in order to map entities mentioned in a linguistic input onto an event structure in memory, one needs to identify those entities with the slots in the representation. Since many representations will be concrete rather than purely abstract, this will have the effect of putting the entity into a role with respect to that event. Thus, by mapping into a scenario, predictability of the behaviour of a given entity is secured at the same time as preventing a possible interpretation explosion. After all, *John* could be almost any manner of man on any manner of mission. Indeed, to say that we have understood a text, such role-placement seems to be essential, at least for the key actors involved. The problem is, *when* does role-placement take place? The above results suggest it does so relatively rapidly.

Role-assignment has its humorous side. Freud (1952) quotes a joke which is quite pertinent to our argument:

> The prince, travelling through his domains, noticed a man in the cheering crowd who bore a striking resemblance to himself. He beckoned him over and asked:
> 'Was your mother ever employed in my palace?'
> 'No, Sire,' the man replied. 'But my father was.'

The whole essence of this story's logical pattern is based upon the assumed roles of feudal lords (having bastards is normal) and feudal ladies (having bastards is not normal).

If entities mentioned in a text may be mapped into role slots, as the evidence suggests, then the scenario itself must contain relational information, such as representations of actions relating the entities to one another. These actions should comprise the programmatic component of the scenario. In Chapter 4, we described an experiment by Garnham (1979) which lends support to this aspect of the scenario theory. He presented sentences like 'The housewife cooked the chips' to a number of subjects, and later carried out a cued-recall test. He found that the cue 'fried' produced better recall than did the cue 'cooked', even though the latter cue was the word actually used in the example sentence. For this to happen, the original sentence must have evoked a scenario containing a representation of the action frying chips.

Janice Keenan (1978) carried out a study using the reading-time technique which also has a bearing on this aspect of the scenario theory. In the following pair of sentences, it is clear that the state portrayed in (2′) results fairly directly from the event portrayed in (2):

> (2) Joey's big brother punched him again and again.
> (2′) The next day his body was covered in bruises.

In contrast, (2′) can only result from (3) if we can find a suitable path to connect the two:

> (3) Joey went to a neighbour's house to play.

(2′) The next day his body was covered in bruises.

Keenan used sets of materials like these spanning four levels of rated 'relatedness' (how well the second sentence follows on from the first) — an example is shown in Table 6.3.

Table 6.3   Examples of sentence pairs used by Keenan (1978).

Level 1   Joey's big brother punched him again and again.
The next day his body was covered in bruises.

Level 2   Racing down the hill Joey fell off his bike.
The next day his body was covered in bruises.

Level 3   Joey's crazy mother became furiously angry with him.
The next day his body was covered in bruises.

Level 4   Joey went to a neighbour's house to play.
The next day his body was covered in bruises.

She found that reading times for the second sentences decreased monotonically with the assessed level of their relatedness to the antecedent.

It is possible that part of Keenan's results derive from scenario contents. For example, a scenario of a larger child battering a small one may well have as part of it the outcome of the poor recipient being injured. This would speed up the integration of a sentence mentioning bruising. However, this sort of scenario-based prediction must have a limit, and it seems likely that even beyond this limit reading-time differences can be obtained. Thus, Keenan's example 4 gives longer reading times than 2 or 3, although it might be considered far-fetched to assume that 'bruising' slots would be the outcome of any scenario made available by the context sentence. We have already presented some illustrations and an experiment to show that in the case of verbs, the representation for *dress* may contain a slot for *clothes* but not slots for related entities like buttons or zips or material. This does not mean that the scenario is of no value when the reader encounters such related entities; it simply means that a new slot has to be produced to form a bridge between the extant representation and the current input. The amount of processing required to do this will clearly be a function of the relationship between what is already there in the representation and what has to be related. The more complex the inference chain to be produced at the time of reading, the longer the reading time will be.

The results which have been described in this and the preceding sections fit naturally into our second way of thinking about a text. A text serves to set up a search in long-term memory for a model of a recognizable episode or situation (the scenario) into which it will fit. One of the consequences of this is that entities become represented with respect to a certain role — a role which defines the behavioural expectations and limitations of that entity within that scenario. Another consequence is that the scenario will contain representations implying individuals, not explicitly stated in the text, but which form a normal part of the episode and situation. In this way, the field of potential referents comes from two sources — scenario information (which is implicit) and newly input text information (which is explicit). This parallels the situation where a speaker in a conversation is able to refer both to entities previously stated in the conversation and to entities in the immediate perceptual environment, which may, of course, be thought of as a further domain of reference.

B. Scenario Selection and Specificity of Description

In the first section of this chapter we contrasted a view of comprehension based primarily on extraction of a propositional text-base with a view based on seeking out and using substantial knowledge structures called scenarios. It was argued that the experimental results from a variety of studies were consistent only with the scenario-based view and did not favour the, perhaps more parsimonious, alternative. However, it could be argued that we have only concentrated on that side of scenario-based comprehension which is obviously advantageous to the reader. For instance, we have suggested how mental scenarios allow the reader to interpret references to predicted events or entities in a relatively straightforward way, at the same time as providing an effective framework for integrating the different statements in the text. It is with the initial selection of a scenario that the problems arise; once the reader has access to the appropriate knowledge structure, comprehension may proceed easily. But obviously if no such structure can be retrieved or perhaps an inappropriate one is selected, then comprehension must falter. Understanding the mental mechanics of scenario selection is therefore of some importance to any scenario-based theory. Though we will leave detailed discussion of this problem to later in this chapter, we will now consider one issue which does seem to be of some importance in relating language to knowledge retrieval, and this is the form of description used for entities mentioned in a piece of text.

The general line which we take is that it is important when introducing any key entity into the text to do so with a suitably specific description in order to facilitate retrieval of relevant information from long-term memory. We shall begin with a brief outline of what psychologists know about specificity of description.

1. The choice of noun-phrase

For a variety of languages, Berlin (1972) describes five different levels of reference:

(1) Unique beginner	e.g. plant, animal	
(2) Life form	e.g. tree, bush, flower	
(3) General name	e.g. pine, oak, maple, elm	

(4) Specific name   e.g. ponderosa pine, white pine, Jack pine
(5) Varietal name   e.g. Northern Ponderosa Pine

In general, people feel the generic name to be the preferred level to use in referring to an object, and in every language Berlin considered there were more categories at this level than at any other. Rosch (e.g. 1977; Rosch and Mervis, 1975) argues that Berlin's generic level is of fundamental significance because it is the level at which members of the same class bear a high degree of resemblance to each other, while members of different categories bear a very low degree of resemblance to one another. This is based on the premise that objects are perceived in terms of attributes, and attributes tend to be clustered. Objects within a single category usually share perceptual attributes with each other, whereas objects in different categories usually bear little perceptual resemblance.[1]

Rosch *et al.* (1976) examined this issue empirically, and found that by the criterion of how *distinguishable* entities were, generic-level names relate to more distinguishable items than do more specific names. On the other hand, when common attributes are considered, there is a tendency for the amount of overlap between entities to increase with specificity. At the generic name level, therefore, categories have the highest amount of overlap for the smallest loss of discriminability. In this way, Rosch argues that there are good reasons why certain forms of description are preferred over others.

One important aspect of specificity clearly relates to distinguishing the appropriate referent from a field of potential referents. If there is only one car in the family, we could easily say 'The bananas are in the car'. If there are three, we would have to identify the *particular* car, as in 'It's in the sports car' or 'It's in the Volkswagen'. The general rule of thumb suggested is to select the simplest description which distinguishes the intended referent from the implicit set of alternatives (e.g. Clark and Clark, 1977; Grosz, 1977). Indeed, this principle is related to one of Grice's maxims for successful communication (maxim of quantity), in which the communicator be as informative as possible without supplying misleading details. If we think of label selection as being dependent upon first identifying the referent entity, then certain attributes of the individual selected will be more important than others, and these will determine the way in which a label is selected. Clark and Clark (1977) suggest that for many stereotyped everyday situations, the *basic-level* term will be selected (Berlin's generic level).

Such an idea bears a relation to the scenario theory. Suppose a speaker or a writer wishes to refer to 'a tank' which he has in his communication plan. He will probably refer to it as 'a tank' and not as 'a vehicle'. The reason is that the listener or reader will have an idea of the properties of tanks, the sorts of things they can do, the situations in which they are to be found, etc., in his long-term memory. A 'tank' enters into a more *constrained* set of typical situations than does a 'vehicle'. In terms of finding a suitable scenario into which a given utterance can map, we might say that the likelihood of finding one will be higher if a basic-level term is used, because it will be a more effective retrieval cue for long-term memory. Notice that all we are really saying is that, just as in normal conversation an appropriate level of specificity enables the listener to identify the correct referent from a set of alternatives, so in *reading* the level of specificity will influence the probability of retrieving a particular scenario. This argument holds independently of Berlin and Rosch's discussions of the evolution of natural categories, but can be related to it in essence.

The present authors (Garrod and Sanford, 1977) found some evidence for difficulties in reading time which appears to be compatible with the idea that specificity facilitates scenario selection. Subjects had to read a single sentence containing specific (exemplar or generic-level) or general (class or 'life form') noun-phrases. They then had to answer a Yes/No question based on the sentence. An example of a *general* sentence might be:

(4) The vehicle came trundling round the bend

in which case an example of a corresponding *specific* sentence would be:

(4') The tank came trundling round the bend.

Tank in sentence (4') corresponds to the 'generic name', while *vehicle* corresponds to the 'life form' category. On seeing a picture of a tank trundling round the bend, (4') is the form people would normally select to describe the event (Glucksberg *et al*, 1975).

Measures of reading times for sentences like (4) and (4') showed that the specific sentences were read some 188 msec *faster* than the general sentence. This was despite the fact that for this particular batch of materials used, the frequency of occurrence in the language for the specific terms was in fact lower than it was for the general terms. How is one to explain this finding? One explanation is in terms of selecting a suitable scenario — a general term cannot serve to retrieve episode structure of any detail from long-term memory, and therefore is in a sense less well understood. Understanding of a general statement may not go far beyond the explicit propositions of the sentence itself, whereas a specific statement may well be more easily mapped into a scenario rich in default information, serving to facilitate later comprehension. Of course, this is only one view based upon a single piece of experimental data. On the evidence presented up to this point, other explanations are possible. However, when one considers the interaction between specificity of description and anaphora, it is possible to give a more detailed appraisal of the various alternatives.

2. Specificity and ease of reference

It is usual in discourse to introduce an individual at an appropriately specific level, and then to refer to it by less specific descriptions and ultimately by means of a pronoun. In general, the rule is to select a noun-phrase at an appropriate level of description when the individual is first introduced, and on a subsequent mention to refer to it at a more general level. Consider, for example, the following sentence pairs:

(5) A *bus* came trundling round the bend.

(5′) *The vehicle* almost flattened a pedestrian.

and

(6) A *vehicle* came trundling round the bend.

(6′) *The bus* almost flattened a pedestrian.

Given that we read these pairs as though 'vehicle' and 'bus' are anaphoric, pair (5) sounds more natural than pair (6). We might speculate that this is because it is normal to introduce an entity by describing it at the required level of specificity in the first place (as in (5)) rather than further specify it for no apparent reason at a later point (as in (6)). Indeed, the different orderings of *bus* and *vehicle* in (5) and (6) have an effect on how long it takes to read (5′) and (6′). In an experiment using the sentence-reading paradigm and materials like those above, sentences like (5′) were read some reliable 227 msec faster than ones like (6′) (Garrod and Sanford, 1977).

Now there are several interesting explanations possible for this result. The most trivial one, readily dismissed, is to suppose that target sentences mentioning specific noun-phrases are slower because specific noun-phrases tend to occur with a slightly lower frequency of usage in the language than do general noun-phrases. In a previously cited experiment in which the target sentences were read in isolation, those containing specific noun-phrases were read more rapidly. So, the specific target sentences are slower only in the presence of the antecedent context. There are three remaining kinds of explanation. One is that the specific-to-general transition is stylistically acceptable for accidental or historical reasons of usage, while the general-to-specific is not. The less acceptable form may then give rise to slower reading times because people are not used to seeing transitions in that order, and for no other reason. The second explanation is that the specific-to-general transition conveys no new information about the individual of interest at the stage of target sentence. Calling a *tank* a *vehicle* tells us nothing new. On the other hand, calling a *vehicle* a *tank* does tell us something new, and it is quite plausible that the incorporation of this new information into the memory representation of the passage could be time-consuming, and lead to the observation of longer reading times for target sentences in the general-to-specific condition. Indeed, this was the theory which was emphasized in our original analysis of the results (Garrod and Sanford, 1977, 1978; Sanford and Garrod, 1978).

This second view is consistent with the Given-New contract (Chapter 5). To specify something to a greater extent after an initial reference is to mark out new information. This can have amusing consequences — for example, it is perhaps the basis of a form of one-upmanship in which new information is unexpectedly introduced, as in:

(7) Q: I'm hungry; where can I get a meal?

(7′) A: They serve an excellent caviare at Il Tramonto.

Under normal circumstances, the question is not aimed at eating caviare — the new information (mediated through caviare being part of a meal) is that *the answerer eats it*.

There is also a third and very different possibility. Suppose that when we use a noun-phrase initially, a more specific phrase makes it somehow easier to integrate subsequent information which is coreferential than is the case when we use a less specified antecedent. In this case, it would not merely be the introduction of extra information in the target sentence which produced the increased reading time, but the specificity of the antecedent which mattered. The rationale for such an explanation could take several forms. For example, prior mention of a general term, such as 'vehicle', could be thought of as opening up a wide range of potential anaphors ('the entire class of vehicles'), while the use of a more specific term, such as 'tank', might open up a relatively small class of potential anaphors ('vehicle', 'it', and 'the class of tanks'). If part of the mapping process included a matching search between the potential anaphor set and the given anaphor, then the process could take longer for the larger set. Indeed, in tasks demanding the direct evaluation of class-membership statements there is some evidence to suggest that larger classes lead to longer evaluation times (Landauer and Meyer, 1972). Alternatively, we could entertain an explanation of a different kind, based upon the nature of the representation of the initial sentence resulting from specificity differences, as discussed above. A specific term in a sentence, as in:

(8) The tank came trundling round the bend

could lead to the retrieval of a mental scenario embodying default concepts about the behaviour of tanks, the kind of circumstances which might lead to the production of such a situation, etc., using the reader's knowledge of episodes and situations. A less specified individual (substitute 'vehicle' in the above sentence) could lead only to retrieval of a more poorly defined scenario, or even to no scenario at all, with the reader awaiting further information before seeking one. If it is assumed that a well-formed scenario facilitates integration, then we have an explanation for faster comprehension following on from more highly specified antecedents.

These speculations really break into two main classes of potential explanation: the first set ascribes the latency effects to the information content of the critical noun-phrase in the target sentence, and the second set ascribes them to the representations set up by the antecedent. In order to determine which view is the correct one, the authors carried out an experiment in which, rather than simply having general-to-specific and specific-to-general transitions, general-to-general and specific-to-specific were also included (Sanford and Garrod, 1978). If *antecedent specificity* is the critical variable, then the general-to-general transition should be slow like the general-to-specific transition. If the *target specificity* is the critical variable, then the general-to-general transition should be faster than the general-to-specific transition, since in the latter case extra information is conveyed in the target. The details of the experimental conditions, example materials, and reading-time results are given in Table 6.4.

Table 6.4 Sample materials used in the specificity experiment and mean reading times for the appropriate targets in msec.

Condition	Example	Mean target rt
S–S	The vehicle would not get up the hill. The lorry was overloaded. Was the lorry going down the hill?	1493
S–G	The lorry _____ The vehicle _____ Was the lorry_____?	1511
G–G	The vehicle _____ The vehicle _____ Was the vehicle _____?	1567
G–S	The vehicle _____ The lorry _____ Was the lorry_____?	1578

It is quite clear that it is antecedent specificity rather than additional information (target specificity) which is important in determining target reading times. A general antecedent has a relatively retarding effect on reading times for targets, regardless of whether the anaphor in the target is a repeat of the general noun-phrase or a more specific noun-phrase. Obviously, these results cannot be explained in terms of the information of the critical noun-phrase in the target sentence.

Thus far the results are compatible with the scenario explanation, but they are also compatible with an explanation based on the range of potential anaphors. A general term like *vehicle* has many more class members than does a specific term like *tank*. Some additional analyses of the data suggest that this second, lexical-level explanation is inappropriate with the present materials.

The materials used had the critical noun-phrase in two positions — either in the topic position, as in:

(9) The *lorry/vehicle* came trundling round the bend

or in the comment position, as in:

(10) Mrs. Dupont dropped the *carrot/vegetable*.

As we shall argue in the next chapter, there are good reasons to suppose that topics and comments have different functions. Specifically, for the present discussion, topics are generally thought of as being what the sentence is *about*

124

(Hornby, 1972; *vide* Chapter 7). In the context of scenario-retrieval, it may be suggested that the individual the sentence is thought to be 'about' psychologically is likely to be the principal retrieval cue in searching for a suitable scenario.

When the effect of antecedent specificity is examined in the light of a division of materials into topic and comment, the results show that the effect is restricted to individuals in the *topic* position. The mean reading times are shown in Figure 6.2.

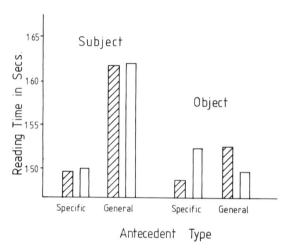

Figure 6.2   Reading times for targets in either topic (subject) or comment (object) position as a function of antecedent description. Cross-hatched bars indicate specific targets, while open bars indicate general targets.

Such a finding enables one to rule out the lexical-level explanation based on the range of potential anaphors. According to this theory the effect should be present, regardless of whether the antecedent was in the subject or the object position. Furthermore, the implication is that the process of mapping one lexical item onto another in anaphors is *independent* of the process producing the specificity effect, since mapping has to occur in both cases but the specificity effect is present in only one of them.

Parenthetically, other evidence can be cited to substantiate these two points. In Chapter 5 we discussed an experiment showing a conjoint frequency effect with materials like:

(11) The $\left\{\begin{array}{l}\text{robin}\\\text{goose}\end{array}\right\}$ was very tame.

(11') The bird would sometimes wander into the larder.

Consider this observation in the light of the idea that a small range of anaphors is produced by a specific antecedent. Since *robin* or *goose* in (11) would be represented in the sentence as *bird*, this being one of the small set of would-be anaphors, we would *not* expect to find a conjoint frequency effect. Of course we did find one, and this fact casts doubt on the range-of-anaphors explanation of the specificity effect. In fact, the magnitude of the conjoint frequency effect was the same regardless of whether the order was specific-to-general or general-to-specific. This too is consistent with the idea that lexical mapping and the mechanisms behind the specificity effect are independent.

3. Specificity and scenarios

If the representation of a text used for comprehension were merely some sort of propositional breakdown of each segment of language input, then one would not expect the pattern of results described above. Whether a lexical item is a label for general class or a more specific exemplar should make no difference to integration time in the case of simple anaphora. In fact, lexical mapping should be easiest when the antecedent and anaphor are the same. This is clearly ruled out by the data. Even an explanation of a more sophisticated kind, involving differential set size, is ruled out by the fact that antecedent specificity only had an effect with the present materials when the critical noun-phrase of the antecedent was in the subject position.[2] We are therefore pressed to consider the effect in terms of a more complex representation of the antecedent, going beyond the superficial propositional content of the sentence. We can now look at this in the scenario terms which were used in the introduction to this part of the chapter. What sort of information is associated with a term like *vehicle*? According to the strong cognitive economy argument (Chapter 2), all general information about *vehicles* will be stored with the *vehicle* node, and only information specific to *buses* would be stored with a specific item like *bus*. However, in Chapter 2 we noted that such a viewpoint was not really tenable. In the first place, to the extent that cognitive economy may characterize the storage of knowledge in human beings, it is only 'weak' economy. In the second place, it is impossible to list all exemplars of a category — some exemplars apparently may not be listed with the category node. Multiple-category nodes seem to be called for. One may know that a gnu is an animal, but may not know (directly) that an animal has as one of its exemplars a gnu. We would like to suggest that in the present context, when a statement about *a vehicle* is encountered only a very limited amount of information is actually accessed in long-term memory. Of course, we cannot say at this stage just what that information might be, but it may be little more than:

Is (vehicle, something to travel in)

Has (vehicle, exemplars (at 103, 104, 105, . . . *N*, and others))

(where the numbers refer to locations of exemplars in memory).

On the other hand, most of us know a great deal about buses, trucks, tanks, etc. Noun-phrases at this level of specificity are the most familiar form of initial description, and we would argue that they have the greater amount of information associated with them. Thus, in order to integrate a new sentence into an existing input about *a vehicle*, or *a specific vehicle*, trundling around the bend, one needs access to the properties of the vehicle, the situations in which it might be found, etc. Many of these properties will be *immediately* available from a scenario based on the specific vehicle, but they will have to be computed on the spot if the general term *a vehicle* has been used. In particular, if both antecedent and anaphor are expressed as *vehicle*, then a general knowledge search, possibly based on the event as a whole, would have to be set up on encountering the second sentence. If the anaphor is a specific term, this may provide another way of accessing the required information, but it will still be utilized at the time of encountering the anaphor, and so will be time-consuming.

Here we should point out a difficulty relating to this interpretation. What does it mean when we say one may have access to a scenario for *a tank trundling around a bend*, but not for *a vehicle trundling around a bend*? While one may well have representations of birthday parties, eating out at a restaurant, or skiing, for most people it seems less likely that one has a specific scenario for a tank trundling around a bend. It is a unique event, not a stereotyped situation. If there is no ready-made scenario, the answer must lie in *scenario construction*.

What one almost certainly does have is a representation of a tank. It will consist of properties of tanks, including tanks on the move, both formal and idiosyncratic. A representation of this kind may be thought of as a *species* of scenario, but an *object* scenario rather than a situational one. However, one can still use the object scenario to constrain one's interpretation of a tank trundling around a bend. What we are suggesting is that this does not make sense with *a vehicle*; not enough extra information is available. So, in the *tank* example, the predominant information available is the properties of tanks; 'trundling around the bend' is secondary.

Such an argument may give a clue as to why the specificity effect only worked with the critical antecedent noun-phrase in the topic position. As we shall see in the next chapter, principal entities in a situation are usually topicalized. Provided the topic noun-phrase is sufficiently specific, it would make sense for the processor to construct or select a scenario based on this, because principal entities will tend to recur in later sentences.

There are a number of other important issues related to the specificity effect when interpreted in terms of scenario construction. With writing in general, not all texts will necessarily draw upon preexisting scenario structures, but they may still be intelligible at some level. For example, when a student first embarks upon a new subject of enquiry, he may have certain key summary propositions brought to his attention. From the point of view of his teacher, each of these propositions may well carry with it complete mental scenarios — networks of implications, unstated individuals, and procedural components. From the student's point of view, he is dealing with bald, superficial propositions. In a real sense, his understanding probably consists of little more than being able to hold these propositions in memory and being able to draw conclusions from them in a syllogistic sense.

In an experiment in which reading times were taken for two passages of equivalent propositional content, and in which an equal number of entities were mentioned, it was found that reading about a familiar topic was easier and faster than reading about an unfamiliar topic (Kintsch *et al.*, 1975). From the present point of view, the problem with the unfamiliar passage may be related to the extent to which parts of the text allow access to related scenario structures in long-term memory. The well-worked material will simply evoke more preexisting scenarios which will then be available to assist integration, and this will give a subjective impression of something which is well understood and familiar. Indeed, the notion that rich memory structures facilitate text integration parallels the oft-made observation that rich representational structures aid the learning and recall of otherwise simple materials, such as paired associates or lists of words (e.g. Bower, 1972). The whole essence of the mnemonic is that a new input (say, a list of words) is mapped into a preexisting memory structure which can itself be accessed easily when required.

C. Scenarios: Their Nature and Some Problems

The scenario is an information network called from long-term memory by a particular linguistic input and, as should be apparent from the preceding discussion, it may vary in complexity. At one extreme the scenario may be very simple, containing only minimal information about an entity or event. At the other extreme, a very rich scenario may incorporate programatic detail about expected sequences of events, default specifications on expected entities, and other explicit constraints which will be introduced in the next chapter. In brief, there should be many varieties of scenario, just as Minsky hypothesized many varieties of frame. However, in all cases the basic principle is one of enabling the knowledge of the reader to be used in such a way as to allow for direct interpretation of entities or events predicted by this knowledge. To the extent that any text conforms to the predictions, it is readily interpreted, to the extent that it does not, it will be more difficult to understand. For a scenario to be of any use to the reader, it must obviously be appropriate for the text being read. But how does the reader select the appropriate scenario?

1. Appropriateness and cues for selection

An appropriate scenario can be defined as one which is going to be of most use in interpreting subsequent text. That is, it has the greatest predictive power. As will be argued more thoroughly in Chapter 9, the success of scenario-based comprehension depends upon the writer employing suitable descriptions to elicit appropriate scenarios at the right time. If this is not done, the reader may select an inappropriate scenario, leading to comprehension difficulties, as exemplified by our example ((1), (1'), (1")) of John the schoolboy/maths teacher/janitor. We shall begin by discussing the kind of descriptions which may lead to the selection of a scenario. To simplify the exposition, consider a case where a scenario is selected in the absence of any prior context.

What would be sufficient to select a scenario representing eating in a restaurant? Suppose one encountered the following statement in isolation:

(12) Barry was feeling hungry.

It would not be reasonable to suppose that this alone would select the scenario. It is too general a statement of Barry's disposition; he could do a variety of things. For example:

• Make a salami sandwich
• Have an Indian meal
• Go to the kitchen
  Etc.

Or we may even learn that he hadn't eaten for a day, or that he was on a strict diet.

Consider another statement of disposition:

(13) Barry wanted a meal in a restaurant.

At first sight, this might look sufficient, because it mentions *restaurant* explicitly. However, once more, a variety of actions are possible:

• He borrowed ten pounds from a friend.
• He settled for a sandwich at home.
• He made a date with his friend for Thursday.
  Etc.

In other words, disposition statements such as these simply reflect goals which may be resolved at some subsequent point in the text. The descriptions do not seem to be specific enough to isolate any particular scenario.

Now let us turn to an isolated description which does seem to evoke the scenario:

(14) The waiter brought the soup.

Such a statement portrays an action which is central to the scenario, and the action involves someone *(waiter)* who fills a definite role slot in it. The crucial thing appears to be that the scenario is singled out by the intersection of these two pieces of evidence. Neither piece of evidence is quite sufficient by itself. For example:

(15) The soup was put on the table.

Such a description again appears to be too general to elicit a scenario representing eating at a restaurant. Similarly,

(16) The waiter smoked a cigarette

is hardly sufficient either. However, (16) does appear to be more constraining than (15). But notice that although it is more likely that *the waiter* is in a restaurant than anywhere else (e.g. at home), any story continuing from this point could be about the restaurant from the point of view of the waiter — for instance, 'the hard life', 'lack of customers', 'after closing', etc. Each of these are just as specific as 'eating at a restaurant', and quite different, although they may have some defaults in common, such as physical setting.

In summary, in order to elicit a scenario, a piece of text must constitute a specific *partial description* of an element of the scenario itself. In the example considered above, it appears that it is important to pick an action from the scenario and a reference to an individual filling a role slot in it. Such a conclusion is similar to that reached by Schank and Abelson (1977) in their discussion of script selection in computer programs.

Beyond this, there are certain psychological issues which have, as yet, received little attention. Certain descriptions of actions are so general as to be applicable to a wide range of situations, and are thus unlikely to be sufficiently selective to call up a particular scenario representing that situation. For instance, 'John opened the door'. Other descriptions may normally only apply to a few, or even one, situations. Accordingly, these would be more likely to select a representative scenario. Which events and roles are central to a situation depends upon the interests of the individual reader. For instance, for a reader keen on horse-racing, a sentence like:

(17) The riders lined up

may be sufficient to call up a 'horse-racing' scenario. On the other hand, for someone less interested in horse-racing, a sentence like the following might be necessary:

(18) The jockeys lined up the horses.

In contrast, for someone interested in foxhunting, (17) could well invoke a foxhunting scenario, while (18) would invoke the horse-race scenario. There are thus two complementary aspects to scenario selection: the specificity of description of roles and actions, and the interests of the reader, which would be reflected in the availability of various scenarios.

2. Discourse-based constraints on selection

The examples given above were treated as selection in the absence of any other information. This is relatively unusual. In most cases during reading, the reader has other information at his disposal, such as the title of the book, previous scenarios encountered in the text, and the unique information provided by the text itself which has been interpreted through the previous scenarios. This additional information provides another constraint in the selection of a scenario: indeed, selection can be viewed as the outcome of an accumulation of evidence from various sources, both from the current text and from the memory structure for previously encountered text. Let us outline two important types of information in the memory structure which assist in restricting scenario selection.

One type of information present in a wide range of texts is that of spatio-temporal setting: it is extremely rare in a text that events are described in the absence of such setting. Indeed, almost all situations are restricted in time and space. A scenario representing 'getting a haircut' will contain default information to the effect that it is during the day, and in a barber's shop, which has a limited spatial area. To illustrate the way in which spatio-temporal constraints restrict the scenarios likely to be accessed, consider the case of people stranded after an air-crash in Alaskan wilderness. Under these circumstances, the sentence:

(19) Barry was feeling hungry

would lead to a restricted set of possible solutions, including, perhaps, cannibalism. Notice that if a person sat down to write a list of ways of satisfying hunger without such a restriction on setting, the chances of thinking of cannibalism would be quite low. If, in the air-crash story, cannibalism had already been mentioned, this information, together with sentence (19), may well be sufficient to invoke a scenario relating to cannibalism.

Characterization is a second type of constraint based on memory representation which is commonplace in stories and novels. For instance, in reading a novel, models are built of the personalities of the people involved just as with learning the character of a newly made acquaintance. The models consist, in part, of representations of predispositions. For example, one of our colleagues regularly lunches in the Department of Psychology on sandwiches. One day he said he was feeling hungry, and that he was going to have an Indian meal. This was sufficiently surprising to cause comment from some others who were present. The expectations associated with him were not met by his stated intentions. A trivial example such as this indicates the way characterization serves to constrain the goal-method possibilities in the memory-representation which one person has of another. With the most rigid personality, it seems likely that feeling hungry and wanting to do something about it may lead to only one expected method of achieving the goal. In other words, although we initially suggested that in general there may be a large number of methods for coping with a given stated goal, in practice there may be rather severe limitations on those which would have any predictive power. Referring to a given character in a piece of writing may serve to constrain the range of possible scenarios which will be called upon. Under some circumstances, the constraint may be sufficient to call upon a single scenario, depending upon how predictable the person is from the way he has already been described. On a view like this, an important part of our memory for a novel is a restricted set of methods for the different characters in different situations.

The evidence we have presented for this point of view is limited and anecdotal. However, there is little doubt that general expectations about people's behaviour limit the information that is typically retrieved from memory. For example, one test of creativity consists in having subjects make lists of the uses of certain well-known objects: for instance, a brick, a milk-bottle, etc. Liam Hudson (1970) describes an experiment in which school-children were asked to complete uses-of-objects tests on three occasions, once as themselves, once role-playing *Higgins*, and once playing *McMice*. A character description was given of Higgins and McMice. Higgins was portrayed as an emotionless intellectual, and McMice as an uninhibited, somewhat shocking, bohemian artist. The children were much more fluent when playing the roles of Higgins and McMice than they were in their own right.

Apart from helping in scenario selection, characterization should also serve to control default assignments in scenarios. For example, if we know that Joe Brown always plays five-a-side soccer on Thursday afternoons, then reading that

> (20) It was Thursday afternoon, so Joe went off to play football

should call up the football scenario with a five-a-side default (even if the reader does not have a special scenario for five-a-side football).

D. Summary

At the outset of this chapter, we contrasted two views of the comprehension process. One we described as a text-based propositional account, in which inference-making only occurred when necessary, and was thus instigated by a currently encountered problem sentence. The other we described as the scenario-based account, in which aspects of the discourse served to identify a specific scenario, representative of the situation of interest and which provided an extended domain of reference. The evidence presented in Section A provided support for this second point of view.

When a scenario has been selected, it is used as an interpreter for incoming text which maps into the role slot and action representations. We shall refer to this direct interpretation process as *primary processing*. If no current scenario is available, or if the current one is inappropriate as an interpreter for new input, then primary processing will fail. Either the system will have to 'hold off', in the manner suggested by Schank and Abelson (Chapter 3), or a search for a new, more appropriate scenario will have to take place. We shall refer to seeking a new scenario, or any other type of bridge-building activity instigated by a 'problem' sentence, as *secondary processing*. In Sections B and C of this chapter, some of the variables influencing secondary processing were discussed.

In any normal informative text, processing may be seen as a balance between the primary and secondary modes of interpretation. Without a scenario, and associated primary processing, no local topic of discourse would have been established and comprehension would falter. Without secondary processing, no new information would become represented in the mind of the reader. Primary processing can be thought of as automatic and rapid, whereas secondary processing would be time-consuming, and thus provides a mechanism for capturing the attention of the reader and controlling the flow of the message of the writer. In the next chapter, we shall discuss some of the more dynamic aspects of comprehension, and describe the means by which any particular text gives rise to primary and secondary processing. In Chapter 8, a more detailed theoretical framework is outlined in which these two aspects of processing are integrated.

Notes

1. Of course, there are exceptions to this. Once a category becomes technically defined, it can contain very different members. For instance, a 'whale' and an 'elephant' are both mammals (cf. Lakoff, 1972b, for a discussion).
2. Examination of the materials indicated that whether they were in the subject or object position there were no overall differences in animacy or set size.

CHAPTER 7

Dynamic Aspects of Text-Processing

Up to now we have been concerned with the idea that a language input searches out a suitable interpretive scenario from long-term memory. This then serves to augment the reference space beyond those individuals, or events, explicitly mentioned in the text. The major emphasis has been on the role of implicit information in a system of textual reference. This concentration on reference to things implicit might mislead the reader into thinking that reference to things explicit is a straightforward process. In fact, a whole variety of problems come to the surface when one looks at explicit reference, and it is to these that the present chapter will be addressed.

As a starting point, let us note that during reading, or more obviously during conversation, all things previously mentioned are not always equally easy to refer back to. It would be absurd to suppose that every individual mentioned in a long piece of discourse is available for direct reference. There is a limitation of some sort on the range of entities and events which can be easily referred to at a given time. For the writer, there is a problem of ensuring that those things which he wants the reader to focus his attention upon are actually in focus. This problem is overcome in the fluent writer by his felicitous use of the language's repertoire of devices of emphasis. For the linguist, the problem is to ascertain what these devices are, and contemporary linguists (e.g. Chafe, 1976; Li, 1976) have paid considerable attention to this. For instance, they have developed the concepts of *staging* or *topicalization* as an approach to emphasis (e.g. Grimes, 1975), with perhaps the most intuitively appealing account coming from Chafe (1972). Chafe introduces his discussion of emphasis by drawing an analogy between a text and events in a play, as they unfold upon the stage. In the same way that the setting, range of characters, and so on, give a specific point of view to our interpretation of the play, so it is with text. On reading a text it is immediately apparent that certain information is of central importance, while other information is not. We might think of this as reflecting the difference between the major characters or events in a play and the props which the actors use to help portray them. In fact, the writer of a text is able to realize this kind of distinction by indicating for any piece of the text a topic and then relating all the other information (sometimes called the comment) to this. It is important to realize that the distribution of emphasis may constantly change as the text unfolds. What is the dominant topic, in the foreground at one point, may be relegated to the background later on.

There are clearly several issues here bearing complex interrelations to each other. In the present chapter we shall examine some of them from an information-processing point of view, and end with a discussion of a fairly wide range of phenomena.

We shall begin by examining the idea that even in short texts, all individuals are not equally accessible under all circumstances, but that their accessibility bears a sensible relationship to the structure of the paragraphs in which they appear. In particular, we shall illustrate this with a study on pronominal reference, and shall relate the findings to the idea that text-processing has, as one of its important elements, operations occurring within a limited-capacity working memory.

The second question to be examined is how scenarios enter into this. In the previous chapter we treated scenarios in a static sense. In this chapter we shall put forward the view that scenarios themselves shift in and out of attentional focus given the appropriate language input. By doing this more evidence is obtained in support of the scenario itself.

A. Working Memory and Text Integration

One intuitively attractive idea is that the ease of making a coreferential mapping depends upon the availability of a memory representation of the individual at the time it is required. It seems reasonable to assume that all previously mentioned individuals, events, and episodes will not be equally accessible at any given time, but that only a relatively small subset will actually be on stage at particular points while reading. Such a view would fit nicely into what is known about memory for information which is actually being used in current processing — so-called 'working memory' (Baddeley and Hitch, 1974; Baddeley, 1976). Working memory is conceived of as a mental workspace of limited capacity, this capacity being shared between the data being processed and the information-processing operations themselves. Experiments by Baddeley and Hitch indicate that competition between storage and processing does indeed occur, and that short-term memory for items such a digits can be detrimentally influenced by processing linguistic information (e.g. by carrying out tasks involving the transformation of sentences or the comprehension and retention of prose). It seems plausible that during text comprehension, only some information will be immediately accessible if a limited working memory has to share processing with memory for events already encountered. To the extent that one does not forget what a text is about, information not in workspace must be thought of as being in some other memory store, or stored in a different form. Of course, plausible as all this may be, we need to see what bearing it may have on text integration.

1. Chafe's concept of foregrounding

The linguist Chafe (1972) provides an interesting analysis of reference problems which has a direct bearing on our argument. He suggests that, at any point during the comprehension of discourse, there are certain concepts which are in the foreground of the mind of the reader:

> ... we might think of what is going on in a discourse as if it described states and events unfolding on a stage. We could then say that at any particular point in the discourse there are certain things 'on stage'. It is whatever is on stage that I am calling foregrounded. (Chafe, 1972)

When a thing is foregrounded, references to it (in a spoken discourse) are generally characterized by being spoken in a low pitch and amplitude. Emphasis (usually but not inevitably higher pitch and amplitude) is appropriate only for bringing items *into* foreground.[1] In written text, foregrounding is best revealed by pronominalization: using a pronoun rather than a noun to refer back to an antecedent individual can be thought of as the written equivalent of 'low stress, low amplitude'. According to Chafe, pronominalization is effective only when the antecedent is foregrounded. If the antecedent is not foregrounded, using a pronoun will seem odd, even if an unambiguous mapping can be made. This idea can best be illustrated with some snippets of text. Take the sentence:

(1) The donkey kicked its owner on the leg.

This could be followed by (2) or (2′) without any difficulty:

(2) Then it ran into the village and hid.
(2′) He was extremely annoyed by this aggressive behaviour.

That one can refer to *the donkey* and *the owner* by means of a pronoun reflects the fact that (1) serves to foreground both of these individuals. However, the introduction of intervening sentences produces difficulty:

(1) The donkey kicked its owner on the leg.
(3) It ran into the village and hid.
(4) He was extremely annoyed by this aggressive behaviour.

He in (4), although unambiguously identifiable, has a distinctly odd ring about it because *the owner* (unlike *the donkey*) is no longer foregrounded.

Foregrounding can readily be interpreted in terms of working memory, with the difficulty of pronominal mapping depending on the availability of the antecedent referent in working memory. The intuition that use of a pronoun is awkward, even in circumstances when it is unambiguous, could result directly from situations where a suitable referent is not immediately available.

2. Topic and emphasis

We shall have reason to refer to the issues of topic and emphasis repeatedly in the remainder of the book. At this point we wish to introduce them by way of a rather specific example in order to illustrate their importance in determining the contents of working memory. To begin with we are concerned to show that for an equivalent propositional content, different surface forms of a sentence do not have equivalent communicative impacts.

At the propositional level, the following sentences are identical:

    (5) The boy is petting the cat.
    (6) The cat is being petted by the boy.

However, a number of studies indicate that they are not equivalent in the effect they have on people. Hornby (1972) showed people sentences like these, and asked them to choose which of a pair of pictures a sentence 'was about'. A typical pair might show a boy petting a dog and a girl petting a cat. With *the boy* in the first noun-phrase position (sentence 5), subjects almost always selected the picture of *a boy doing something* (e.g. petting a dog). With *the cat* in the first position (sentence 6), subjects selected the picture in which *the cat was being petted*, even though it was a girl doing the petting. In short, the initial noun-phrase in the sentence seems to be what the sentence is about. For this reason, initial noun-phrases are commonly referred to as *topics* (Lyons, 1968).

Another illustration of the priority assigned to an initial noun-phrase comes from a study of the way in which pronouns are understood (Broadbent, 1973). Consider a sentence like:

    (7) The feedpipe lubricates the chain, and it should be adjusted to leave a gap half an inch between itself and the sprocket.

Broadbent's study indicated that most people interpret *it* as referring to *the feedpipe* and not *the chain*, although, logically, it could refer to either of these. Of course, as Broadbent indicates, pronoun assignment can be changed by playing with the semantics of the sentence. But in the absence of such cues, assignment seems to be to the earliest part of the sentence. Again, this is consistent with the idea that the opening noun-phrase is what the sentence is about.

Broadbent (1973) and others (e.g. Haviland and Clark, 1974) explain 'topic of a sentence' (what it is about) in terms of the effect it might have on the representation of the sentence in the memory of the listener. The early part of the sentence (topic) is construed as the address to which subsequent information is to be affixed, and the latter part (comment) is information to be affixed to this address. Such an interpretation will explain both why people feel that the early part is what the sentence is about, and why, in pronominal reference, the earlier part of the sentence is selected for the mapping process.

3. Reference experiments and the operation of working memory

It should be clear that by measuring the ease of making a coreferential mapping, a number of these ideas can be examined in the context of multi-sentence text-processing. In the present section we will outline a study of this kind, from the authors' laboratory, carried out by Liz Purkiss (1978). This was aimed at relating both foregrounding and topicalization to pronominal reference, combining what is known of sentence word order with the ideas of Chafe. A representative set of materials used in the study is given in Table 7.1.

Table 7.1 Sample of materials used in the pronominal reference study (Purkiss 1978).

Key noun-phrase in subject position
The engineer repaired the television set.
It had been out of order for two weeks.
* It was only a few months old.
* It was the latest model.
He/the engineer took only five minutes to repair it. (TARGET)
Had the television set been out of order for five weeks?

Key noun-phrase in object position
The mother picked up *the baby*.
She had been ironing all afternoon.
* She would not be finished for some time.
* She was very tired.
The baby/it had been crying nearly all day. (TARGET)
Had the mother been sleeping all afternoon?

Consider first Chafe's argument. When an entity is no longer foregrounded, it can be referred to by an unambiguous pronoun only with difficulty, if our intuitions are correct. Table 7.1 shows target sentences which can either take a noun-phrase form or a pronominalized form. The coreferential pair of interest is italicized in each paragraph. Either one or three intervening sentences ensure that the focus of the discourse have moved away from the noun-phrase of interest. The prediction examined was that pronominal reference should be more difficult than direct noun reference, especially in the situation where there were three intervening sentences. Difficulty was measured using reading time for the target sentence as an index, in a way analogous to that used in the reference experiments described in the previous chapters.

In Table 7.1 there is also a division of materials into *subject* and *object*. *Subject* materials have the noun-phrase of interest introduced in the subject position of the first sentence. In all cases this means they are the first words of the sentence, since all of the first sentences are actives. In the *object* position the noun-phrase of interest occurs at the end of the sentence. In line with the discussion given in Section 2 above, it might be expected that noun-phrases in the *subject* position would be represented as part of the main topic of discourse, and should be available for future reference in working memory. On the other hand, noun-phrases in the *object* position will not be so treated, and should be dropped from working memory more rapidly. If there are the right number of intervening sentences in the experiment, one would expect pronoun difficulties to be greater in the case of *object position* materials than *subject position* materials.

The pattern of results which emerged provided support for both of these contentions (Figure 7.1). In the first place, regardless of all else, delaying a

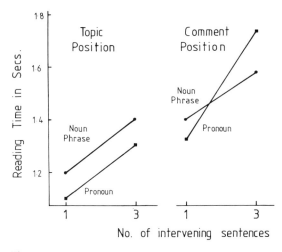

Figure 7.1   Mean target reading times in Purkiss' study.

reference by the introduction of extra intervening sentences produces an increase in the time to read a target sentence, so the availability of the antecedent representation appears to be reduced with an increase in intervening non-coreferential material. Secondly, after an adjustment is made for differential sentence length, references to antecedents in the object position are slower than references to antecedents in the subject position. This fits the view that subject and object do indeed differ in terms of how they persist in working memory. But by far the most interesting evidence for a difference between subject and object emerges from a comparison of targets containing repeat of the critical noun with those containing a pronoun substitution.

Consider first the *subject position* antecedent. Targets containing a repeated noun-phrase are read *more slowly* than targets containing a pronoun, this effect persisting even over the three intervening sentence condition. Pronominal reference is apparently successful, and we would suggest that the individual referred to by the subject of the first sentence *still resides in working memory* — in Chafe's terms, it is *foregrounded*. This, of course, fits in nicely with the view that one usually begins a paragraph by establishing what it is that is to be talked about (i.e. specifying the topic), and consequently expects references to that topic to be made. Turning to the *object position* results, the pattern is very different. Although there is some marginal evidence that after a one-sentence shift in focus a pronoun can still be mapped onto an appropriate noun-phrase faster than the repeated noun-phrase, this is certainly not the case after three intervening sentences. Reference by means of the noun-phrase is now considerably faster. Thus, in the case of the object position materials, one could say that the individual is no longer in working memory, and cannot be addressed by a pronoun without considerable difficulty. In Chafe's terminology, it is no longer foregrounded.

We can now make a number of suggestions about how individuals mentioned in a discourse might be represented in working memory. For convenience, let us refer to the initial sentence in our material as:

$$\alpha - ACT - \beta$$

meaning that α is the subject, related to β the object by some ACT. When one reads a paragraph, α is selected as the topic of discourse, and is assigned a special status. Both α and β have representations in working memory. Continued references to α of the form:

$$\alpha - ACT - \gamma$$
$$\alpha - ACT - \delta$$

have the effect of maintaining the topic α in working memory. However, because working memory has a limited capacity, the representation of β gradually fades, and ultimately remains only in long-term memory.

On the other hand, if the intervening sentences take the form:

$$\beta - ACT - \gamma$$
$$\beta - ACT - \delta$$

the representation of β remains in working memory, but *so too does that of* α, because of its special status as the topic. Eventually, of course, the reader may give up on α as the topic, but its representation obviously persists for a long time in comparison with β, unless this is referred to continuously. This line of argument leads to the prediction that false topics should 'clutter up' working memory, making a text become generally difficult to read and integrate.

Other investigators have produced results which have a bearing on these observations. For instance, Lesgold *et al.* (in preparation, see Perfetti and Lesgold, 1977) used a similar reading-time paradigm and materials containing an anaphoric reference in the form of a repeated noun-phrase. The introduction of topic-change sentences between the antecedent and anaphor again produced a longer reading time for the target sentence (containing the anaphor).

4. Some additional factors in pronoun assignment

While these results, and their interpretation, offer a simple but significant bridge between certain linguistic approaches to reference and a psychological approach, there is much more to interpreting pronouns than has been suggested here. For instance, in all but a few of the examples considered above, the pronoun references could be described as unambiguous and plausible. There only was one antecedent to which the pronoun could be assigned while retaining agreement on gender or number. In many cases of pronoun usage there may be a variety of syntactically possible antecedents, yet there is usually only one which is picked by the reader.

In this section we will attempt to broaden the discussion of pronominalization to take into account some of the additional factors involved, and then use this to build up a more general psychological account of what is happening when the reader encounters a pronoun in text. It is useful to begin by reviewing the major factors which have been discussed by both linguists and computer scientists when considering pronominalization. Apart from considerations of topic, or separation of pronoun from antecedent, which have been alluded to earlier, there are two other major factors which affect pronoun assignment: syntactic factors and semantic/pragmatic factors.

The syntactic factors have been extensively quoted in the literature on transformational grammar, and like most syntactic matters are best characterized in terms of restrictions or filters which rule out certain constructions. The simplest of these is the agreement rule for gender and number, whereby a pronoun has to agree in number and gender with its antecedent. More complicated rules concern reflexives and backward pronominalization. In the case of a reflexive, the rule is simply that the pronoun must refer back to some antecedent which is the subject of the same clause. With non-reflexive pronouns this is ruled out. In the case of backward pronominalization, the rule is that this can only occur when the pronoun is in a subordinate clause which precedes the main clause. Thus in sentence (8) below *he* can refer to Fred while in sentence (8') coreference is ruled out.

(8) Although *he* could not swim, Fred jumped in to save Mary.

(8') *He* jumped in to save Mary, although Fred could not swim.

What is most apparent about the syntactic restrictions on pronoun assignment is that they are all determinable on the basis of lexical cues in the input. In the case of the reflexive and gender restrictions, the cue is in the form of the pronoun itself; in the case of the backward pronominalization constraint, it is in the subordinating conjunction which precedes the pronoun. From the point of view of the processor, this means that on the basis of a minimal interpretation of the sentence it is possible to rule out a large number of potential antecedents on purely syntactic grounds.

When one turns to the remaining factors involved in pronoun assignment, it is not possible to draw up such a tidy list of constraints. This is mainly because they result from the reader's general interpretation of the text, rather than operating through superficial cues in the immediate environment of the pronoun. The first set of factors result entirely from the reader's interpretation of the prior text, and include such things as topicalization and recent emphasis. They are perhaps best summarized in terms of heuristic rules which may aid the processor in assigning a pronoun reference. Common examples of such rules include: (1) the current topic is more likely to be an appropriate antecedent than others, (2) proximal expressions are more likely antecedents than distant ones, and (3) repeatedly referenced prior concepts are more likely to be relevant antecedents.

This set of heuristic rules, together with the syntactic constraints mentioned earlier, have been widely used in text comprehension programs which carry out pronoun-antecedent matching as part of their comprehension task. For instance, Norman *et al.* (1975, p. 202) describe a program which goes through a serial testing procedure, after some initial tests for reflexivity. First, tests are made to find a match onto 'the topic under discussion', which is defined as a term which was either previously pronominalized or was the subject of the previous sentence. They are checked for number and gender. If neither meets the number and gender constraints, preceding propositions are searched, starting with the most recent. Norman *et al.* claim that an appropriate assignment is made in about 90 per cent of all cases. Of course, it is doubtful whether human readers *always* make initially correct assignments, and the result the program achieves suggests the method to be reasonably accurate. Similar heuristics and cues are used in other programs, for instance that of Winograd (1972).

These heuristics relate sensibly to the limited-capacity, working-memory hypothesis entertained earlier. Topicalization and amount of intervening material both have an effect on the ease of pronominal reference. We might say that the capacity of working memory is allocated more to the topic than to other entities, but that with new material coming in, capacity is increasingly allocated to the new material. The way in which allocated capacity of working memory might relate to topicalization and amount of intervening material is illustrated schematically in Figure 7.2.

It seems reasonable to suppose that faster mappings would be achieved in cases where the storage space in working memory is greatest. Thus a topic noun-phrase will be addressed much more rapidly than a comment noun-phrase. Let us add one other idea to this: that a pronoun-to-noun-phrase mapping takes place *before* any semantic interpretation of the result occurs, whenever possible. If both of these ideas are correct, we have an easy way of explaining cases like (7) in which a logically ambiguous pronoun receives a single allocation acceptable to all readers.

Let us summarize the position presented up to now. There seem to be two components involved in pronoun assignment. The first derives from topicalization and recency — both factors which will have influenced the

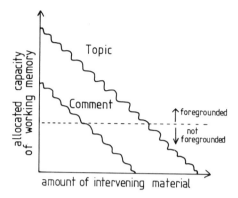

Figure 7.2 Schematic representation of how degree of foregrounding and associated working-memory allocation might relate to time since mention for topics and non-topics.

reader *before* the pronoun is encountered. This component gives a *prior* weighting to the various possible antecedents, and serves to restrict their number. The second component enters into pronoun resolution only at the time when the pronoun itself is encountered. It derives from lexical and syntactic information, either in the pronoun (number, gender, reflexivity) or in its immediate vicinity (clausemate constraint, backward pronominalization). This component serves to filter out illegal assignments from the previously restricted set of possible antecedents.

However, these mechanisms alone cannot account for all cases of pronominal assignment. For instance, consider the following example from Wilks (1975):

(9) Give the monkeys the bananas although they are not ripe because they are hungry.

The assignments of the two *they* references depend upon our knowledge of monkeys and bananas. Other examples depending on general knowledge are:

(10) Simon lent money to Jim because he needed it.
(11) Simon lent money to Jim because he was generous.

He receives a different assignment in these two sentences, but this can only be done on the basis of working out the implications associated with 'lending' and 'being generous'. To the extent that utterances like those are commonplace, they do demonstrate that it is not sufficient to have a processor working on the basis of recency and topic heuristics alone. In terms of the scenario-based account, discussed in the previous chapter, we might say that an adequate pronominal assignment must lead to a representation in which the actions of the entity described by a pronoun fit the role specification of the tentative antecedent.

5. Does mapping precede interpretation?

The question therefore arises as to how and when inferences and direct mappings are used. Quite obviously, inferential processes will always be used when necessary, otherwise an integrated interpretation of the discourse would not result. But the question remains of how inferential processes and direct mappings combine to enable the reader to identify the antecedent of a pronoun efficiently.

A number of studies on pronoun assignment decisions demonstrate that it is not always necessary to use general knowledge about the overall meaning of a sentence before a mapping can take place (e.g. Caramazza *et al.*, 1977; Ehrlich, 1979; Springston, 1976). Consider the study by Kate Ehrlich. Her task involved presenting subjects with sentences and asking them to respond with a key when they had decided to which noun-phrase a particular pronoun referred. Example sentences are given in Table 7.2. With sentence (a), subjects

Table 7.2   Sample sentences for Ehrlich's (1979) pronoun assignment study.

(a) Steven blamed Frank because he spilled the coffee.
(b) Jane blamed Bill because he spilled the coffee.

prefer to assign *he* to *Frank*, but clearly have to do this on the basis of situational knowledge. Spilling coffee is usually bad, and from general knowledge that Frank is doing something bad there is a reason for Steve to blame him. *He* is therefore assigned to *Frank*. With sentence (b), the same argument applies, except that there is only one possible mapping anyway, since *he* cannot refer to *Jane* because of the gender restriction. If inferencing were always used before assignment took place, we might expect the assignment to take as long with (b) as with (a). If gender checks occur prior to inferencing, we might expect (b) to be handled faster than (a). Measurements of choice times indicate (b) to be faster than (a), from which we might conclude, along with Ehrlich, that mappings based on gender cues occur prior to inferencing. Obviously, if gender cues cannot enable an unambiguous mapping to take place, other information must be used. We suggest that topic mappings also occur before inferencing is used, otherwise ambiguous examples like (7) would always give an undecided reading. Finally, if topic mappings do not help, inferencing may be used, possibly being invoked by the analysis of later sentences.

Ehrlich's results suggest that readers use general (as opposed to lexical) knowledge only when gender does not identify a unique referent. Similar arguments for the use of lexical cues early in processing come from the work of Springston (1976), who demonstrated that both gender and reflexivity produce faster assignments than when inferences are needed.

According to the framework proposed in this and the previous chapter, it is therefore possible to draw up a summary of the factors influencing pronoun assignment in terms of where they enter into the real time processing of the reference. In Table 7.3 such a summary has been laid out. The factors which

Table 7.3.

Time of operation relative to encoding the pronoun	Influencing factor	Origin of influence
Pre	Topicalization, emphasis, & recency	Within the working-memory system
At encountering	Lexical and syntactic information	Lexical analysis which filters out antecedents on the basis of genders
Post	Coherence of the text with respect to general knowledge	Checks on scenario role assignments

influence the assignment before the pronoun is encountered are loosely summarized as topicalization and recency. As we have argued, these can be best understood in terms of a limited-capacity, working-memory buffer, with topics and recently mentioned items taking up a larger proportion of the memory space. On encountering the pronoun itself, syntactic and lexical factors come into play, and on the basis of these it is possible to make some sort of mapping onto an item represented in the working-memory buffer. Finally, after such a preliminary mapping has been made, it is possible to check its plausibility in terms of the built-in constraints on the scenario into which the entity is also mapped. If this is in question, then another mapping will have to be tried (presumably a time-consuming process).

The extent to which this last process will involve drawing new inferences is still a moot point. One would think that in many cases it will follow directly from the scenarios evoked by the current input and the prior text, but this need not always be the case. To see how scenario role information could be used to help in plausibility checking, it might be useful to consider an example:

(12) John bought the car from Bill because *he* needed the money.

In sentence (12) most people will assign the pronoun to Bill rather than John, although there is a natural tendency in all such sentences to assign it to the subject noun-phrase. The reason for choosing this assignment is presumably because by buying Bill's car John is giving him money, and since Bill needs money this is plausible. Most of this information can be incorporated directly into the miniscenarios associated with the two verbs. In other words, one might represent 'buy' in terms of some formulation like:

X buy from Y
X gives money to Y
(Outcome: Y has *more money* than before)
and 'need':

Y needs X
Y does not have X
(Resolution: Y has X).

Assigning the 'Y' role to Bill rather than John will therefore match the outcome of the first event with the resolution of the second; if the assignment were otherwise, this satisfactory matching would not have occurred. In fact, if one replaces the conjunction 'because' with 'although', which requires such a mismatch, the opposite assignment becomes the plausible one, as is illustrated in sentence (13) (see Ehrlich (1979) for further details).

(13) John bought the car from Bill although he needed the money.

In other words, it is quite possible that reassignment on the basis of inference need not entail making very complex bridging inferences at the time of reading, but follows in a direct way from information available in the scenario.

Resolving a pronominal reference can therefore be seen as occurring in both the primary processing mode and the secondary processing mode, as outlined in the previous chapter. In many cases, adequate pronominal resolution can be made at the time of parsing the sentence, on the basis of factors originating both before the sentence is encountered (i.e. topicalization and recency) and at the point of encountering the pronoun (i.e. syntactic restriction). This kind of resolution will occur in primary processing, within the constraints of local topic. On the other hand, there are cases, like those discussed above, where the appropriate antecedent is not discovered at this time and resolution may only occur through secondary time-consuming processes. We would suggest that such a use of pronouns is at best inelegant and, as we will argue in Chapter 9, represents inconsiderate discourse, since the primary function of the pronoun is to mark reference within the constraints of local topic.

B. The Status of Individuals and the Dynamics of Scenarios

Our analysis of the pronoun studies leads to a number of interesting questions. What happens to the representation of an individual when it is no longer foregrounded: how is it stored and accessed? Secondly, is it just the number of intervening sentences which affects availability in working memory? Thirdly, and perhaps less obvious, how does the analysis of foregrounding relate to the idea that language operates through calling up scenarios from long-term memory? We shall attempt to link the answers to these questions by reference to another study of the nature of the scenario; in this case we are interested in the dynamic aspects of scenarios — how they are changed by the appropriate cues in a text.

1. Principal actors and scenario-dependent entities

For the purposes of the present discussion, we shall distinguish between principal actors and scenario-dependent entities. Principal actors need not be just people but could be any loosely animate thing, like a ship or a tank for example. In a simple story, a principal actor will move from situation to situation, goal to goal, etc. As this happens, it is constantly related to scenarios which come and go depending upon the content of the text. Within these scenarios, which provide the extended reference domain, other auxiliary entities will have a place too — like 'waiters' in 'restaurants', 'snow' in 'skiing', 'hairdressers' in a 'barber's shop', etc. These auxiliary entities only have relevance to the scenario in which they occur, unless the text specifically indicates otherwise. We shall therefore term them *scenario-dependent*. To illustrate, consider the following brief passage:

(14a) John Brown decided to have a haircut.
(14b) He went into the barber's shop and had a new style.
(14c) The hairdresser advised him well and he was pleased.
(14d) Because he had time to spare, he later went to the cinema.
(14e) The film was a rather poor western.

It is plausible to assume that two scenarios predominate in this story, 'barber's shop' and 'cinema'. Being the principal actor, *John Brown* is relevant to both scenarios. On the other hand, *the hairdresser* is not relevant to the 'cinema' scenario. Indeed, we may find it quite surprising to learn:

(15) The sheriff looked like the hairdresser.

What we are suggesting is that perhaps *the hairdresser* is rather more difficult to access if we have shifted away from the scenario on which he depends. Indeed, it seems more natural to write:

(15′) The sheriff looked like *the hairdresser at the barber's shop.*

In contrast, John Brown remains foregrounded, and easy to refer to.

2. Indirect scenario switches: time and space constraints

In the example given above, the shift in scenario is made explicit by the text. However, imminent change of scenario can be indicated in more subtle ways — any serious violation of the default information in a scenario could serve to indicate that it is no longer appropriate. Indeed, this is one of the mechanisms suggested by Minsky (1975) for discovering whether a current frame is inappropriate.

A clear-cut example of a potentially serious violation can be found in part of the programmatic component of certain scenarios. We would argue that if scenarios contain script-like information, then they will also contain default information about the spatio-temporal range over which they operate. For instance, consider the scenario which might be associated with a football match. By its very nature, a football match occurs in a limited space over a limited period of time, which should mean that language cues indicating events *outside* of these limits are understood as being *outside of that scenario*. That is, the current scenario would be signalled as inappropriate. Perhaps a sufficiently extreme violation might make the scenario less accessible, so that the background information it contained might not be so readily available for reference. This notion provides the basis for an empirical test. Using the reading-time technique, it should be possible to check accessibility of background information to discover whether scenarios are still prominent after various language inputs. Let us consider a concrete example:

(16a) Tom Smith really needed a haircut.
(16b) He went to a fashionable new barber's shop.
(16c) A beautiful assistant cut his hair.
(16d) Five hours later he was not so pleased with himself.
(16e) She was obviously not employed for her skill.

The assistant in sentence (16c) fills a role in the barber's shop scenario. We suggest that sentence (16d), containing the critical time reference *five hours later*, puts Tom outside of the barber's shop scenario, and consequently *she* in sentence (16e) should be hard to relate back to the beautiful assistant. By contrast, the same *she* should be easy to relate back if the critical time change falls within the range of time a person normally spends in a barber's shop — for instance, *five minutes later* or *one hour later* should pose no problems, because the appropriate scenario would still be available. Of course, in this or any other case, individual 'tracks' of the program may have different time ranges. If it were a ladies' hairdresser, and the specification were *having a perm*, five hours may not put us outside the range at all!

3. An empirical investigation of indirect scenario switches

In our laboratory, Anne Anderson has carried out a self-paced reading experiment to investigate the way in which time changes alter the availability of both principal actors and scenario-dependent characters for subsequent anaphoric reference. As we have indicated, the first problem was to estimate the time range associated with the critical programmatic component of a given scenario. She began by having a number of judges estimate the maximum time associated with stereotypic events such as 'having a haircut', 'eating in a restaurant', etc. From these data it was possible to obtain a reasonable estimate of the time boundary on a normative basis. The time shifts which she used in her experiments were based on these normative data, with the critical changes being either well inside or well beyond the range boundaries.

Once these time changes had been worked out, it was possible to generate passages like that shown above (16a–c) according to a simple formula. Each passage has a key topic character or set of characters who are the principal agents or actors in the situation. These are essentially independent of the scenario, in that although they fill a role in it, their relevance to the passage does not depend upon it being the appropriate scenario. In the example given

148

above, the key topic character is *Tom*. At the same time, each passage introduces an entity which *is* dependent on the scenario, in that it fills a role whose existence is predicted by the scenario *(the beautiful assistant)*. By having both types of potential antecedent entity, it is possible to obtain a measure of control over any general reading-time effects for sentences which refer to them.

A sample passage type from the experiment is given in Table 7.4. The scenario here is a birthday party, being introduced by both the title and the context. The topic characters are the children, and the scenario character the entertainer. For the time-change sentence there are two possibilities — either a time change within the normative expected range (one hour) or outside of the

Table 7.4   Example of materials used in Anderson's time-change study.

The birthday party
The children were all enjoying the party.
There was *an entertainer* to amuse them.
No expense was spared to make the party a success.

$\left\{ \begin{matrix} One \\ Five \end{matrix} \right\}$ hour(s) later energies flagged. TIME CHANGE

Scenario-dependent	Organizing the games had exhausted him.
Topic	Playing the games had exhausted them.
	TARGET SENTENCES

---

normal range (five hours). Following this, there are two alternative types of target sentence, one referring to the topic character and the other to the scenario-dependent character. Finally, after reading these sentences in the self-paced reading situation, subjects had to answer two questions: one question referred to the key topic character and the other to the scenario-dependent character.

With this experiment a number of predictions can be made and tested, if our initial reasoning is correct. First, if the time cue is beyond the expected scenario range, then references to scenario-dependent individuals should be more difficult to resolve, given that the scenario is dropped as the interpretive mechanism. On the other hand, references to the key topic character should not be rendered more difficult, because that individual is not scenario-dependent. These differential effects should be reflected in the reading times for the two target-sentence types. As a second check on this point, a similar differential should appear in the times to produce Yes/No answers to questions about the text: the time to answer questions referring back to scenario-bound individuals should be long after a large shift because the scenario will no longer be in working memory, but references to the topic character should not be affected. The pattern of results shown in Figure 7.3 indicates that both of these predictions are upheld. Reference to the bound

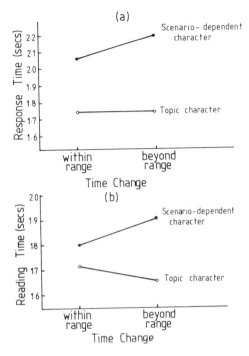

Figure 7.3 (a) Response times for questions referring to scenario-dependent and topic characters after a time change within or beyond the scenario limits. (b) Reading times for corresponding target sentences.

individuals is adversely affected by the large time shift. In contrast, reference to the key topic individual is not so affected, hence the results cannot be attributed to some general influence of time change on any subsequent sentences. The effect is clearly restricted to the scenario-dependent individual. It is also worth noting that the targets which refer to the key topic individuals are processed faster than those referring to scenario-bound individuals. This is exactly what we would expect on the basis of the studies described earlier, showing the dominance of the key topic in the working-memory representation.

Let us now turn to the time-change sentences themselves. Up to the time change, comprehension proceeds by developing and then instantiating the scenario. All that is encountered can be related to the scenario. But the time change, if beyond the scenario range, should violate the scenario specification, and the interpreter must note this fact and (as we have seen) alter the status of the scenario structure itself with respect to the current contents of working memory. In addition to closing off the current scenario, it is also consistent with our argument to suppose that the processor will be set up to seek new scenario structures, or be set up for other bridge-building operations.

Accordingly, one would expect that when a sentence with a time change beyond the scenario range is encountered, reading time will be longer than it would be for a time change within the scenario range. In fact, the data bear out this prediction. An analysis of the reading times for the sentence containing the time shift reveals that shifts beyond the scenario boundary do indeed take longer to process, as shown in Figure 7.4.

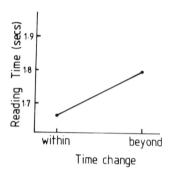

Figure 7.4   The effect of time change on the reading time for the sentence in which the time change itself is introduced.

We consider the time-shift study to be of particular importance, because it seems to reveal many things at the same time. First, the results tell us something about the status of the various individuals mentioned in the text. The scenario can be thought of as a supportive background structure, representing default and explicit entities, but nevertheless a background structure. It enables an interpretation of the behaviour of the principal (topic) characters to be made. Scenarios may change, but until explicitly signalled, principal actors remain dominant even when the scenario-dependent individuals have been removed from the centre of attentional focus. This difference in referential availability is a psychological manifestation of text coherence. Texts cohere into a causal chain because they represent a series of encounters (e.g. scenario changes) largely from the point of view of the topic characters.

Second, although simple, it is quite startling on many accounts to find that a time shift beyond the bounds of an episode's expected limit should reduce the ease of the anaphoric mapping of episode-bound characters. Such a finding would rule out any simple explanation of working memory in which it is merely the number of intervening individuals mentioned which determines whether a previously mentioned individual is still present. It suggests that the availability of individuals represented in working memory is jointly dependent upon their nature and the presence of a supportive scenario.

Finally, the data support the argument that scenarios are modular in nature. A text could be thought of as activating a handful of concepts which are associated with the words in it. So, for example, *entertainer* might be activated on reading the word *party*, thus making *entertainer* more accessible for reference than it would otherwise be. However, such a view does not provide a good explanation of how *entertainer* could instantly become less accessible given a large time change. The only way this can be handled is if the working representation contains time information about the programmatic components of an episode, and if the availability of referents can be instantly reduced when the time information does not fit the expected range associated with the situation. To preserve an argument not based on scenarios, it would be necessary to suppose that part of the associative dependents of *entertainer* includes time-range information general to entertainers. However, it is almost a truism that the time range over which an entertainer might operate is entirely dependent upon the situation in which he is working. This is equivalent to saying that for the time cue to influence the referential availability of the entertainer, scenario information is being used.

Temporal statements are cues that a scenario may not be of any further use as a contextual support structure. Similar arguments may be made for spatial statements. For example, if we encountered a statement:

Three miles away . . .

when reading a passage about a party or a hairdresser's, this might well cue the need to set the action in a new scenario as soon as the enabling information becomes available.

At this point, it might be tempting to think of scenarios as being amenable to the rules of foregrounding, in much the same way that explicitly introduced characters are. After all, there seems to be evidence that the referential accessibility of scenario-dependent entities can be affected by whether the scenario is currently in the processing 'foreground'. However, to describe a scenario as foregrounded seems somewhat contrary, since it quite obviously constitutes the 'background' for text comprehension. Instead of this, we will introduce the notion of 'focus' (cf. Grosz, 1977) to describe the active state of a scenario. If a scenario is currently active, we will say it is in 'focus'.

By focus we mean that the scenario both as an interpretive structure and domain of reference is currently available to the processing system. From a phenomenological point of view, we might say that when a scenario is in focus a scenario-bound entity is more likely to be in the mind of the reader than when the scenario is no longer is focus. In fact it is possible to test this experimentally.

Consider a situation where the reader is given an incomplete passage like that shown in Table 7.5 overleaf and is asked to complete it, what sort of completions would one expect? If one simply considers the characters that a reader might choose to mention in the completion sentence, one would naturally expect that characters in current focus would be likely to appear, with foregrounded characters, such as the topic, being at the top of the list. This means that when such a passage ends with a time change beyond the scenario range, one would expect a drop in the likelihood of mentioning scenario-bound characters, but there should be no such effect with topic characters.

Table 7.5.

At the cinema
Jenny found the film rather boring.
The *projectionist* had to keep changing the reels.
It was supposed to be a silent class.

Ten minutes
Seven hours later the film was forgotton.

Topic =   Jenny
Scenario-bound = Projectionist

A further study by Anne Anderson was based on just such a continuation experiment using materials of this sort. Her basic results are shown in Figure 7.5. In the figure is shown the number of continuations which mention either

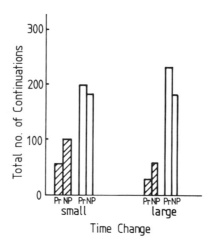

Figure 7.5 Number of continuations mentioning topic character (white bars) or scenario-bound character (cross-hatched bars) as a function of size of time-change sentence. (From Anderson, unpublished data.)

the topic or scenario-bound character under conditions of either a large or small time change sentence. Two things emerge from the data. First, that the subject is much more likely to produce a continuation sentence mentioning the topic than one mentioning the scenario-bound individual. This follows from our previous observations about foregrounding and topicalization. But what is most significant is the fact that the time-change manipulation only affects mentions of scenario-bound characters; with a time change in violation of scenario range, the proportion of mentions of the scenario-bound characters drops by 50 per cent. This latter result is quite in line with the hypothesis that the scenario is no longer in focus and its domain of reference is thereby no longer immediately available to the processing system.

Interestingly enough, the continuation data also tell us something about the relative foregrounding status of the topic and scenario-bound characters. It is possible to separate out those continuations in which a pronoun was used to identify a previously mentioned character from those employing a noun-phrase; the data are shown in Figure 7.5. As one might expect, references to the topics are typically made with pronouns, whereas references to the scenario-bound characters are typically definite noun-phrases. Although both topics and scenario-bound entities may be in current focus, only the topic is foregrounded.

4. The distinction between implicit and explicit focus

The primary aim of this chapter has been to characterize the processes underlying the referential resolution of entities which are recoverable from the prior text. The factors which determine the ease of resolution can be summarized according to their origin. First, they may derive from the structure of the text itself, and may be described in terms of foregrounding. Principal actors, which are usually introduced early in the text, and are topicalized within the sentence, are highly foregrounded. In addition to this, recently mentioned items tend to be more highly foregrounded than those which have not been mentioned recently. The way in which foregrounding affects ease of resolution is reflected both in the time taken to identify the antecedent and in the relative effectiveness of pronouns and noun-phrases as anaphors. Pronominal reference leads to more rapid resolution for fore-grounded antecedents, whereas noun-phrases have the advantage for antecedents which are not topics, or have not been mentioned recently.

The second factor has its origin in the role which the antecedents played in the reader's interpretation of the text. Entities which were solely dependent upon a specific scenario will only be readily available for reference if that scenario is still in focus. On the other hand, principal actors, which are seen as independent of any specific scenario, are not affected in this way.

Both of these factors are dynamic in that their effects will be changing as the reader progresses through the text. Thus, at any given point in reading, there will be a limited set of foregrounded items which were mentioned explicitly in the text, in conjunction with a particular scenario. This currently available domain of reference comprises the *focus* of the reader at any given time. Further properties of the focus system become apparent when one considers reference to information which has not been explicitly mentioned.

In the previous chapters we introduced the concept of the extended domain of reference to explain a reader's ability to interpret references to entities implied by the text, but not mentioned explicitly. It was argued that such an extension comes about through the reader's use of scenarios. For instance, as has already been pointed out, it is possible to make situational references of the following sort:

(17) Mary dressed the baby.
(17') *The clothes* were made of pink wool.

The definite noun-phrase *the clothes* serves to identify an entity in that extended domain of reference set up by the verb *dressed*. Although the experiments described in Chapters 5 and 6 show that such references can be resolved as easily with implicit as with explicit antecedents, it is now appropriate to emphasize the difference in processing in the two cases. A major difference emerges when one considers the use of pronouns in each case. While it is admissible to say:

(18) Mary put *the clothes* on the baby
(18') *They* were made of pink wool

one simply cannot say:

(19) Mary dressed the baby.
(19') *They* were made of pink wool.

In fact, pronouns can never be used to identify implied entities in the extended domain of reference.

This example points to the fact that one needs to maintain a clear distinction between the domain of reference derived from explicitly mentioned entities and that derived purely from the current scenario, although both may be in focus at the same time. To this end, we will refer to entities mentioned in the text as being in *explicit focus*, so long as they are represented in working memory. In contrast, the extension of the domain of reference provided by the current scenario will be described as being in *implicit focus*. In the next chapter, we develop the argument that these two types of focus represent different partitions of working memory, and can be characterized, psychologically, in very different ways.

Note

1. Note the way in which foregrounding fits in with Halliday's Given–New distinction.

CHAPTER 8

Focus, Mapping, and Memory: A Processing Framework

In the second section of this book, we have attempted to discuss, in some detail, a number of specific issues which relate to how a reader may resolve references. Chapter 5 concentrated on the process of resolving anaphoric references, with special emphasis being paid to the circumstances in which antecedents are sought for such references. In Chapter 6, the discussion broadened to include arguments about how the reader might utilize his knowledge, to help produce a unique interpretation of any piece of text. Here, it was argued that the reader has two main tasks: first, he has to select an appropriate domain of knowledge which corresponds to his assumptions on what the text is about, and, second, he has to use the mental model or scenario that he has selected in order to guide his interpretation of subsequent sentences in the text. In terms of reference resolution, the scenario will enable the reader to map certain references which have no explicitly mentioned antecedents directly into his representation of the text. Finally, in the previous chapter, we returned to a discussion of the main factors which enter into resolving references to antecedents mentioned previously. Our conclusions here were that topicalization and foregrounding of the antecedents were critical variables in determining the reader's ability to resolve subsequent reference. Furthermore, consideration of pronominal reference led us to argue for a clear separation between those domains of potential reference which derived from explicit mention and those deriving from the evoked scenario.

The aim of the present chapter is to develop a processing framework which will accommodate the various observations which we have made in these three chapters, and hopefully also lead to a clearer understanding of the relationship between knowledge access and comprehension in the human reader.

A. Memory Partitions and the Active Processor

In Chapter 1, we posed the problem of how a piece of text might be described in such a way as to enable it to make contact with knowledge. Up to now, the argument has been concerned with specifying the nature of those knowledge structures which are going to be of most use in interpreting text at any given point in reading. This poses the psychological problem of how a system might make the appropriate structures available. One way of looking at this problem is in terms of the dynamics of memory addressing. Not surprisingly, any account of interpretation based on knowledge must ultimately be framed in terms of how the appropriate information is found. For instance, with the resolution of references, the problem may be construed as one of finding the appropriate referent in memory. Similarly, lexical interpretation can be viewed as a process of seeking from memory the appropriate semantic representation for the word in question. Thus, if we are to produce a psychologically fruitful framework for understanding knowledge access during comprehension, it will be necessary to consider how a reader's memory might be organized to help him recover this information. However, as Miller and Johnson-Laird (1976) quite rightly point out, this task is rendered difficult because psychologists interested in memory have not usually concerned themselves with the problems of comprehension. The present approach will therefore be to use the findings on text-processing as a basis for identifying operationally distinct components of memory, rather than trying to develop an account based solely on existing distinctions. However, wherever possible we will try to relate this account to the more general conclusions psychologists have come to concerning memory organization.

Before launching into the task of describing a memory system for comprehension, let us consider in a little more detail the steps which a reader must go through in the process of interpreting a sentence.

If we were to imagine the processor faced with a sentence like the following:

(1) He gave Mary the present

how might it go about interpreting such a sentence? Once the initial perceptual problem of identifying the words in the text is overcome, most theorists would suggest that the primary task is one of parsing the input into syntactic and semantic categories. From a purely syntactic point of view, the outcome of a parse, in our example sentence, might be something like:

He = pro = noun-phrase = subject of sentence.
Gave = verb = verb of the sentence.
Mary = proper noun = indirect object of sentence.

The = article
\right\} = noun-phrase = direct object.
Present = noun

In order to come up with this classification, the processor does not need access to knowledge except in the limited sense of knowledge of lexical and syntactic categories and the combinatorial rules of syntax. However, as was argued in Chapter 3, the parsing system will need to go much further than this if a semantic analysis is to be produced. For instance, it will have to select a semantic representation for the verb *give* and assign the subject to the category *agent*, the indirect object to the category *recipient*, and the object to the category *object*, wherever these slots arise in the representation. Furthermore, the processor will have to determine what it is to which the various noun-phrases 'he', 'Mary', and 'the present' refer. It is at this point that memory access is called for.

From the point of view of any linguistic processing system, it is useful to think of the various elements in the sentence as directives to the processor to carry out certain operations; this is perhaps best illustrated in parsing systems such as the Augmented Transition Network (e.g. Eisenstadt, 1979; Kaplan, 1975; Johnson-Laird, 1977). Thus, when it comes to describing the semantic side of the process, one might characterize certain of these operations in terms of memory access. So, for instance, when the processor encounters the category 'verb of the sentence' in a parse, this would lead to the action *find in memory a semantic representation for the verb*, or when encountering a pronoun to the action *find in memory a referent matching this pronoun*. At the same time, any language-processing system will have to be able to construct semantic representations in memory which reflect the outcome of the parsing process. Thus, once the verb representation has been retrieved, it will be necessary to map tokens onto this for the referents recovered for the various noun-phrases encountered in that sentence. So, in the example sentence given above, the referent retrieved for *he* would be mapped into the agent slot in the verb representation, the referent for *Mary* into the recipient slot, and so on.

In terms of memory, the comprehension process can therefore be thought of as one of both *retrieving* appropriate information and *constructing* a unique representation of the text. The retrieval process may be specified in terms of three variables:

(a) The domain to be searched.
(b) A given partial description of the information to be found.
(c) The type of information to be returned.

Let us describe these three in some detail. First of all, the domain to be searched has to be restricted in some way. For example, if the problem is to find a referent for the pronoun 'he', as in the example given above, a search of all memory would be fruitless, since it would return every male entity. For a search to be effective, it would have to be restricted to what we have been calling *explicit focus*. So, in searching for a referent for 'he', the domain (a) must be restricted to something corresponding to explicit focus. The partial description (b) may be found in the semantic specification of the pronoun itself, i.e. 'entity, male, singular'. Thus, what is to be returned is the identity of a unique male, singular entity to be found in explicit focus.

Of course, searching for pronominal referents provides a relatively simple example. However, we will argue that in each case of memory addressing postulated, (a), (b), and (c) must be specified, and it is to this problem that the bulk of this chapter is directed. But in addition to the retrieval process, there is the problem of constructing a representation of the text in question. Construction may also be specified in terms of three variables:

(a) The domain of memory where the construction is recorded.
(b) A description of the information to be incorporated.
(c) The type of structure to result.

Thus, in the case of the pronoun reference described above, the retrieved referent and the new information conveyed by the sentence that the pronoun is in will become combined into a coherent structure within some partition of memory. In order to expand upon both the processes of retrieval and those of construction, we need to distinguish between a number of partitions of memory.

Let us define a memory partition as independently addressable, and capable of being treated by a processor as a distinct search domain. We would like to suggest that a minimum of four of these is necessary in order to describe memory access during comprehension, and that they are based on psychologically defensible divisions. The first distinction is between search domains which we have described as *in current focus* and those not in current focus. In Chapter 7, it was argued at length that, at any given time, certain information can be accessed rapidly and easily, while other information is more difficult to retrieve. The easily accessible information can be considered as being in the dynamic partitions of memory, since the contents of the partitions change as the text unfolds. By contrast, both general knowledge and the long-term representation of the text are relatively stable. Let us say that these are represented in static partitions of memory.

A second distinction which is independent of the first is between memory representations that derive purely from interpretation of the text and those which comprise knowledge from other sources. In the case of the dynamic partition of focus, we have argued in Chapter 7 that it is necessary for the processor to have two distinct search (reference) domains within this: explicit focus, comprising representations based on entities mentioned in the text, and implicit focus, comprising scenario-based representations. A similar distinction has to be made for the static partitions. It is important to retain a separation between memory for the text itself and other general knowledge. The relationship between the two distinctions and the partitions of memory is illustrated in Table 8.1. There is a relationship between these partitions and distinctions made in other areas of psychology: for instance, between short-term working memory and long-term memory (e.g. Baddeley and Hitch, 1974). Such a distinction appears to be revealed by a wide range of cognitive tasks, and corresponds to the difference between dynamic and static partitions in the present scheme. The second dimension corresponds in some ways to Tulving's (1972) distinction between 'semantic' and 'episodic' memory. On this view, semantic memory represents our general knowledge, dissociated from the specific situations in which it was acquired, while episodic memory refers to knowledge of particular episodes, in which information regarding how it was acquired is also retained. While acknowledging the similarities between the distinctions we are suggesting and those above, we shall simply

Table 8.1 The four memory partitions defined in terms of the static/dynamic distinction and whether or not the information they contain has its origins in the text or the knowledge-base of the reader.

	Dynamic	Static
Text-based	Explicit focus	Long-term text memory
Knowledge-based	Implicit focus	Long-term semantic memory

refer to the four memory types which result as *partitions* of memory. To summarize, the four partitions are:

Partition 1. Explicit focus. This may contain representations of entities and events mentioned in the text. It is of limited capacity, as discussed in Chapter 7.

Partition 2. Implicit focus. This is a currently selected subset of general knowledge which corresponds to the current scenario.

Partition 3. Long-term memory for the discourse — a specific subset of episodic memory.

Partition 4. Long-term semantic memory, or the knowledge-base.

In the next section of the chapter, it will be suggested that the semantic side of text understanding can be framed in terms of retrieval and construction processes operating within the constraints of these four partitions of memory. While there is a wide range of processes which may be described as 'semantic', we will restrict our discussion to one major class, that of interpreting reference. One basic stage in comprehension is the retrieval of word-sense information. At the other extreme, comprehension would be severely limited if the final result of semantic processing were not a coherent representation of the entire text. Between these two extremes must lie the mechanisms for constructing a unique model of the things being talked about and the relationships which exist between them. This is the fundamental problem of reference, and it is to this that we shall restrict our discussion.

Problems of reference have two major aspects. For any entity which is mentioned in a text, there must be some referring expression. Such expressions can take a variety of forms: for instance, pronouns, noun-phrases, both definite and indefinite, or even whole clauses. One of our concerns is to explore how these expressions could serve as processing directives, and so enable the reader to construct a unique configuration reflecting the relationships amongst the things mentioned in the text. Such an approach could be construed as an exercise in producing a procedural semantics of reference. The second aspect of the reference problem is the way in which the text as a whole seems to refer to recognizable events and episodes, of which the reader has general knowledge. The configuration of entities has to be mapped into general knowledge if the significance of a text is to be understood.

In Section B, we begin with a discussion of the nature of focus, based largely on the conclusions drawn in the previous chapters. This leads on to how a processor might use forms of referential description to instigate retrieval and construct operations within focus. This discussion will be largely analytical, attempting to define the necessary and sufficient conditions for the occurrence of such operations. We will suggest that the operations constitute the primary level of semantic processing, arising directly out of the parsing process. When references cannot be resolved in focus, other, more complex, processes are called for (which we have termed secondary processing). Such secondary processing is analysed in a later section, where it will be argued that it arises from failures in processing at the primary level.

Throughout Section B, the basic elements for a system of referential interpretation emerge, and this leads to an account of how a mental model of a discourse is constructed in the mind of the reader. In order to illustrate how such a system might work with a complete text, a short example is considered (Section C). Finally, the relationship of text-processing to memory for text is discussed in Section D.

Although much of this chapter is necessarily analytic, the claims made arise from the sort of problems which were highlighted by the empirical investigations described in previous chapters: for instance, claims about strength of representation, foregrounding, and the reality of scenarios. Our aim is to outline a system which is both sufficient to carry out the necessary processes and at the same time defensible, or at least testable, through standard experimental procedures of the kind described throughout the book.

B. Retrieving from and Constructing in Memory

1. The nature of focus

The two partitions of focus, explicit and implicit, have only one aspect in common. They serve to provide a retrieval domain which incorporates the information most pertinent to understanding the text at any given time. In some sense they embody the current 'topic' of the text. The utility of focus is computational — it provides a narrowed domain in which a search for referents begins. As workers in artificial intelligence are keen to point out, it is essential to constrain any search for potential referents if the search is going to take place in a reasonable length of time, or indeed if it is to be successful at all on many occasions (e.g. Grosz, 1977; Hirst, 1979). The potential success of a search can be looked at in terms of the *partial description* variable. Thus, as we have seen, pronouns provide such limited partial descriptions that they would lead to search procedures returning every entity which matched the description (sex, gender, number). Similar arguments can be made for simple noun-phrases. If the phrase 'the man' is introduced at some point in a text, then an unconstrained search for a referent made on the basis of this description would return a representation for every entity having this description. For this reason, it is necessary to constrain the likely search domain in order to limit referential ambiguity. In the previous chapters, evidence was provided in support of the claim that referential search for pronouns must be restricted to explicit focus, and that referential search instigated by definite noun-phrases be limited only to the focus partitions (partitions 1 and 2). For example, when some character is interpreted as playing a role in a scenario this must come about through a search of implicit focus.

Beyond providing restricted search domains, it must be argued that explicit and implicit focus have very different properties. Explicit focus must consist of representations of things mentioned in the discourse. Such representations we shall call *tokens*. Thus, when a new entity is mentioned in a text, a *token* for it is constructed in explicit focus, and when the reference resolution results from a search of this partition, the return of the search process is *a note that the partial description matches a specific token*. On the other hand, implicit focus is more complex structurally, since it consists of scenario representations, made up of slots and default specifications, bound together by relational programmatic information. When a reference resolution results from a search of implicit focus, there will be no token corresponding to its partial description, but there may be a slot corresponding to it in the scenario. Thus, the return of a successful search will be a note that the partial description matches a *slot* in implicit focus. In order to incorporate the linguistically 'new' entity into the memory representation, a **CONSTRUCT** operation will be carried out consisting of:

(a) **CONSTRUCT** (*in* explicit focus, *on basis of* partial description, token) and

(b) **CONSTRUCT** (*in* explicit focus, *on basis of* implicit focus slot, role description in scenario).

Thus, whenever implicit focus is implicated in a search procedure (which it usually is), the consequent **CONSTRUCT** results in a mapping between a token in explicit focus and the scenario itself. Suppose, for instance, that 'the waiter' is introduced as a linguistically 'new' entity which is represented as a role slot in the current scenario. The resulting structure in explicit focus would be:

Role 1

Waiter ——————— Scenario 1

where scenario 1 is a token specifying the address of (say) a 'restaurant' scenario in long-term memory. Of course, for such a mapping to come about, scenario 1 must have been currently singled out in implicit focus.

These arguments may be justified on psychological grounds. At the descriptive level, explicit focus can be thought of as containing tokens of entities mentioned in the text. However, the *representation* of the tokens is defined by the properties of explicit focus. A token points to a computational space in explicit focus, and the size of the space is the realization of the degree to which the entity is said to be foregrounded. The rules of foregrounding, described in the previous chapter, characterize rules operating on the computational spaces labelled by the tokens in explicit focus. As we argued, highly foregrounded entities seem to take priority in terms of mapping (or the **RETRIEVE** operation, as we shall now call it). This is quite reasonable, since the computational space available for comparing partial descriptions with tokens will be greater in the case of highly foregrounded entities, and thus the comparison should be more rapid in these cases.

If, as we suggest, explicit focus is a short-term store of limited capacity, then the amount of information held in it must, of course, be limited. Accordingly, we suggest that explicit focus only contains tokens and scenario pointers.[1] As new tokens are added, old ones will gradually diminish in terms of the computational space to which they point, until, eventually, they are no longer in focus at all.

Quite by contrast, implicit focus 'contains' current scenario information. There is no reason to suppose any capacity limitation here if implicit focus is thought of as a partition of long-term memory which is simply currently privileged in terms of ease of access. Thus, searching implicit focus may be construed as just a special kind of long-term memory search, which is severely constrained by the context. One way of characterizing this type of constrained search is in terms of filters imposed on the processor; filters which direct the search only within the currently focused partition of memory. So, for instance, if the processor needed to interpret the noun-phrase 'the waiter' while reading about someone in a restaurant, the search instruction might look like 'find the role "waiter" at locations in long-term memory partition RESTAURANT', where RESTAURANT corresponds to an address for the reader's 'restaurant' scenario. According to such an account, having a certain scenario in implicit focus simply means attaching the filter associated with that scenario to any search instructions which the processor might carry out. That is to say, the search domain 'implicit focus' is really an address in a partition of long-term memory. This principle corresponds to what Grosz (1977) has called a *focused search*. In the next section we shall describe the *partial description* in more detail, so that an example of focus in operation can be presented. For the moment, let us simply list some of the issues which arises from our discussion, and which will form the basis of the elaborations:

(a) How do various forms of reference — definite descriptions, indefinite descriptions, pronouns, restrictive relative clauses, etc. — set up tokens or match other tokens currently in focus?
(b) How are events which do not match scenarios handled?
(c) What kind of structure finally results from the operation of focus, and how does this relate to memory?

2. Forms of addressing focus

Focus may assist in the problem of search for referents, but this is only the start of the issue. Of primary concern is how the processing system comes to find referential resolutions in current focus (or, failing that, in long-term memory). Let us start by considering the apparently straightforward case of definite nominal reference. How does this category serve to instruct the processing system?

There are two major subcategories of definite reference: the simple, nominal pronoun (e.g. 'he', 'she', 'they', etc.) and the definite noun-phrase. Let us assume that whenever a definite reference is encountered, the processor will execute a retrieval operation of the following sort:

RETRIEVE   (a) *domain: focus*
(b) *partial description: noun-phrase (or pronoun) decomposition*
(c) *return: token identity* (if explicit focus), *slot identity* (if implicit focus).

In this formulation, one of the major characteristics postulated for definite references is that the search domain is restricted to current focus. However, the particular partitions of focus employed will depend upon the subcategory of the description. For example, simple nominal pronouns will only refer to individuals in explicit focus, as argued at length previously. Thus, for the pronoun 'she', the **RETRIEVE** operation may be specified in the following way:

RETRIEVE   (a) *domain: explicit focus*
(b) *partial description: -male, singular*
(c) *return: identity of matching token*

Although the partial description which may be derived from such a pronoun is minimal, **RETRIEVE** will be successful because the search domain will contain a very restricted number of tokens. On the other hand, in the case of a definite noun-phrase, the partial description available will be more informative, and, as was seen in the previous chapters, may address implicit as well as explicit focus. By being able to address the whole of focus, a definite noun phrase thus enables the processor to retrieve role slots as well as tokens.

The rationale for a processing distinction between pronoun and noun-phrase presumably arises from the differential payoff of the simplicity of checking a partial description against potential candidates and the size of the set of potential candidates. This leads to a simple empirical prediction. If the search domain for a pronoun is smaller than that of a noun-phrase, and the partial description for the search operation is simpler, then referential resolutions on the basis of a pronoun should be faster than a resolution based on a substituted noun-phrase. This can be related to the strange effect of using closely continguous anaphoric noun-phrase repetitions. Thus, (2′) seems strange to most readers:

(2) The donkey kicked its owner.
(2′) Then the donkey ran down the street.

It is much more appropriate to use a pronoun (*it*) in (2'). At the empirical level, evidence has already been presented which supports the view that the pronoun would give more satisfactory access to the explicit partition. In Purkiss's experiment (Chapter 7), when a pronoun reference was used for antecedents assumed to have a representation in the explicit partition, the dwell-time on the target sentence was actually shorter than it was when a repeated noun-phrase was used. This would follow if, on encountering a pronoun, the processor was set to deal only with the explicit partition.

When a **RETRIEVE** operation is successful, the return will be either the identities of tokens (in explicit focus) or role slots (in implicit focus). In order to integrate the new information associated with the mention of description, a further **CONSTRUCT** operation must take place. If the entity being mentioned already has a token in explicit focus, then the new information is simply attached to this token. If the reference only retrieves a role slot, then a new token for the entity is set up in explicit focus, and an identity mapping is made into the appropriate role slot. The outcome of this process may be represented as a token for the entity connected to a token labelled with the scenario address. The connection could be represented as an arc labelled in terms of the role specification to be found in the scenario. In this way, all **CONSTRUCT** products are deposited in explicit focus. This is consistent with our previous arguments, since **CONSTRUCT** operations produce the representation of the content of the text itself.

Other forms of reference beside definites can be analysed in much the same way. So far, only definite descriptions have been considered. Let us now consider how similar analyses can be applied to indefinite descriptions of the form A (n) + noun (phrase). This latter form of description is most typically used in a situation where the entity being introduced is new, as in:

(3) John kicked *a football* along the street.
(3') When it bounced off a car, *the football* broke a window.

In (3) the *football* in question is newly introduced, and in (3') it is given.

Before discussing some of the complications of definite and indefinite descriptions, let us characterize this formulation in terms of how definite and indefinite could serve to instruct the processor. We have suggested that on encountering a *definite* description, the priority strategy used by the processor is to **RETRIEVE** a unique individual from current focus (explicit or implicit) which fits the description and carry out the appropriate **CONSTRUCT** operation. On the other hand, with an *indefinite* description, the priority strategy used is to set up a token of what is being described and **CONSTRUCT** this token within explicit focus. In both cases, tokens in explicit focus would be tied to role slots in implicit focus wherever possible. So, in the case of example (3), *a football* signals a new token to be **CONSTRUCT**ed in explicit focus. At the same time, the complete action is represented in implicit focus, and the indefinite *football* is tied to the scenario of 'John doing the kicking, etc.'. When *the football* is encountered in (3'), the processor does not

CONSTRUCT a new token, but assigns the information predicated of *the football* to the original 'football' token in explicit focus. However, new tokens are set up for *a car* and *a window*, and these are bound to a newly evoked scenario in implicit focus, which was retrieved by the entire event description. The two scenarios are linked by *the football* (and, possibly, by *John*, but this is not important for the moment).

Although at first sight this analysis seems to capture the essential difference between definite and indefinite descriptions, there are a number of problems. Let us first consider a case in which a token is already available in explicit focus, but in which the indefinite article is still used:

(4) Three Englishmen, an Irishman, and a Scotsman were having a discussion.

(4') An Englishman said 'it made a change not to be outnumbered'.

In this case, (4) should CONSTRUCT three tokens for 'Englishman', one for 'Irishman', and one for the 'Scotsman'. According to the account up to now, the phrase *an Englishman* should act as an instruction to the processor to CONSTRUCT a new token 'Englishman' in explicit focus. But the example is clearly handled in a yet more complicated way. Most readers of this pair of sentences are struck by the fact that the phrase *an Englishman* could possibly refer to one of the three 'Englishman' tokens already in explicit focus. What is striking about (4') is that it seems to be rather curious, or even ambiguous. The term *an Englishman* could refer to yet another (new) entity, and thus require another token to be set up. The ambiguity of this example is interesting, in that it shows how an indefinite description does not *simply* result in a CONSTRUCT operation for a new token, but also seems to involve a RETRIEVE for any token in explicit focus. Indeed, the ambiguity would usually be handled in different ways, since it is more natural to say:

(5) *One of the Englishmen* said that it made a change not to be outnumbered

if the objective is to RETRIEVE one (unspecified) token from the existing set of tokens, or:

(6) *Another Englishman* said it made a change not to be outnumbered

if the objective is to set up a new token. Indeed, in an informal study in which a small number of informants were asked to choose between (4') and (5) as a way of expressing the situation where a new token need not be introduced, all informants chose (5) as the best way of doing it. We would suggest, therefore, that the indefinite in this case does cause the processor to try to CONSTRUCT a new token, but that *if possible* the token is tentatively identified as being one and the same as an existing token. To circumvent the first stage, in normal discourse, format (5) is used rather than (4').

In this way, the expression one of + definite noun-phrase could be represented as shown below, provided the appropriate tokens are in explicit focus.

RETRIEVE: (a) *domain: focus*

(b) *partial description: noun-phrase (or pronoun) decomposition*

(c) *return*: if from explicit focus, *any one token identity*

On the other hand, the expression *another + noun-phrase*, with suitable referents in explicit focus should produce the following

RETRIEVE: (a) *domain: explicit focus*

(b) *partial description : noun-phrase (or pronoun description)*

(c) *return: identities of matching tokens*

and

CONSTRUCT: (a) *domain: explicit focus*

(b) *information to be incorporated: token and identity tag (based on matching tokens retrieved)*

(c) *resulting structure: labelled token.*

To return to our original ambiguous example (4) and (4′), if the reader entertains the possibility that *an Englishman* might refer to one of the set of existing tokens, then the implication is that indefinites in themselves do not simply serve as instructions to **CONSTRUCT**, but have a **RETRIEVE** component also. There is both experimental justification for this assertion and, as we shall see shortly, it is a logical requisite of the use of the indefinite.

In the study carried out to look at straightforward anaphora (Chapter 6: Garrod and Sanford, 1977, 1978), one condition used a semantically related but non-coreferential pair of noun-phrases:

(7) The tank/bus came trundling round the bend.

(7′) It almost hit a vehicle.

In this case, the presence of a conjoint frequency effect on (7′) was taken as a sign that subjects were checking whether *a vehicle* was coreferential with *the tank/bus*. Thus, it would appear that semantic overlap precipitated an attempt to check for coreference, even in a syntactically unfavourable environment. Nevertheless, ultimately, a new token has to be created for *a vehicle* in explicit focus, because it is the only way (7) and (7′) can be integrated.

In general, indefinite references to entities having tokens in explicit focus will result in setting up a new token, recognizing that it is a new entity, regardless of the curious and strained examples considered above. However, other cases show that it is a good strategy to search in focus for a referent, even with indefinite descriptions. It is particularly clear with the next case.

Let us examine the situation in which only *slots* are available in *implicit* focus. Consider first the use of the indefinite article:

(8) John was hungry and so he went into restaurant.

(8′) A waiter gave him the menu.

Such a case is basically straightforward. A new token, 'waiter', is set up in explicit focus, and is mapped into implicit focus. Although the waiter in question is unspecified, the 'waiter' role occurs in many places in the restaurant scenario, and the set 'waiters' occurs in the general set of roles within the scenario too. Thus, the token 'waiter' maps into the scenario easily, given the specific action description of 'John being given a menu'. In this case, a definite description would cause no problems either, as in:

(9) The waiter gave him a menu.

This is because the action as a whole singles out one *particular* waiter — the one who is interacting with John.

Thus, in the examples described above, both definite and indefinite descriptions introducing the *waiter* have the same end result — a token is set up in explicit focus, together with a mapping into a role slot in implicit focus. So even with a definite description, if there is no existing token in explicit focus, one will be constructed.

Despite these apparent similarities, the two forms of reference do have different processing implications. These arise through a difference in priority of the **CONSTRUCT** and **RETRIEVE** operation which they instigate. For the successful primary processing of an indefinite, it is *necessary* that a new token is set up whether or not any existing token or slot is retrievable. On the other hand, for the definite description, it is the successful retrieval which is necessary whether or not a new token needs to be constructed. With a definite description there is no point in first *constructing* a token in explicit focus since there may be one there already. With the indefinite there is no point in first trying to RETRIEVE a token or slot since a new one will have to be CONSTRUCTed in any case.

3. Addressing outside of focus

The cases discussed above assume that referential resolution can be successful because there is either a token in explicit focus, or a suitable slot in implicit focus, or both. In any piece of discourse, this need not be the case, and when such resolution is not possible, *secondary processing* is called for. We have just argued that there is a difference in the priority of **RETRIEVE** and **CONSTRUCT** operations with respect to focus, when using definite and indefinite descriptions. The distinction is made equally clear when one considers addressing outside of focus.

Once a search has to take place beyond the boundaries of current focus, the number of potential returns becomes very large if the partial description conveys little specifying information. The significance of this can be illustrated by way of a fairly close analogy. Suppose a man to be making an arrangement to meet his wife. He gives her an address, perhaps 'I'll meet you at the end of Hope Street'. This reference can only be resolved if she knows that he means 'Hope Street, Glasgow', and not any other 'Hope Street'. The partial description 'Hope Street' is adequate only if the search domain is restricted to Glasgow. A much longer partial description would have to be used if there were more alternatives available — 'Hope Street, Birmingham, Alabama', for example. So it is with long-term memory reference. Even with relatively recently evoked scenarios, simple noun-phrase references to entities implicit in them can rapidly become awkward, as in:

Peter decided to go to the cinema.

He was shown to his seat, a good one, and enjoyed the film.

Later he had a meal, and went home to work.

He couldn't concentrate on the work, so he watched TV.

The lady newscaster reminded him of the usherette.

The phrase *the usherette* seems decidedly awkward, although it can be resolved. We would be more likely to find a greater specification more acceptable, as in *the usherette at the cinema*. In a longer piece of discourse, it may need to be still more specific, as in *the usherette at the cinema he went to earlier*, for instance. All of this suggests that the *restrictive relative clause* is an appropriate formulation for achieving successful reference resolution outside of current focus. Furthermore, the noticeable thing about the restrictive relative clause is that it can contain sufficient information to activate an entire scenario, either new, or (as in the example above) a previously used scenario which now forms part of the long-term memory representation of the discourse.

We shall now consider how relative clauses might be handled within this framework. Consider the clause:

(10) The man who brought the soup . . . .

This may be interpreted in two distinct ways: either as a restrictive relative clause, or as a non-restrictive relative clause. In the first case (restrictive), it can be seen as singling out a particular man, and in the second case, as telling the reader something new about a man. The distinction is made clear when we look at the **RETRIEVE** operation which may take place on encountering such a clause. If a unique token for 'a man' already exists in explicit focus, then the processor will return with the identity of that token when executing a **RETRIEVE** operation for the initial noun-phrase *the man*. The new information *(who brought the soup)* can then be attached to this token. This exemplifies the non-restrictive resolution of the clause. In contrast, if no unique token for 'the man' is in explicit focus, then the initial **RETRIEVE** operation will fail, and the remaining information in the clause will be added to the existing partial description to augment it. In this way, the clause is used in a restrictive manner.

In this second case, the operation of **RETRIEVE** now becomes a secondary search process. The discovery of the restrictive property serves to instigate a search for resolution on the basis of the augmented partial description. When the description does not match anything in focus, the more detailed specification can serve as an adequate retrieval cue for entities which only have representations in the static partitions of memory. In this way, secondary processing is seen as being instigated through a failure of a **RETRIEVE** operation at the primary level. This can be illustrated by considering an example in which an indefinite noun-phrase is followed by a relative clause:

(11) A man who brought the soup . . . .

In this case, the only available interpretation of the clause is that it is non-restrictive, providing only attributive information to be attached to the token set up by the noun-phrase *a man*. This comes about because a successful **RETRIEVE** operation is not a necessary condition for the success of primary processing with indefinite descriptions.

To return to the restrictive case, the advantage of a long partial description is that it enables referential resolution to take place when there would be too large a number of possible referents with a shorter description. The augmented partial description is made possible because, in a secondary process, use can be made of partially interpreted information from an entire sentence or more. This is one major distinction between **RETRIEVE** operations at the two levels, because with primary processing only a simple noun-phrase serves as the partial description.

Secondary processing will take place in any situation where primary-level descriptions are inadequate to select a unique referent. Thus, if a text had contained mentions of two Englishmen, one with red hair and one who had black hair, then 'the Englishman' would not be an adequate description to make a selection, and primary processing would fail. However, if the description 'the Englishman who had red hair' were used, secondary **RETRIEVE** processing would return with the identity of the appropriate token. With longer texts, as we argued in Chapter 7, and shall elaborate later, we may assume that there may no longer be suitable tokens for a particular individual in focus, even though that individual may have been mentioned before. In such a case, the appropriate search domain would be the static, long-term memory partitions. So, for instance, it may not be adequate for us to write 'Schank's statement' if we have not been writing about it sufficiently recently for it to be in focus. Rather, we would have to say to which *particular* statement we were referring. The longer partial description which would be given in this way should be sufficient to enable the reader to retrieve the appropriate information from memory.

Another major function of secondary processing is the selection of scenarios for implicit focus. At the outset of reading a new piece of discourse, the reader will have no scenario in implicit focus. Consequently, any entities or actions mentioned will necessarily fail when primary **RETRIEVE** operations are attempted. While **CONSTRUCT** operations will guarantee the establishment of token representations, in order to interpret the text adequately (*vide* Chapter 6) a scenario must be selected. As in the case of the restrictive relative clause, discussed above, the configuration of entities and actions may provide an augmented partial description for a secondary **RETRIEVE** operation resulting in the return of an address for a scenario of which the description is a partial match. So, for example, with the initial sentence:

(12) The waiter brought the soup

none of the entities mentioned will find a suitable token or slot in focus. New tokens will be set up in explicit focus as a result of **CONSTRUCT**, but the failure of the primary **RETRIEVE**s for both noun-phrases should be sufficient to instigate a secondary **RETRIEVE** with a partial description corresponding to the entire event (i.e. roles + action). As we have previously argued in Chapter 6, such an event description may match a particular element in the scenario representing 'eating in a restaurant'. In this case, then, the return of the **RETRIEVE** will be the address of this particular scenario, which may then be used as a search filter to guide subsequent **RETRIEVE**s, which would then be at the primary level. Of course, as we pointed out in Chapter 6, the amount of information in a partial description which is sufficient to return a scenario address will vary widely, but additions to the description, based on the text, will continue to be made by the processor until such a return is obtained. Again, secondary processing is seen as arising through failures at the primary level.

One kind of failure at the primary level which is of particular importance happens when some new event is described which cannot map into a current scenario. Given a sufficient description of the event, the secondary **RETRIEVE** which would result from this should lead to a return of the address of a new scenario, or a specific subset of the existing scenario, and will serve as a new basis for interpreting incoming text.

We are now in a position to summarize the main points. The major problem which we set out to examine was the relationship between comprehension and memory. This is most clearly seen in reference resolution, which is characterized above in terms of **RETRIEVE** and **CONSTRUCT** operations. We have argued that these operations require four specific partitions of memory in which to locate or deposit information, and that certain linguistic cues (e.g. pronouns and definite and indefinite articles) serve to guide the manner in which **RETRIEVE** and **CONSTRUCT** take place. In describing these processes, we have suggested that it is important to distinguish between primary- and secondary-level processing.

Primary-level processing can be directly linked to the operation of a syntactic parser, which identifies such basic categories as noun-phrase and verb-phrase. So, for instance, when a noun-phrase is identified, this will lead directly to primary semantic processing, which is aimed at both resolving reference in focus and constructing representations in focus. Such processing will be rapid, because the search domain is limited to two small partitions, and is, of course, achieved on the basis of short descriptions which are immediately available. In terms of a more general view of text comprehension, primary processing is processing within the constraints of the local topic of the discourse itself, embodied in the focus partitions of memory.

Failures of primary processing instigate secondary processing. References which remain unresolved at the primary level become part of the partial description on which secondary-level **RETRIEVE** operations can now be based. The search domain for secondary **RETRIEVE**s is large, comprising the entire memory space, and typically, returns are found in the static partitions. Thus secondary processing is both slower than is primary, and longer partial descriptions are required for its success. Taking a general view of comprehension once more, secondary processing provides the means by which new topics can be introduced, or earlier topics reintroduced to current focus.

4. Matching problems in reference resolution

Explicit focus has been characterized as the working memory space which serves as repository for new information conveyed by the text. One of the main ways of representing this information is through *tokens*, which raises the question of how a token should be labelled. The following illustrations suggest that the answer must lie in the relationship which a noun-phrase bears to the current state of focus. Consider first the introduction of a person described as *a waiter* in the context of a scenario which is unrelated to restaurants. The new information in this case will be existence of a person who is a waiter, and could be represented as a token for the person with the qualifying information 'is a waiter' attached to it, the whole complex residing in explicit focus. Now consider a similar case, but in the context of a restaurant scenario. The structure in this case will be a token for a person, connected to the scenario token by a role defining arc, as described above. The point is that attributional information which cannot be handled by the current scenario is represented in explicit focus. This treatment of the distinction between attributive and purely referential descriptions is analogous to some of the arguments about restrictive and nonrestrictive relative clauses, made earlier.

For our third example, we shall consider a hybrid case, in which part of a noun-phrase serves to identify a role-slot in implicit focus (the *noun*), and part of it is purely attributional (an *adjective*). Given a 'restaurant' scenario in implicit focus, a reference to 'a *handsome* waiter' would result in a token and role mapping for the *waiter*, but *handsome* would not be accommmodated. After all, there is no slot for *handsome*: waiters are not necessarily, or perhaps even normally, characterized as being handsome. Thus the information 'is handsome' will be attached to the token in explicit focus. Such adjectival qualifications are often used to emphasize the entity qualified, or to bring the reader's attention to some aspect of that entity. This is intelligible in terms of the theory of foregrounding.

We suggest that qualifying information of the kind described above serves to boost the degree of foregrounding of the qualified individual, thus providing a basis for emphasis within the constraints of working memory. In our initial discussions of foregrounding, it was suggested that tokens point to computational space in explicit focus. The greater the space to which a token points, the greater the degree to which it can be said to be foregrounded. Now, in the case where attributional information has to be represented in explicit focus, this effectively increases the foregrounding of the token to which it is attached.

The implications of this can be tested empirically. Anything which is foregrounded is more readily available for reference, and is more likely to be referred to by a pronoun (Chapter 7), and this should apply to entities which are foregrounded through specifying information, if the present arguments are correct. A useful way of testing the idea is through the passage continuation task, discussed in the preceding chapter. Such a study has been carried out by Anne Anderson. Two matched sets of passages were prepared along the following lines:

(13) *The bus journey*
Mrs. Grey was travelling by bus.
A (teenage) conductor collected the fares.
The bus jolted and rattled as it went.
After two hours joints still ached.

The scenario-based character in this is the conductor. One group of subjects encountered the passage without the qualifying adjective *teenage*, while the other group saw the passage with it in. A total of 40 such passage pairs was used with a total of 53 subjects. They were asked to write brief continuations of each of the 40 stories.

In terms of the discussion of foregrounding above, the adjective should have the effect of reinforcing the representation of the scenario-bound character, bolstering its foregrounded status. The prediction for continuation should therefore be that an adjective will increase the likelihood of the scenario-bound character being mentioned. Anderson's results showed that the topic character (*Mrs. Grey* in this example) was more likely to appear in continuation than the scenario-bound character (1185 *versus* 333 mentions), but that of the 333 mentions of the scenario-bound character, 181 followed on from adjectival modification and only 152 from unmodified noun-phrases, a reliable difference. The results thus appear to bear out the contention that adjectives increase foregrounding status.

Given these results, questions about predictability in general may be raised. Consider some of the roles which might enter into a restaurant scenario: *customer(s), waiter(s), wine-waiter, chef, cook(s), dishwasher.* Now if a person were asked to list different roles in a restaurant, it is highly unlikely each of these would come to mind equally easily. Some may be omitted altogether. Obviously, some roles seem more likely to be important elements of a scenario than others. According to the argument made for the adjectives, while the important roles would not be strongly foregrounded when mentioned, less important roles might well be, on the grounds that they cannot be so readily accommodated by the scenario. As before, this idea translates easily into empirical predictions, both for continuation and reading time. A relevant study has, in fact, been carried out within the reading-time situation.

One empirical test is that it should be easier (take less time) to resolve a pronominal reference to a weakly predicted role-filler than to a strongly predicted role-filler. Again, the baseline is that principal characters should be the easiest to refer to. But a further prediction can be made. In the previous chapter it was shown how scenario-dependent characters lose in foregrounding when the relevance of the scenario is contra-indicated by an appropriate time-change reference. Now this effect should be most readily detected with poorly predicted scenario-dependent role-fillers, because they will be the only ones which can lose much so far as foregrounding status is concerned. Strongly predicted role-fillers, being only weakly foregrounded, should have less to lose, and show a rather weaker effect.

Anne Anderson has examined these proposals empirically. She produced sets of scenario-dependent characters which were either highly or poorly predicted. A large group of subjects were asked to write down characters which they would expect to find in a list of stereotyped settings. Characters mentioned by everyone served as the highly predicted group; characters not mentioned but nevertheless relating directly to the situation served as the poorly predicted group. Typical examples are — *restaurant*: *waiter* (good), *dishwasher* (poor).

Using these examples in materials like those in her earlier reading-time experiment, she recorded the reading times for target sentences after small or large time changes. The mean reading times are shown in Figure 8.1. As is suggested in the figure, the only reliable effect of a large time change occurs with the poorly predicted scenario-bound characters. This is exactly as would

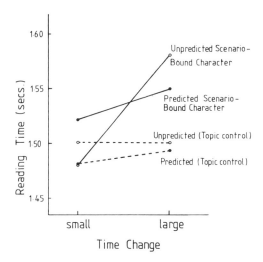

Figure 8.1 Mean reading times for sentences containing references to predicted and unpredicted scenario-bound characters after large or small time changes. Also shown are the reading times for topic control sentences (from both the predicted and the unpredicted reference group).

be expected if it is only poorly predicted entities which are represented in explicit focus. While the reading times for subsequent reference to predicted entities are numerically greater than the topic reference control, this effect is not quite reliable in this experiment. However, the overall pattern of results is exactly as predicted.

5. Event resolution and scenario mismatches

Up to now, we have considered the resolution of nominal references only, although actions have been mentioned *en passant*. In a situation where a new sentence describes an action which is part of a scenario, this can be readily interpreted by the operation of primary processing. So, if a discourse were about a visit to a barber's shop, and the sentence

(14) The assistant cut John's hair

were encountered, tokens for *John* and *the assistant* would be mapped into the appropriate role slots. In this case, the mapping would be into that part of the scenario representation where the programmatic act of 'barber cuts customer's hair' was represented. No new token or representation of *cut* would be incorporated into explicit focus, because the entire character–action complex can be simply represented as mappings. The significance of the sentence — the way it is understood — comes about simply through these mappings. If a subsequent sentence were to be:

(15) Then she held up the mirror for him to see her work

a new set of role mappings would be produced, connecting the same tokens to the programmatic act representation of 'barber holds up mirror for customer to scrutinize his work'. So it would be for any perfectly predicted event.

However, when an action does not fit the scenario (as must often be the case), the **CONSTRUCT** operation must be rather different. Suppose that the sentence had been:

(16) The waiter ate John's soup.

In such a case, primary **RETRIEVE** operations would successfully return token identities for *the waiter*, *John*, and *soup*, but the entire action would not fit a programmatic element in the scenario.

Just as an adjective which cannot be assimilated into a scenario serves to foreground the individual qualified by that adjective, so it should be with whole events which do not match a scenario specification. A mismatch should receive a fairly strong representation in explicit focus, and consequently should produce more continuations, as illustrated in the adjective experiment described above. At the present stage, this prediction has not been examined empirically. However, in a later section it will be argued that foregrounding strength is reflected in what is remembered in a piece of discourse, and it has been established that events which do not fit script-like scenarios are remembered better than events which do (Bower *et al.*, 1979; cf. Chapter 4).

The relation between implicit and explicit focus is therefore a complex one. While explicit focus is primarily taken up with representing foregrounded information not already represented in implicit focus, it is also true that the processor will always attempt to map the explicitly focused information into some scenario in implicit focus. If this cannot be done at all, some new scenario is sought until there is a possible mapping. Thus, mismatches with implicit focus will tend to lead to its modification. Under these circumstances, the original scenario may be totally displaced (as when there is a complete change of scene) or, more commonly, it will incorporate in some way the new scenario as a subpart or specification on the original. In this way, the implicit focus partition may be changed or extended or further specified as a result of incompatible inputs. It is this set of mappings between explicit and implicit focus which corresponds to the mental model of the text built up by the reader.

C. Focus in Action — An Example

Up to this point we have sketched out the mechanics of reference resolution in terms of the different ways in which referential descriptions are given in a text. Each case was considered in isolation; in this section we shall illustrate and summarize our ideas on how the complete memory system might operate in building up a final, long-term memory representation of a complete piece of discourse. This we shall do in order to illustrate a number of issues: first, to show how representations are built up in explicit focus, secondly, how these map into implicit focus, and finally, to show how the long-term representation arises from explicit focus.

While much of what is said clearly follows from the discussion in this and other chapters, there are occasions when essentially *ad hoc* assumptions about processing have to be made. In some cases this is simply because there are aspects of the parsing system which have not been discussed, such as how it should deal with sentential connectives or how it should handle temporal information. The general approach taken is to assume that anything in the linguistic input can be treated as a directive to the parsing system to take some action, and in these cases a suitable action is proposed. So, for instance, if the system encounters the string '. . . x so y . . .', we make the assumption that it treats 'x' as the 'cause of' or 'reason for' 'y'. This might be questionable, but such assumptions are needed to illustrate the less arbitrary aspect of the system.

There are, however, some cases where the arbitrariness of assumptions derives from limitations in the framework itself. For instance, when discussing the content of any scenario which might be evoked by a statement in the example, one inevitably enters the realm of speculation. The main reason for this is that while the structure of human knowledge is something which is in principle specifiable (see Chapter 2 for instance), its content is bound to be subject to a wide range of individual variations. We will often suggest that a certain statement evokes a scenario containing certain information; in all such cases we assume that the processing system is acting like a hypothetical reader who would possess such a scenario. However, as will be pointed out, there are many cases where the particular scenario evoked would be dependent on the background or inclination of the reader being modelled. While this is clearly a limitation, we believe that it is the only realistic way of recognizing the fact that readers with different background knowledge will, in fact, interpret the same text in different ways.

In presenting the example, the text will be built up a sentence at a time, while the relevant actions of the processing system are discussed. The first sentence is:

(17) Mary was dressing the baby.

On encountering this, any primary **RETRIEVE** on the basis of the noun-phrases and verb-phrase will fail, because there will be nothing in focus. Thus, the processor will combine the entire action into a new partial description, and use this as the basis of a secondary **RETRIEVE**. This should return a scenario (call it scenario 1) for 'someone dressing a baby', with tokens for *Mary* and *the baby* mapped by identity relations into the appropriate role slots. Figure 8.2 gives a representation of this. The token for *Mary* is printed with a bold

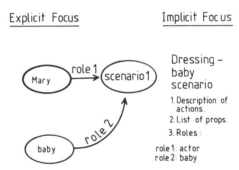

Figure 8.2   Hypothetical state of explicit and implicit focus partition after interpretation of the sentence: 'Mary was dressing the baby'.

surround: this convention represents the degree of foregrounding or workspace allocated to this token. It is greater than that allocated to the token for *the baby*, because *Mary* is the topic of the sentence (*vide* Chapter 7). The role mappings point to the token for the scenario itself, and this token consists of the address of the part of long-term memory where the scenario information is to be found.

Once focus is set up in this way, primary processing **RETRIEVE**s are now possible. By this means, subsequent inputs may be interpreted in terms of focus when appropriate. Suppose the discourse continues:

(17) Mary was dressing the baby.

(18) When she had finished, they went to the shops.

Faced with (18), the processor attempts interpretation at the primary processing level, starting with the first clause. The word *when* is assumed to serve as a primary directive to treat whatever follows as fixing a reference at some (as yet unknown) point in time. The pronoun *she* is a directive to **RETRIEVE** a suitable token identity from explicit focus, and *Mary* will be identified. The verb-phrase *had finished* should recover a lexical structure with a slot for 'some action' which is the action being terminated. Although there is no such action mentioned explicitly in the current clause, one can be found by a secondary **RETRIEVE** in current focus combining *Mary* and some (as yet unspecified) action in which she was a participant. The return of such an operation will be scenario 1, together with the mappings of 'Mary' and the 'baby' in it.

The verb-phrase *had finished* heralds the end of one episode and the start of another. The main event of scenario 1 is now tagged as being in the past — in fact, it is a special case of the time-change device discussed in the previous chapter. By definition, the new time reference is beyond the range of the current scenario. The main clause *they went to the shops* gives rise to a mixture of primary and secondary processing. The pronoun *they* instigates a **RETRIEVE** in the domain of explicit focus, and matches the tokens for *Mary* and *the baby*, but the event *went to the shops* does not find a match in focus. Thus the entire main clause becomes a partial description on the basis of which a new scenario may be identified.

The result of all this might be to produce a new representation like that shown in Figure 8.3. The total scenario in this situation might well have two

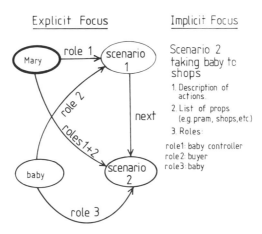

Figure 8.3   Hypothetical state of explicit and implicit focus after: 'Mary was dressing the baby. When she had finished, they went to the shops.'

components: one based on standard procedures for looking after babies while out at the shops, the other based on standard procedures for what happens at the shops. It is therefore a *hybrid* rather than single scenario. Of course, if a reader is familiar with the situation, a ready-made module might be available. And if the reader has never had any dealings with babies, the baby aspect may be entirely missing. Only experimental tests with references to implicit focus, using people of different backgrounds, would be able to solve this problem. In essence, such tests are possible.

The pointer connecting the token for scenario 1 to the token for scenario 2 is labelled *next*. This is a simple connection to which we have given an arbitrary label, but which nevertheless conveys temporal progression and would arise from the change in temporal reference described above.

Suppose the next sentence to be:

(19) She was thirsty, so she sat down in a cafe.

Again, the mapping of *she* is straightforward. The stative *was thirsty* implies a goal and an antecedent. The function word *so* is interpreted by the processor as heralding an action or state following upon the existing state, and finds its match in the action *she sat down in a cafe*. As yet, this has no referential resolution. There is no primary-level resolution available for being thirsty and the subsequent action, but as a partial description for a secondary **RETRIEVE** there is ample information to return the location of a scenario for 'a customer in a cafe':

Being thirsty (precondition)

Sitting down in a cafe (setting plus event).

Because the pronoun *she* has been identified with the token *Mary*, role mappings are made between the new current scenario and *Mary* (customer identity). The result might be represented as shown in Figure 8.4.

The multiple-role arrows connecting *Mary* to the 'cafe' scenario represent *Mary* being mapped into the stages of the programmatic components which have been made explicit. The pointer connecting the nodes for scenarios 2 and 3 is labelled 'next', again to indicate the sequential nature of the actions.

The state of explicit focus is now interesting. Mary has been mentioned again twice and *the baby* has not, so *Mary's* allocation of workspace has gone up relative to that of the baby, and it should now be more difficult to refer to *the baby* than before. Furthermore, the workspace allocated to the scenario 1 token will have diminished, because it has not been used, and the workspace allocated to the token for scenario 2 will also be less than that allocated to the scenario 3 token, because scenario 3 is currently in use. It might be helpful at this point to make the difference clear between scenario tokens, in explicit focus, and the current scenario in implicit focus. Explicit focus contains a record of scenarios previously used (in the form of their addresses), whereas the current scenario in implicit focus provides the processor with the current primary implicit search domain. It is only through the current scenario that incoming text can be interpreted at the primary level. Note, however, that

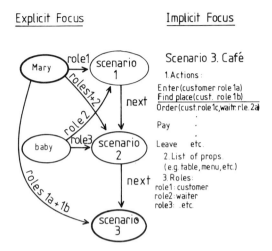

Explicit Focus   Implicit Focus

Figure 8.4 Hypothetical state of explicit and implicit focus after: 'Mary was dressing the baby. When she had finished, they went to the shops. She was thirsty, so she sat down in a cafe'.

previously activated scenarios may still be recoverable through secondary processing, using scenario tokens as part of the partials description.

Because of the limited capacity of explicit focus, at some point the tokens of explicitly mentioned individuals and tokens for scenarios will have no more workspace allocated to them. At this stage, all that is left of them is a long-term memory representation. We shall consider how transfer to long-term memory occurs in the next section. Let us assume that the scenario 1 token is no longer in explicit focus, add another sentence to the discourse, and consider the result. Suppose the sentence to be:

(20) She was served by a handsome Italian waiter.

The mapping of *she* proceeds as before. *Getting served* and *a waiter* are both identifiable referents through implicit focus, and so further role mappings are entered between *she* and the scenario and a new token set up in explicit focus for *the waiter* and the scenario. *Handsome Italian* is a constraint which cannot be interpreted by anything in focus, and so it is entered into explicit focus as an attribute of *waiter*. The result is shown in Figure 8.5.

By now, scenario 2 has not had its status in explicit focus reinforced; nor has *the baby*. The emphasis is on *Mary*, scenario 3, and *the waiter*. *The waiter* is relatively highly foregrounded because of the attributions connected to him, which *have to be* represented in explicit focus since they cannot simply be accommodated by the scenario. The tokens for scenario 2 and *the baby* are either about to lose or already have lost any status in explicit focus. They remain only in long-term memory.

Most of the defensible aspects of our account have already been exhausted

180

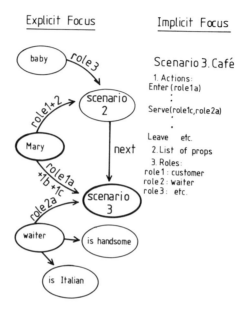

Explicit Focus

Implicit Focus

Scenario 3. Café
1. Actions:
Enter (role1a)
:
Serve(role1c,role2a)
.
Leave etc.
2. List of props
3. Roles:
role1 : customer
role2 : waiter
role3 : etc.

Figure 8.5   Hypothetical state of explicit and implicit focus after: 'Mary was dressing the baby. When she had finished, they went to the shops. She was thirsty, so she sat down in a cafe. She was served by a handsome Italian waiter'.

by this example, and even at this stage we have introduced a number of *ad hoc* assumptions which are merely plausible within the framework being offered. Nevertheless, the example serves to make the relationships of foregrounding, focus, scenarios, and reference as clear as possible at this stage. We shall continue more generally, highlighting some of the broader problems which emerge from thinking of text-processing in this way.

At this point, some evaluation of our treatment of the example is called for. First of all, processing at the primary level is more readily described because it is not subject to substantive individual variation. A failure in identifying the referent of a pronoun, for example, is not a case of misunderstanding the message of the writer, but is rather a complete failure to comprehend. Such a case is nicely exemplified by a piece of nonsense from Lewis Carroll's *Alice in Wonderland*:

(21) I gave her one, they gave him two,
    You gave us three or more:
    They all returned from him to you,
    Though they were mine before.

On the other hand, the nature of secondary processing is much more difficult to specify, since it is determined by the reader's interests, knowledge, and skill. For example, when we mentioned 'Mary going to the shops', we arbitrarily suggested that this invokes a scenario representing going to the shops. Indeed, for some readers, this may be the case. For others, the information may simply be represented in explicit focus, until subsequent information is combined with it to provide a suitable partial description to evoke some other scenario. Thus, one degree of freedom in the account results from individual variations in the efficacy of a description in retrieving a scenario. A second degree of freedom results from the content of any scenario which is retrieved. As we mentioned earlier, for some readers, a specific scenario may include not only 'going to the shops', but also 'with a baby'. Such differences carry important implications for subsequent processing. If a later reference is made to 'the baby being cold', it would be easily interpreted if a suitable scenario were available, but would require more complex processing if one were not. It is for these reasons that in discussing any particular example, descriptions of secondary processing will be more speculative than descriptions of primary processing.

D. The Focus System and Long-Term Memory Representation of Text

When the comprehension framework was first outlined at the beginning of this chapter, a distinction was made between the dynamic partitions of focus and the static partitions of long-term memory. We proposed that the latter partitions contained, among other things, knowledge representations (scenarios) and a long-term representation of the interpreted text. In this section, we will make some suggestions about the nature of the memory representation of the text once interpreted.

As was pointed out in Chapter 4, studies of memory have traditionally been used to draw inferences about processes of comprehension. Here we shall examine the rather obvious, but different, notion that memory patterns can be predicted on the basis of the comprehension process itself. Our method will be simple, taking the focus framework as the basis for a comprehension process and attempting to derive from this some sort of long-term representation which might be expected to survive. In fact, this is a reasonable proposition, since it is clear from looking at the type of memory access which occurs naturally during reading that some long-term representation of the prior text is needed for comprehension of the current material to take place.

1. Explicit focus and memory

Let us begin by supposing that the long-term representation of a discourse is a record of the structure unfolding in explicit focus. So, returning to the example discussed in the previous section, a representation based on the four sentences of the passage might be that shown in Figure 8.6. This structure consists of entity and scenario tokens, plus a number of pointers which specify the roles of entities in the various scenarios. As we have been at pains to point out, scenario contents themselves will not be directly represented in explicit

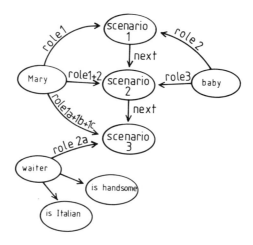

Figure 8.6 Hypothetical long-term memory representation of the example text considered in Section C.

focus; however, it is clear that the long-term representation will need to be able to make contact with this information during recall or recognition. Such contact is achieved because each role-pointer has as its target terminal the scenario token representing the address of the scenario itself. Thus, the whole long-term structure could serve as a key for the retrieval of scenario information, bringing it back into implicit focus when required. In effect, the long-term representation would be both a repository for information (as in the case of the tokens) plus a plan for retrieval. So far as giving any specific explanation of how text memory comes about, the account which we are suggesting really makes only one point: part of what is remembered will have its origins in the prior contents of explicit focus, whereas another part will reflect the original contents of implicit focus, and so be reconstructed from general knowledge.

However, there are a few other assumptions to be made before any valuable memory predictions can be proposed. The first assumption is that everything (or virtually everything) which is processed in explicit focus will in some way be recoverable from the long-term memory representation. This might at first seem unreasonable, since recall for text is notoriously sketchy, reflecting the gist of the passage rather than its detail (cf. Chapter 4). However, as McKoon (1977) demonstrated, errors in *recognition* memory for texts as long as 200 words were really quite low, even when subjects had read as many as 32 paragraphs. Of course, this does not mean that everything is equally easy to recover. As McKoon found, 'important' parts of the text were more rapidly recognized than unimportant parts. This would suggest that the strength of representation (in terms of accessibility) is not uniformly registered in explicit focus.

Our second assumption derives from this point. It is that transfer of a structure to long-term memory can only occur while that structure resides in explicit focus, and that the strength of representation of any element will be a direct function of how long it remained there. Of course, the time over which anything resides in explicit focus is a joint function of foregrounding and usage, as we have already argued. Thus, a particular explicitly mentioned entity gains in foregrounding every time it is mentioned, and drops in strength when other things are mentioned instead. Oft-mentioned entities reside in focus longer, and therefore their representations will give rise to stronger representations in long-term memory.

Similar arguments apply to scenario tokens. The strength of representation of a particular scenario token should depend upon the length of time over which the scenario itself is used in processing. It does not matter whether the scenario is called in and out of implicit focus from time to time as the text unfolds, or whether it is simply used once for a great deal of contiguous processing. This assumption is at the heart of our suggestions concerning the manner in which 'gist' memory might be explained.

Consider a text in which one particular scenario has been used more often that the others, and in which certain characters have been mentioned more often than others. The proposed long-term memory representation would be a connected structure comprising all tokens that were in explicit focus. But the dominant scenario and characters will be more strongly represented, and so will be more likely to be retrieved in recall, or more easily accessed in subsequent reference. It will be apparent that in many respects this account is similar to that of Kintsch and van Dijk (1978; also Chapter 4): the strength of representation depends upon the degree of involvement of any token in the comprehension process itself.

There is a little evidence in the literature which supports the particular account which we are giving above. Black and Bower (1979) studied the recall of texts which were especially constructed to consist of a number of discrete 'episodes'. They found that the recall of the main events of one episode was independent of the content of the other episodes and that recall of the main event in a particular episode was higher if there were a larger number of subsidiary propositions relating to it. In terms of the dominant scenario hypothesis, repeated use of a scenario (through repeated subsidiary references to it) should bolster the status of its token in explicit focus and hence in long-term memory. At this crude level, at least, the results of Black and Bower conform to our expectations.

Much work remains to be done on the relationship of recall patterns to foregrounding. But it is striking that the various cases of gist recall discussed in Chapter 4 could all be interpreted in these terms. For example, principal goals in goal-oriented stories are better remembered than subgoals (Thorndyke, 1976). A good example of a story dominated by goal structures is 'the old farmer and his stubborn animals' (Table 8.2). The principal scenario in this story embodies the main goal — the farmer trying to get a stubborn donkey

Table 8.2.

The old farmer and his stubborn animals (after Thorndyke, 1975b, 1976)

(1) There was once an old farmer (2) who owned a very stubborn donkey. (3) One evening the farmer was trying to put his donkey into its shed. (4) First, the farmer pulled the donkey, (5) but the donkey wouldn't move. (6) Then the farmer pushed the donkey, (7) but still the donkey wouldn't move. (8) Finally, the farmer asked his dog (9) to bark loudly at the donkey (10) and thereby frighten him into the shed. (11) But the dog refused. (12) So then, the farmer asked his cat (13) to scratch the dog (14) so the dog would bark loudly (15) and thereby frighten the donkey into the shed. (16) But the cat replied, 'I would gladly scratch the dog (17) if only you would get me milk'. (18) So the farmer went to his cow (19) and asked for some milk (20) to give to the cat. (21) But the cow replied, (22) 'I would gladly give you some milk (23) if only you would give me some hay'. (24) Thus, the farmer went to the haystack (25) and got some hay. (26) As soon as he gave the hay to the cow, (27) the cow gave the farmer some milk. (28) Then the farmer went to the cat (29) and gave the milk to the cat. (30) As soon as the cat got the milk, (31) it began to scratch the dog. (32) As soon as the cat scratched the dog, (33) the dog began to bark loudly. (34) The barking so frightened the donkey (35) that it jumped immediately into its shed.

---

into its shed. This scenario is cued by the main goal (3) and two methods of attack (4) and (5). These methods are the kind which might be anticipated as being obvious methods, and so would not be greatly foregrounded. However, the scenario token itself would be, since it is essential for the interpretation of (4) and (5). Bringing in the dog (9) is an unusual method, and so would be more strongly foregrounded, although it still plays a method role in the initial scenario. Even the events bringing in the cat refer back *explicitly* to the original scenario (in (14) and (15)). So half of the story content requires the principal scenario for its interpretation. The remainder of the story makes no explicit reference to the scenario. Now, if the reader tries actively to relate each successive subgoal to the main scenario, the scenario will be used over and over again. If he does not, the principal scenario will lose its foregrounded status as each remaining goal is interpreted.

From this point on the story is more complex from the processing point of view. It could be construed as a series of scenarios, switching in and out as each problem is posed and a method tried to achieve each goal. For instance, it may call in a scenario for 'getting milk from a cow'. However, in Chapter 6, it was argued that simply describing a goal would not generally serve to invoke a scenario unless strong constraints on methods were operating. Accordingly, each problem statement could be considered as being strongly foregrounded in explicit focus, since it does not evoke or map into a scenario in implicit focus. When it becomes clear how the farmer proposes to resolve the problem, this may bring in a scenario such as 'getting hay from a haystack' or 'getting milk from a cow', but such scenarios would have a limited lifespan. It is clear from this that the principal goal will be better remembered than the subgoals, simply on the grounds of foregrounding the associated scenario token.

Obviously, many of the details of this account are quite speculative, but a few general principles serve to differentiate the approach from one based on a story-grammar. The extent to which a hierarchical relationship is found between goal level and recall should depend upon the extent to which each goal has an associated scenario. Specifically, it should depend upon the amount of processing which is mediated by each associated scenario. One of the problems with the particular story considered above is that the scenarios which may be invoked cannot be readily defined. By designing stories appropriately, however, the use of particular scenarios could, perhaps, be controlled systematically so that goal level (in story-grammar terms) and scenario dominance may be assessed independently as sources of recall effects.

A further way in which the present account relates to memory depends upon the foregrounding which results from only partial matches in the resolution of primary **RETRIEVE** operations. In our discussions of this (Section B.3) it was shown that an adjectival qualification of an entity having a possible return to be found in focus leads to the entity being more highly foregrounded than it would be if the description was not so qualified. So, on the present argument, such qualified descriptions should be better recalled than descriptions not so qualified. A recent experiment carried out in our laboratory tested this prediction (McDonald and Tweedie, 1980, unpublished). Twenty short stories were constructed around situations which were likely to have script-like scenario representations in memory. Each story introduced a scenario-dependent entity: for example, in a *funeral* scenario, *coffin* was the dependent entity. After seeing the stories, subjects were asked to reconstruct them. Three separate conditions were used: no adjectival modification (e.g. the coffin), an adjectival qualification considered to be consonant with the cultural norm (e.g. the *wooden* coffin), and an adjectival qualification considered to be unpredicted by the cultural norm (e.g. the *red* coffin). The experimental hypothesis was that the unpredicted qualification should be more fore-grounded than the other two, and so, in recall, should be better remembered. The results showed that adjectival modification does indeed increase the probability of recalling the entity itself, and unpredictable qualification has the greatest effect of all (the differences between all paired comparisons were statistically reliable). Furthermore, an examination of conditional probabilities indicated that while recall of the adjective was almost always accompanied by recall of the entity which it qualified, the recall of an entity was more likely to lead to recall of the adjective if it was unpredicted than if it was predicted.

Let us consider these findings in the light of two theories of retrieval. In the first, it might be supposed that adjectival modification gains advantage at recall because it is represented as an additional proposition in long-term memory. If a search of long-term memory is a search for text-based propositions, then it is plausible that two propositions containing a common element increase the chances of finding that element over a representation containing only one proposition. Clearly, such a view will not accommodate the present results. It is not merely adjectival qualification which increases recall probability, but it is the predictability of the qualification with respect to the background situation which has that effect. According to the view developed earlier, the intermediary between recall and predictability is foregrounding. Similar results, but for entire events which are not predicted by scenarios, have been reported by Bower *et al.* (1979), and were discussed in detail in Chapter 4.

The central point we wish to make in this section is that what is recalled will be a joint function of the state of explicit focus giving rise to the representation and also of the accessibility of scenarios. While the long-term (episodic) memory of a text may gradually decay, the scenarios which have been used to construct that representation will not, since it is, by definition, general knowledge. In other words, one would expect the degree of distortion towards normalization in recall to increase over time, a finding highlighted in some of the earliest studies of discourse memory (cf. Bartlett, 1932). Furthermore, one would expect scenario-based recall to be all or none for any given episode, since it is simply the accessibility of the scenario which can be affected by decay, not its content.

2. Evaluating a focus-based theory of text memory

In Chapter 4, three main criteria were used to assess the adequacy of the various models of memory for text: (a) the extent to which they predicted 'gist' remembering, (b) the extent to which they explained distortions in what is remembered, and (c) how much contact they made with processing accounts of comprehension. The present account clearly satisfies (c): it is based on an account of processing discourse, albeit one that is incomplete in some respects. Also, like most schema-based theories, it satisfies (b). Recall is, at least in part, dependent upon interpretive scenarios originally used to comprehend the discourse. Such scenarios provide many of the inferences which experiments have shown to be so easily confused with what was in the text itself. Furthermore, scenarios will have a specifying effect — so that 'cooked the chips' will be confusible with 'fried the chips'. It remains for us to comment further upon 'gist' remembering.

Obviously, to the extent that particular scenarios dominate a discourse, it can be argued that they, and the way in which they relate to one another, provide the gist. Given a range of strengths of representation of each scenario token, subjects asked to produce a summary may be expected to assemble an answer based upon the highest strengths. Such a hypothesis, although simple, carries an interesting implication. If a writer produces a discourse in which there is more detail than gist, and does this by using a particular scenario continually, then the reader may not easily be able to assess what the gist is. It may be reflected in comments of the type, 'Well, I thought it was about X, but it seemed to turn out to be about Y'. Such muddy discourse structures, and the effect they have on readers, have received little, if any, attention from psychologists, who generally use only good discourse structures. (Exceptions to this are usually artificial, as in Thorndyke's (1976) manipulations, or those of Kieras (1978), to be discussed in the next chapter.)

Using strength as a guide to gist also seems a plausible strategy for deciding what a subject would say was the local 'topic' at various points in reading a discourse. In such a case, it might be argued that the immediate topic is to be found in the current focus configuration, and that a subject's description of what the current topic is will be determined by the tokens in focus which have the highest foreground strength.

E. Concluding Remarks

In this chapter, we have proposed a general framework for text comprehension in terms of memory access, and given a detailed account of how reference can be handled within this framework. It could be argued that reference is only one aspect of comprehension. After all, there are a multitude of stages between seeing the letters on a page and finally understanding what is written there. Not least among these is the task of converting the input into some sort of mental currency. We would not want to give the impression that these stages are in any way unimportant; however, there are good reasons for concentrating on the higher level operations here. In the first place, there is a considerable literature already available on the lower level processes in reading. In fact, the vast majority of work in psycholinguistics is directed towards problems of translating a string of letters or speech sounds into some form of mental representation, and this work is readily available elsewhere (cf. Clark and Clark, 1977; Rumelhart, 1977, for recent reviews).

However, there is a more important reason for attempting to describe the comprehension process in terms of higher level operations like resolving reference. In order to make any sense of a psychological process, it is necessary to have some idea of its goal, what it is that the process is directed towards, since this should constrain the nature of the lower level processes. We would suggest that the ultimate goal in understanding a piece of discourse is to relate it to some hypothetical or real state of the world — in other words, to determine to what it is that discourse refers. It is with this in view that the framework was proposed, and to this extent it might form a coherent system in which to evaluate other aspects of comprehension.

Note

1. This is not always true, but generally so. Exceptions are discussed in later sections.

CHAPTER 9

Goals and Constraints in Readers and Writers

The previous chapter was concerned with the elements of a model for the processes of comprehending written discourse. The present chapter is more discursive; the issues considered illustrate the explosion of questions which arise when broader aspects of comprehension are considered. However, the main theme is essentially straightforward. When a writer writes, he has to tailor his words to his audience, and at the same time convey his message as clearly as he is able. He faces a range of stylistic problems, problems of structuring his paragraphs, as well as those of structuring the entire discourse. The intelligibility of a discourse is determined by constraints on the reader — we shall argue that these may be identified in terms of the account developed in this book. To a large extent, the effectiveness of a discourse from the writer's point of view depends upon his success in producing the right model in the mind of the reader. Thus, to be basically misunderstood, and yet considered coherent, is of little use to almost all writers. When one considers the writer, he will be working within the constraints of processes which determine writing behaviour. There is no existing account of the writing process to match current views about reading, but some possibilities are discussed in this chapter. Writing is likened to conversation, which has been better analysed from the point of view of the communicator's intentions.

Later in the chapter, some simple aspects of the question of style are discussed. We shall begin to ask what it is that underlies 'poor style'. The analysis is in terms of our arguments about focus, foregrounding, etc., and it is proposed that style in general can be considered in terms of psychological information-processing models. All of these things are largely without direct empirical support; our aim is simply to show the sensible possibility of such an analysis.

Finally, reading depends upon the attitude and competence of the reader. Research on this point is discussed.

A. Conversation and the Reader–Writer Gap

The aim of conversants is usually to put over a particular point of view. What they say depends upon the knowledge of the other conversants. Similarly, in writing, the aim is to put over a particular point of view as clearly as possible. Let us expand upon this point.

1. Dialogue, models, and intentions

Nowhere is the contractual nature of communication more intuitively obvious than it is with dialogue. In order to communicate efficiently, speakers and listeners have to cooperate with one another in various ways. Speakers try to be informative, clear, and unambiguous; and listeners anticipate that speakers will be doing this. Grice (1975) suggests that such cooperation can be embodied in four maxims for efficient conversation:

> (1) Maxim of quantity. Contributions should be as informative as possible, but not overinformative.

An example of a breakdown due to failure to abide by this maxim is illustrated in the interaction below (from Clark and Clark, 1977):

Steven: Wilfred is meeting a woman for dinner tonight.
Susan: Does his wife know about it?
Steven: Of course she does. The woman he is meeting is his wife.

> (2) Maxim of quality. Contributions should convey propositions which the speaker believes to be true.
> (3) Maxim of relation. The contribution should be relevant to the aims of the conversation.
> (4) Maxim of manner. Contributions should avoid obscurity and ambiguity.

These maxims do not provide a description of the processing constraints in conversation, but they do serve to highlight its contractual nature. Failure to make contributions relevant, for example, is often at the heart of children's games with language:

Father: Do you know the time, Jimmy?
Jimmy: Yes.

The maxims form the basis of what Grice calls 'conversational implicatures'. For instance, take the following interaction:

William: We seem to have run out of milk.
Mary: There's a shop around the corner.

Superficially, all Mary has done is to make a statement that *there is a shop around the corner*. However, more than that, William will assume:

> (a) Mary thinks the shop probably sells milk, and
> (b) Mary thinks the shop is probably open.

If William is to make use of Mary's utterance, he has to make the implicatures (a) and (b).

Grice's maxims can be related to the scenario-based theory of comprehension which we have developed in this book. For instance, the maxim of quantity relates directly to the question of specificity discussed in Chapter 6.

When Steven asserts to Susan that *Wilfred is meeting a woman for dinner tonight*, he is using a noun-phrase (*a woman*) which underspecifies 'Wilfred's wife', so that any scenario elicited in the mind of Susan (or the reader of the interaction) is unlikely to assign 'Wilfred's wife' to the 'escort' slot, even if his wife is thought of at all. Similarly, maxims (3) (relation) and (4) (manner) may both be construed as requiring the speaker to relate new utterances to any existing scenario-based model in an unambiguous way. As we have seen, the ease with which information can be related to extant or prior scenarios determines the efficiency of the recipient's comprehension.

Rather than discuss the complexities of the cooperative principle at work in conversation, our aim here is to use these few illustrations to show that each participant in a dialogue must have a number of *mental models*, which guide the form of his conversational acts. Sources for further discussion (which are extensive) include Clark and Clark (1977), Searle (1975), and Austin (1962), in addition to Grice's own work.

The importance of mental models in conversation can be illustrated by considering a situation in which participant A wishes to convey a message to participant B. In order to do this appropriately, he must have his own model of the message he wishes to convey (call this A's source model). But he must also have a model of what he believes B already knows (call this A's model of B's knowledge state). The form of his communication act, his choice of wording, and the amount of background he introduces will depend upon his model of B's knowledge state. For instance, if he believes that B knows no background, then he will have to fill in a great deal of detail, otherwise B will not retrieve a suitable referent scenario, and will not be able to interpret the message properly.

Just as A has a model of B, so B will have a model of A, and background knowledge to rely upon in interpreting A's utterance. Conversation can then be thought of as A trying to isolate a scenario in B's current focus, and this is, of course, an important starting point or component of A's source model. To the extent that A's utterances successfully isolate an appropriate scenario for B, B is understanding A in the way which A intends. If A cannot do this, corrective conversational interactions will have to take place until a common referent scenario is established.

A neat illustration of understanding on the basis of different models has recently been provided by Wilson (1978; also Johnson-Laird and Garnham, 1978):

Tom, Dick and Harry are presidential advisers, and they are discussing whether or not it would be safe to hide some presidential tapes in a particular room of the White House. Tom and Dick are both privy to the information that a member of the Russian Secret Police is making a clandestine visit to see the President, and that he will be staying in the room in question. Harry does not know of the visitor, and should not know. Tom believes that Dick has forgotten this fact, and

he wishes to alert him to it without giving the game away to Harry. Tom says:
'A guest of the President will be staying in this room'.

In this case, for Harry, the comment merely means that some guest will be staying there, but no specific guest. For Dick, Tom's intention is that it will be a sufficient partial description to elicit a scenario relating to the specific guest, about whom Tom believes he has forgotten. Although background knowledge makes the utterance intelligible to both, the scenarios they invoke are different, and hence the entities available for further reference are different. In normal conversation, Tom would make a more direct utterance, of course — the example illustrates the point that Tom should be as specific as he can dare to be. The primary aim of most conversation is to focus upon a common domain of reference, but is it possible to elicit reference domains at will given knowledge of different listeners' knowledge states.

Control over the form of an utterance thus depends upon each speaker's model of the other speaker's knowledge state. The appropriate use of reference and emphasis can enable a particular speaker to control the focus of attention of one of the other participants. Half-truths can be considered as elements of discourse which fit two different models equally well, and in which one speaker's intention is to deliberately bring up the 'wrong' model in the mind of the listener.

To summarize, in conversation, the principle of cooperation is paramount. In telling a half-truth, the teller trades on the fact that the listener will assume that the principle is being adhered to. When it is obviously not, it is clear that the communication being undertaken is not a simple conversation but has a significance beyond the domain of pure linguistic expression.

2. Writing

As with conversation, writing also has a contractual basis. As we have been at lengths to show, one primary aim of good writing is to produce an appropriate reference scenario in the mind of the reader at the right time. Suppose the writer to have a source model of a situation and message at the outset of his writing. His objective is then to produce a written discourse such that the message is interpreted by the reader in terms of a model resembling the writer's source model. Interpretation in terms of some other model would be no use at all, except perhaps as a deliberate literary trick. For instance, recently British television carried an advertisement for a make of television receiver known as 'Bush'. The advert began with a picture of a conventional living-room. One off-stage voice began with 'I've got a new Bush in the living-room'. At this point, it became apparent that the picture of the living-room was the 'mind's eye' of the second off-stage character: a large indoor shrub suddenly appeared in the corner of the room. The advert continued in this vein, with the shrub in the 'mind's eye' performing the feats which the other off-stage voice was attributing to the television set. Up to a point, an appropriate model does not prevent comprehension, but comprehension is nevertheless inappropriate. Of course, understanding in terms of a seemingly inappropriate model may sometimes be forced deliberately by a writer. Thus, the actions of some character in a novel may seem to be determined by Plan X, and at some later point in the book it becomes clear that he was really operating under Plan Y. But such 'inappropriate' models are really quite appropriate from the writer's point of view. His problem is still to ensure that the reader first selects a scenario appropriate to Plan X, and then switches to one for Plan Y at the right moment.

Hence, the task facing a writer has much in common with that of a participant in a dialogue. The fundamental difference is that there is no opportunity for corrective dialogue after the final draft has been produced, and to engender a truly inappropriate model in the reader may make comprehension impossible, or at least lead to misunderstandings of the writer's ideas. There seem to be two methods which are used in writing that are analogues of corrective dialogue. First, the writer himself can read over what he has written, and this may serve to isolate some of the more obviously muddled areas of exposition. Second, the writer usually has some other persons read his work, and this provides a second corrective stage at which to catch parts of the discourse which do not produce a clear model or reference scenario.

Besides isolating appropriate reference scenarios, the writer is faced with problems of poor, inelegant, and difficult expression. How are we to begin to develop a psychological theory of what it is that characterizes poor or difficult discourse? One obvious way is in terms of the processing rules and constraints governing *reading*. In terms of the model outlined in Chapter 8, poor style could be reflected in such things as inadequate control over fore-grounding, under- or overspecification of partial descriptions in **RETRIEVE** operations, inadequate scenario selection, and inadequate cues indicating a change in implicit focus. At present, there is very little empirical work exploring the style–comprehension interface, other than work on the problem of awkward reference, which we shall discuss in the next section.

The problem of isolating appropriate reference scenarios in the reader's mind corresponds to making efficient use of the rules governing secondary processing. Besides doing this, the writer has to produce a discourse which makes efficient use of the reader's primary processing: as we pointed out in the previous chapter, failures in processing at the primary level may result in total comprehension failure. We now wish to argue that much of what is called 'poor writing style' does not necessarily result in complete failures of processing, but often in more complex processing than would a 'good style'. In many cases, failures at the primary level lead to attempts at secondary processing, and these may succeed and result in a coherent discourse model. Consider the brief passage below:

(1) John saw Bill because he was annoyed.

(1') Bill was waving his fist like a maniac at the seminar.

(1") He knew John had lost the manuscript of their important paper.

The resolution of *he* in (1), through primary processing, should be such that *he* is identified as *John* (the topicalization principle, Chapter 7). If such a mapping is made, then a revised mapping must be made on encountering (1') or (1') and (1"). By the end of the passage, it is apparent that *he* in (1) refers to Bill, and not to John. But such a realization is achieved only through secondary processing. The secondary processing results from a failure to be able to accommodate the referents and acts in (1') and (1"), through primary processing, into the model set up by (1). Unless the writer is deliberately trying to produce the 'wrong account' in the mind of the reader, the passage exemplifies a poor (or inconsiderate) discourse structure. Comprehension of the equivalent information could have been achieved much more readily if primary processing predominated: for instance, by ordering the sentences (1'), (1"), (1). Inconsiderate discourse, of the kind shown in the passage above, illustrates the view that reading is easier when primary processing predominates.

Now, it might be argued that such inconsiderate discourse cannot be equated with poor or unclear writing. After all, a writer may have many reasons for wanting to create the 'wrong' model in the mind of the reader, only to change it later. It may be used to introduce an element of surprise: the whole essence of the classic mystery story revolved around shifts in the attributions of actions and motives made to the various characters. We are not denying this. Indeed, it is a potentially rich field of exploration for those interested in the psychology of writing. Rather, we would argue that poor or unclear writing creates ambiguities to no recognizable or appreciated purpose. Mundane examples, at a very local level of writing, include failures of reference which should be resolved at the primary level. Such failures are commonplace, and some discussion of them is given in the next section.

B. Some Local Problems of Discourse Structure

Above, we introduced the rather graphic term 'inconsiderate discourse'. The term was used by Kantor (1977), who concentrated upon difficult (or *'strained'*) pronominal reference. We shall begin with this. Later, we shall move on to a related question — the extent to which discussions of how language is processed rely upon examples which, in themselves, are strained. It will be argued that the significance of such examples may be interpreted within the present theory, and a method of analysing them will be suggested.

1. Two minor but recurrent problems in inconsiderate discourse

Various examples of strained pronominal reference have already been given, especially in Chapter 7. A typical example might be:

(2) The actress, who was appearing in the play, was well known. She was a very experienced actress, and had often appeared on television. She had also been in a few films. *It* was taken off after a week.

In (2), it would seem to be more natural to use the noun-phrase 'the play', rather than *it* in the last sentence. This example parallels those used in Purkiss' experiment on pronouns, and our explanation of the difficulty with the pronouns could be that *the play* is poorly foregrounded (if at all). Consequently, any attempt to retrieve the token 'play' by means of a primary processing directive (a pronoun) will falter. In Kantor's terms, it exemplifies inconsiderate pronominalization.

Kantor's analysis is concerned with identifying a number of factors which influence the ease of pronominal reference resolution. His list follows the lines of our own discussion in Chapter 7: global topic, local topic, and recency are all seen as having a role to play. At the heart of his theory lies what he terms 'concept activatedness'. He claims that the degree to which a concept is activated determines the ease with which it can be referred to by an anaphoric pronoun. Of course, this is similar to Chafe's (1972) concept of foregrounding. But is is even closer to our own view that foregrounding is equivalent to workspace allocation in explicit focus, and is therefore a continuum rather than being simply all-or-none as Chafe seems to suggest. Therefore, strained pronominal reference can be understood in terms of the focus system described earlier. Just as foregrounding can occur to various degrees, being reflected in the ease with which primary processing can occur, so the 'inconsiderateness' of anaphoric pronominal references should lie upon a continuum. Indeed, even if primary processing should fail, the ease and success with which secondary processing may rescue the situation should also constitute part of a continuum of considerateness.

In psychological terms, such an argument implies that considerateness should be *judged* along a continuum. It is not sufficient for one individual to simply classify the use of an anaphoric pronoun as 'good' or 'poor' style — some measure of the degree to which the style is comprehensible is possible. Furthermore, if allowance is made for the view that people may differ in the extent to which certain individuals mentioned in a text are foregrounded, and in the efficiency of secondary processing, then a reference which for some people is difficult to resolve may be easy for others. If this is indeed the case, then (scientific) claims about inconsiderate discourse should be tested empirically. An expansion of this argument is taken up a little later. For the moment, it is worthwhile reflecting upon whether or not an example from Kantor's own work constitutes strained pronominalization:

A good share of the amazing revival of commerce must be credited to the ease and security of communications within the Empire. The Imperial Fleet kept the Mediterranean Sea cleared of pirates. In each province, the Roman Emperor repaired or constructed a number of skilfully designed roads. They were built for the army but served the merchant class as well. Over them, messengers of the

Imperial Service, equipped with relays of horses, could average fifty miles a day. (from Kantor, 1977)

Where is the strained anaphoric pronoun? According to Kantor, it is *they* in *They were built for the army . . . .'*. While it is conceivable that this anaphor may not be as easily handled as others, the authors doubted whether it was a really good illustration of inconsiderate discourse. Accordingly, an informal check was carried out on what 20 judges might find difficult about Kantor's paragraph. They were each given a copy of the passage, and asked to say how it might be improved. Various (albeit few) suggestions were made, and, in the main, these were comments about the construction of the final sentence. No one mentioned the so-called strained anaphoric pronoun. On asking the subjects directly about the pronoun, one out of the 20 thought it to be perhaps a little awkward, but said that he himself had not noticed it at all during his previous careful, critical reading. The point is not that Kantor's *theoretical* claims are wrong, but that his example probably does not do his claims justice.

These findings lend at least some support to the view that one person's criterion is not always sufficient to make a statement concerning considerateness if that statement is to reflect the views of the majority of readers. Since linguists and philosophers often argue over theories from their intuitions about examples, this is a serious issue. It is especially serious since it has been demonstrated that people who habitually analyse language (linguists, psychologists, philosophers) have intuitions which often deviate markedly from those of the everyday consumer (see e.g. Spencer, 1973). We shall raise this again shortly.

Certain other low-level aspects of poor style can be analysed within the focus framework described above. Poorly edited pieces of writing are often beset with the avoidable repetition of certain words, even if the writer has a fund of synonyms at his disposal. Such repetition is generally considered to be disagreeable by readers. Can such things be understood in terms of the theory which we have been developing? An affirmative answer seems likely if consideration is given to the way in which the processor handles incoming text. Close repetition of the names of individuals in discourse means that tokens referring to entities often still reside in explicit focus, and so the processor will try to connect the input with the existing tokens. If they refer to different things, problems are bound to arise. Longer-term usage of very similar labels could create other problems by calling up irrelevant aspects of the long-term representation of the discourse. Having to entertain irrelevant aspects of the discourse will hamper and impede efficient processing.

From the writer's point of view, there are various possible explanations for the tendency to repeat words. One account might be based on theories of processing at the word level: for instance, Morton (1970) argues that when a word is used, it is easier to process in the near future. In other cases, a restricted vocabulary may be the key. In all cases, the effect will be the same so far as comprehension is concerned.

It is beyond the scope of our current enquiry to elucidate still other examples of inconsiderate discourse. Nevertheless, such phenomena are essentially suitable for interpretation within the framework which we have outlined. A theoretically useful possibility is to take suspected cases of inconsiderate discourse and examine them within such a framework. An example of such an approach is presented in the next section.

2. Inconsiderate discourse and accounts of processing

Many of the examples which we have used in the studies described in earlier chapters are undeniably instances of inconsiderate discourse structure. Now, it could be argued that it is impossible to build theories of natural understanding on the basis of examples of inconsiderate discourse — examples which read in strange or unnatural ways. But such an argument is very superficial. Our interest has been in determining what distinguishes references which can be easily resolved from those which cannot. Inevitably, inconsiderate discourse is a label which can be applied to examples where referential resolution is difficult. Any theory of discourse-processing must establish the relation of the normal pattern of discourse to the processing constraints under which a human reader is operating; these limits can only be established by finding examples which tax them.

Arguments based on inconsiderate discourse need not always be sound, however, especially if the way in which the examples are handled is not related to the psychological constraints of the reader. This is important, for within the analytical approaches of philosophy and linguistics, for any example produced to illustrate a theory of language, a counterexample can almost always be produced. However, we would argue that the extent to which the counterexample scores against the theory depends upon the extent to which example and counterexample exemplify considerate discourse.

Some examples used in such arguments are seen as very poorly expressed by most ordinary language users. Consider the following examples, taken from Wilks (1975; see also Hirst, 1979):

(3) John left the window and drank the wine on the table.
(3′) It was good.

In this case, we would argue that *the wine* (or more strictly, 'John's drinking of it') is the topic of (3), and although, logically, *it* in (3′) could refer to *the table*, this assignment does not happen because of the topicalization principle (cf. Chapter 7). In arguing that topicalization may not be an appropriate way of resolving pronoun assignments, Wilks produces the following counterexample:

(4) John left the window and drank the wine on the table.
(4′) It was brown and round.

In this case, argues Wilks, *it* refers to *the table*, for *the wine* cannot be *brown and round*, while *the table* can. For this reason, he suggests that all simple explanations of pronoun resolution based on topic can be rejected.

The major question for the production of pronoun assignment heuristics is whether examples like (4′) are more likely to occur in language usage than ones like (3). If cases like (3′) occurred with much higher frequency, then a heuristic to check topic for mappings before considering mappings based on inference, as required in (4′), would be sensible. Indeed, heuristics similar to this were actually argued for in Chapter 7. But, although psychological data were presented in support of the topic-preference principle, such a principle would not be very useful if (4′) exemplified the commonly used format. However, intuitively (4′) would appear to be a case of inconsiderate discourse, and so should not exemplify a commonly accepted format.

Earlier, it was argued that pronoun mapping which results from knowledge-based secondary processing takes longer to accomplish than resolution based on topicalization, which has its influence through primary processing. Such arguments should apply to the present examples. However, it is not convenient to carry out comparative measures of reading time with single examples, and some alternative index of inconsiderate discourse is called for. One possibility is to use a paraphrase technique: the rationale for this is that different expressions can be used to convey a particular message, and that, given a set of people trying to express the message, some expressions will be preferred over others. Such a preference should be reflected in the number of people choosing a particular format. If a number of people were presented with (4) and (4′), how many of them would choose to change the way it was written, in order to make it more considerate? And which form of paraphrase would be the most common?

The present writers carried out an informal paraphrase experiment using Wilks' material. When a small number of people were asked to choose between leaving the example as it stood or producing a paraphrase, all claimed that a paraphrase would be better. The most popular candidates chosen can be expressed in the following form:

(5) John left the window and drank the wine which was on the table.
(5′) He noticed that the table was smooth and round.

It was deemed better to refer to *the table* by definite noun-phrase than by a pronoun. Of course, this fits the view that Wilks' example is inconsiderate with respect to choosing a pronoun. All subjects preferred the noun-phrase. Two other points emerged. The phrase *on the table* was seen by some subjects as odd, and they preferred the expression 'which was on the table'. This is possibly because the preferred expression serves to highlight *the table* in some way. The final point is that some informants were dissatisfied with the second sentence as a whole. They felt that some form of introductory expression should be used: something like 'He noticed that'. Such discontentment further reinforces the view that *the table* is in no way the topic of the initial sentence, although it is being treated as though it were in (4′). A change of topic to *the table* can only make sense and be considerate if if is explicitly related to the original topic of discourse.

Although this analysis is relatively informal, it suggests a very powerful technique for analysing the unease which some examples seem to induce in readers. Wilks claims that his example rules out any simple theory of pronominal disambiguation based on topic. This is true; after all, his original example is ultimately intelligible. But the paraphrasing technique supports the view that the example is strained, because topicalization is a *major cue* for pronoun assignment. In other words, the fact that a reader eventually understands a strained example like this does not mean that processes entailed are necessarily used in every assignment. Preferences in the order of application of procedures, which comprise processing heuristics, should reflect the processes employed in handling considerate discourse. It is just this sort of distinction which is reflected in the difference between primary and secondary processing.

In conclusion, suspected cases of inconsiderate discourse can be examined within the context of the theory of focusing. Since many factors contribute to the efficacy of anaphoric reference, inconsiderateness should not be thought of as binary, but as a continuum, possibly affecting different people in different ways.

Furthermore, just because an example presented in an argument might be ultimately intelligible, it cannot be argued that the main aim of the processor is to handle such examples. It must be recognized that the writers of messages typically attempt to match the format of these messages to the processing constraints of the readers, and that although 'inconsiderate' discourse *may* be intelligible, it nonetheless makes abnormally heavy processing demands upon readers.

3. Paragraph structure and writer intentions

In the previous section we pointed out how it is possible for a writer to produce inconsiderate discourse through inappropriate use of local devices in the language such as pronouns or underspecified descriptions. However, one finds more discussion in the psychological and educational literature of the relationship between the global structure of a passage and its comprehensibility. This has already been alluded to in the earlier discussion of text memory in Chapter 4. For instance, in Thorndyke's (1976) study, it was demonstrated that a passage such as 'Circle Island' was particularly difficult to understand and subsequently recall when the theme came at the end. This was attributed to the idea that a reader could not use a story-schema to guide his interpretation of the passage. In this section we will consider the various ways in which writers commonly choose to structure paragraphs of text and what effects this choice of structure might have on comprehensibility in general.

Bissex (see Gilliland, 1975) has put forward an informal analysis of paragraph structures which assumes three basic forms. A schematic representation of the classification is given in Figure 9.1. The three basic forms are *inductive*, *deductive* or *balanced*, and derive from the ordering of statements of theme or generalization *versus* other statements of fact, cause,

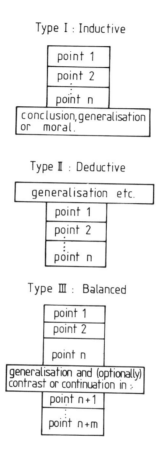

Figure 9.1   A schematic representation of the three types of paragraph structure based on Bissex's classification.

effect or implication. In inductive paragraphs, the writer starts with a number of points which build up at the end to some generalization. In deductive paragraphs, on the other hand, the generalization comes at the beginning and the remainder of the paragraph is used to enumerate examples, arguments in support of it or simply points which follow. Within each of these basic forms there are a number of variants (three for each), so, for instance, inductive paragraphs may be syllogistic or simply structured with the various causes, facts or implications coming before the generalization.

The balanced type of paragraph begins with some points, makes a generalization, and then continues with more detail or possibly contrasting points. A common variant of this type, which Bissex calls the 'classic' structure, is one where a simple main generalization is made, then details are given, after which the generalization may be recapitulated or even abandoned.

While it may not always be possible to fit any paragraph into one of Bissex's categories, since it may be too short to easily classify, the scheme does seem to represent the majority of different types of structure seen in writing (Gilliland, 1975), and is particularly interesting in terms of the importance given to ordering of thematic statements in relation to others. But what implications does this have for the comprehensibility of a passage of text? One way of looking at paragraph structure and comprehensibility is in terms of how different global structures might help or hinder interpretation at the primary level (see Chapter 8), and Kieras (1978) has performed a number of experiments which have relevance to this problem.

Kieras was interested in the effect of two structural factors on comprehension: *initial topicalization* and *coherence*. Initial topicalization relates loosely to Bissex's distinction between inductive and deductive paragraph types, but was described by Kieras in terms of what he called top–down *versus* bottom–up structures, which depend on whether the topic statement comes at the beginning or end. Coherence, on the other hand, relates to the sequence of Given or New statements in the text.

In order to generate different paragraph structures for the same basic text, Kieras took single text-bases of the kind used by Kintsch and created a set of different texts from them. He did this according to two principles of ordering, which he referred to as top-down/bottom–up and breadth-first/depth first. These can be illustrated with reference to the example text-base in Figure 9.2.

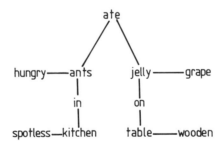

Figure 9.2 Example of text-base used by Kieras (1978) in his reading studies.

The main action in this example is *the ants eating the jelly*, so a top–down passage would start with this statement, whereas a bottom–up one would finish with it and begin with *the kitchen was spotless*. The distinction between depth-first and breadth-first structures derives from the fact that the text-base has two branches, one concerned with descriptions of the *jelly*, the other with descriptions of the *ants*. In a breadth-first passage, propositions from first one branch of the base structure and then the other are presented alternatively. In a depth-first structure, all of the propositions from one branch appear consecutively, and are presented before those from the other branch. Texts illustrating the four resulting structures are shown in Table 9.1.

Table 9.1   *Examples of the presentation orders showing proposition type and Given-New status* (from Kieras, 1978).

Depth-first	Breadth-first
Bottom–up	
n — The kitchen was spotless	n — The kitchen was spotless
g — The ants were in the kitchen	n — The table was wooden
g — The ants were hungry	n — The ants were hungry
n — The table was wooden	g — The ants were in the kitchen
g — The jelly was on the table	n — The jelly was grape
g — The jelly was grape	g — The jelly was on the table
g — The ants ate the jelly	g — The ants ate the jelly
Top-down	
n — The ants ate the jelly	n — The ants ate the jelly
g — The ants were hungry	g — The ants were hungry
g — The ants were in the kitchen	g — The jelly was grape
g — The kitchen was spotless	g — The ants were in the kitchen
g — The jelly was grape	g — The jelly was on the table
g — The jelly was on the table	g — The kitchen was spotless
g — The table was wooden	g — The table was wooden

g or n indicates the Given (g) or New (n) status of the sentence.

These four types of passage vary according to both *initial topicalization* and *coherence*. Initial topicalization is present for the top–down passages but not the bottom–up ones. The coherence, however, depends upon both top–down/bottom–up and breadth- or depth-first structuring. This is illustrated in Table 9.1, where it can be seen that in the top–down passages only the first sentence is *New*; all others are *Given* in that they refer to some earlier statement in the passage. On the other hand, the coherence is poorer for the bottom–up passages and worst of all for the breadth–first bottom–up passage, since only three out of the seven statements actually refer back to the earlier ones.

Using passages of this type, Kieras was able to investigate the relationship of *initial topicalization* and *coherence* with comprehensibility. In one such experiment, he had subjects read the passages a sentence at a time, in much the same fashion as with the reference experiments which we have reported earlier. He was then able to measure both overall reading time and subsequent recall for the different types of passage. The results showed that bottom–up structures were recalled more poorly than top–down structures and that the worst recalled type of all was the breadth-first, bottom–up passage.

The memory results therefore suggest that it is coherence which may account for intelligibility in these cases. However, contrary to Kieras' expectations, he found no reliable differences in the reading times for the various passages. In order to increase the chance of detecting reading effects, he therefore went on to repeat the experiment but with increased memory load. In the high-load condition, sentences from three passages were presented cyclically — one from A, one from B, one from C, another from A . . ., etc. In the other condition, the three passages were presented consecutively before the recall test. Under these rather extraordinary conditions, the expected reading-time differences emerged. Poor orders of within-passage Given–New sentences produced longer reading times; this was particularly true for the New sentences.

While this experiment is somewhat unnatural in terms of conditions for reading, it does suggest that paragraph structure can be related to intelligibility through local considerations such as coherence. Kieras considered that one role of good paragraph structure was to minimize working-memory load, since with the least coherent orderings, new propositions would have to be held in memory until later sentences enabled integration. This would have the effect of both slowing down reading rate and making it more likely that a new proposition should be lost from memory before it could be fully interpreted. While we would agree in principle with Kieras' conclusion, his results are totally consistent with predictions from an account of comprehension in terms of reference and focus. Poor discourse structure makes integration difficult because it taxes the limitations of the focus system and forces the reader to carry out secondary-level processing when this is quite unnecessary.

This, of course, raises the question of whether top–down discourse structures are best from the writer's point of view. After all, many of the categories of paragraph described by Bissex do not conform to the top–down prescription and quite certainly not all naturally occurring paragraphs are of this form. But this does not mean that alternative structures merely exemplify poor discourse? Writers do not necessarily only want to maximize memory performance or reading ease on a given paragraph. They may not wish people to worry about all of the details which they introduce, and so may arrange paragraphs to lead to something which seems to resolve an issue without the details actually being retained. For instance, such a formula would be especially useful in a propaganda speech, where some of the antecedent details may not actually fit the conclusion.

A further consideration revolves around the somewhat loose terms 'interest', 'tension', and 'affect'. Bottom–up discourse structures often seem to be either uncomfortable or exciting to read. If the writer does not seem to be getting to the point early enough, it can rouse considerable feelings of tension in the reader. Provided the point is finally reached and did not become too predictable earlier on this may be cathartic, and lead to a release of tension. It is not difficult to imagine how useful such an effect might be: there is something boring in extreme predictability. To keep the interest of a reader, somehow a balance must be struck. Furthermore, it is not always the *writer* who will be construed as producing unpredictable discourse structures. The attribution of unpredictability could be made to one of the *characters* in a story, for instance. Strange, apparently unmotivated, behaviour in characters can be interesting up to a point, and the writer can trade on the affective aspects of discovery. But again, if it is overdone, then the text may seem unintelligible.

In both the cases of writer and character attributions of unpredictability *versus* predictability, some trade off is called for. At present, there is little to say where the watershed comes. It is a sad fact that the affective aspects of information-processing make little serious contact with the currently available process models (see, for instance, Koestler, 1964, and Mandler, 1975, for two views of the state of the art). Developments in this field must surely appear soon.

C. Reading and the Reader

We now turn from emphasizing the writer to emphasizing the reader. The reader's goal in processing discourse depends upon his intentions. The most basic task is to derive a model of the text in his mind which he finds coherent, and which he believes reflects the model the writer had in mind. To the extent that the writer is skilled, this will happen. Beyond this, various modes of reading are possible. The reader could be analytic, pausing to consider counterarguments to the claims a writer makes; he could be reading simply to get the gist of what the writer says; or he could be reading in order to retain the detail. With short texts of the kind considered in this book, these alternatives are seldom encountered. But with longer tracts of naturally occurring discourse, alternative approaches are manifest. Below, we shall discuss some of these.

Whatever his intentions in reading, the reader must still use the analytical machinery of primary and secondary processing in order to comprehend. To the extent that there are good and poor readers, individual reading skill might be related to the efficiency of this machinery. Such a possibility is outlined in the second section.

1. Strategies in reading

When a particular global reading strategy is employed, one possibility is that the reader uses a guiding *schema* structure to which he tries to relate the text. However, rather than being specifically driven by the text content, as with a scenario, the schema may be an orienting framework based on text-form and intention. An obvious example is reading quickly through a document looking for reference to a particular point — until the key words relating to the point are met, detailed processing does not occur. For instance, many people will have an idea of the layout of a scientific report, and may skim through it looking for reference to a particular theory. Their knowledge of the theory is a kind of scenario structure, and they are trying to relate aspects of the paper to that. Thus, in much the same way that a text-based scenario guides the interpretation of text, so a plan for selective reading can be characterized in this way.

One problem in reading which can be thought of in this fashion is that of reading to retain detail rather than reading for gist. Traditionally this has become known as reading to *learn*, although what is usually meant is reading to learn details. Many experiments have been conducted which show that learning can be enhanced by the introduction of *adjunct questions* into the text from time to time. Such questions relate to the text, and are either put in such a place that they refer to text which has already been read or in such a place that they refer to material which is about to be read.

Rothkopf (e.g. 1968) distinguishes two effects such questions might have. One is that they cause the reader to focus on material relating directly to the questions themselves (question-specific effects), and the other is that they can cause the reader to adopt a more detailed way of reading in general, thus improving 'learning': this latter set of processes Rothkopf refers to as mathemagenic, meaning 'giving birth to learning'. In tests of general learning, Rothkopf (1968) showed that subjects who had adjunct questions about what they had already read performed better than those who had questions relating to what they were about to read, or those who had no adjunct questions at all. In other words, these subjects adopted a deliberate learning strategy in order to retain any facts which might be of importance. Subjects knowing specific questions in advance concentrated only on material relevant to these questions. Of course, both groups who encountered adjunct questions performed better on later tests comprising items relating to those questions. Rothkopf (1968) concluded that questions given after reading segments of discourse produced mathemagenic behaviour.

Rothkopf, amongst others, has carried out an extensive research programme on the ways of controlling reading strategies (see Gibson and Levin, 1975, for a review). But the single example which we have cited serves to show how, in a global way, reading strategy can be manipulated, a potentially important finding from an educational point of view.

Learning from reading is certainly also influenced greatly by the spontaneous activities of the reader. Classifying statements made by the writer and making inferences from what he says are cited by Gibson and Levin (1975) as important activities. Such behaviours amount to exploring the details of scenarios invoked by the writer, and/or relating them to general classificatory schemata possessed by the reader. Ultimately, any form of classificatory or extrapolative behaviour should have the effect of maintaining certain scenarios and entities in explicit focus, so effecting a greater probability of recall at a later date.

Apart from differences in active strategies of this kind, we might suppose that the knowledge and the interests of the reader, whether long-lived or transitory, would have fairly direct effects on the way comprehension takes place. In the previous chapter it was suggested that the scenarios available to readers would depend upon their experience and interests. Thus a detailed scenario for the procedures entering into taking a baby to the shops might exist for a young parent, or an older child in a large family, for instance, but may not be possessed by a middle-aged bachelor.

At the level of information-processing, the consequences of this idea are twofold. First, the more detailed the scenario, the better are the chances of accommodating any new input without having to maintain in explicit focus information which cannot be matched. Second, information which cannot be matched will either be forgotten, have to be rehearsed, or produce a search for a new structure in which it might be accommodated. Accordingly, processing will be inefficient, slow, or both. This, of course, relates back to the writer–reader contract. If a writer wants to put across a message, he is well advised to know the interests of his readers, otherwise his expressions will not evoke the appropriate scenarios. If this is not directly possible, the discourse must be expanded so that the scenarios to which he wishes to refer are memories of the discourse itself. Thus (hopefully), the present writers can now refer to 'the reading-time technique' and evoke a complete scenario in the minds of their readers. At the time of first wishing to refer to this technique (Chapter 5), we went to considerable lengths to explain it in terms of scenarios with which we imagined most of our readers to be familiar.

No matter what the extent of writers' efforts, interests and background will determine scenario availability and the nature of scenario contents. It is likely that everyone reads a novel from their own point of view, and this in turn suggests a relationship between personality and the local mechanics of the reading process. Let us be specific in our speculations. A crime story in which a criminal is sketched, a crime is described, and its detection outlined could evoke different interpretations in different people. Someone who has been involved in a crime of the type described may utilize scenarios which are close to the ones the criminal himself might use. A detective reading it might utilize his vast range of detection-procedure scenarios. More 'average' readers might use scenarios which were built up from previous encounters with the works of the novelist. Finally, in understanding the motivations behind the crime, a social worker might use scenarios relating to its causation which would be different from those used by a person who believed primarily in the simplest version of preserving law and order. Whether specific personality traits can be used to predict something like the ease of specific reference resolution in a particular situation is an intriguing, and not altogether unreasonable, question to ask. But of course, no such data exist at present, beyond relatively crude experiments showing that memory for prose and pictures seems to depend upon the observer's political outlook (e.g. Allport, 1954). Nevertheless, the possibility of linking attitudes and process-models of reading behaviour directly should be emphasized — it becomes feasible when attempts are made to model the interaction of knowledge with discourse-processing itself.

Some of the major factors controlling scenario availability are sketched in Figure 9.3, which makes it clear that both reader and writer alike contribute to the control process. Ultimately, however, comprehension depends upon what is in the mind of the reader. It is the reader's scenarios which have to be utilized in building up discourse-based scenarios.

Once these broader aspects of the problem are brought into view, it is apparent that the processing rules governing scenario accessibility will be

206

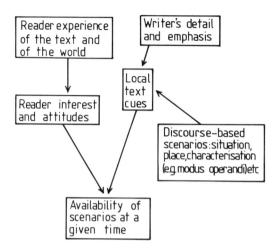

Figure 9.3   Diagram showing the main factors which might enter into scenario availability and their interdependencies (indicated by the arrows).

extremely complex. Schank and Abelson (1977) describe the procedures for activating a script in their system: because part of the system has been implemented as a computer program, they have had to set some specific criteria for this process. The criteria are entirely based upon the text-input, however, depending upon certain combinations of one or more headers, MAINCONS, and subsidiary actions, or props, or roles. But beyond this scenario selection must depend upon other principles of availability. To speculate again, there may be some principle whereby the dominant scenarios used by people tend to be privileged in terms of accessibility over less commonly used scenarios. This is a reasonable principle, but the details of how it might work open up other unexplored realms. This way of looking at reader-goals and individual differences highlights a limitation in the sort of group studies which most contemporary psychologists rely on when investigating reading. The fact that scenarios, as detailed knowledge structures, are almost bound to differ between individuals suggests that any analysis which assumes a common scenario will only really make contact with a structure which is the lowest common denominator of the various scenarios held by the group of subjects. This can easily lead to the mistaken conclusions that scenarios are not well defined or that scenario selection is a probabilistic process. For any given reader with any given text this seems most unlikely, but, in order to verify it, one would need to carry out quite detailed analysis on individual subjects.

2. Limitations in reader skill

In addition to individual differences in knowledge, interests, and reading strategies, it is well known that readers simply vary in *efficiency*. Reading is such an important activity in the modern world, and so bound up with the general process of education, that a great deal of research is aimed at the improvement of reading skill. The aim here is not to review this vast body of work, which would not be possible or desirable in a book of this kind; it is rather to relate the analysis of sources of individual differences in reading skill to the framework presented in the preceding chapters. Those interested in the broader aspects of reading are referred to Gibson and Levin (1975).

Individual differences in reader abilities could originate in any or all of the processes which we have described. Perfetti and Lesgold (1977) describe a number of studies which relate fairly directly to these processes. The most significant of these, carried out by Perfetti and Goldman (1976), relates to the properties of the parser. They classified a group of readers as skilled or less skilled on the basis of a standard reading test (the Metropolitan Reading Test). These subjects took part in a test based on a technique used by Jarvella (1971) to examine verbatim memory for recently presented text. Subjects read stories of 45–50 pages, and on 18 occasions found only a *single word* when a page was turned. Such a word was a cue, and subjects had to say which word followed the probe in the preceding text. In terms of verbatim recall, Perfetti and Goldman found that skilled subjects could remember more words using this probe procedure than could unskilled subjects. This effect was restricted to cases where a sentence boundary intervened between the cue's appearance in the test and its appearance in the preceding text. The investigators concluded that although verbatim recall was poorer in poor readers, they still segmented the text input in the same way as skilled readers. As Jarvella (1971) found, sentence boundaries appear to signal the end of a sample for the processor to work on, and Perfetti and Goldman's results show that this happens in the same way with poor readers. However, beyond this, the poorer reader appears to have a deficit in retaining verbatim information.

It is tempting to suppose that the difference might lie in the capacity of the short-term buffer in which verbatim information is held. However, a further study by Perfetti and Goldman suggests that this is not the case. They performed a similar experiment, using meaningless strings of digits instead of connected text, and found no differences between the two groups of subjects with respect to probe memory performance in this situation. Perfetti and Lesgold (1977) suggest that this means that the short-term verbatim store is *not* smaller in the poorer reader. Rather, they prefer to look at the verbatim store as a *workspace*, in which translation into meaning representations competes for capacity with the storage of verbatim material awaiting translation. One possibility is that these translation operations may be slower in the poorer reader. If this were the case, it should be true that wherever speed is of the essence, poorer readers would be unable to complete processing on a sample. By contrast, if accuracy is important, the poorer reader should be much slower. Perfetti and Lesgold suggest such a possibility, but there is little in the way of evidence to decide the issue at present.

If we return to our own account, the 'translation' stage is extremely complex and multifaceted. Some of the things involved are addressing scenarios, determining whether reference is to implicit or explicit focus, making mappings, setting up new tokens, checking coherence, identifying (sentential) topic, in addition to syntactic parsing. Even this incomplete list is sufficient to show that any general claim about the locus of reading disadvantage could be explained in a number of ways. What would be interesting would be to discover whether poorer readers are slower at all of these things, or just some of them. Enquiries into reading disability could be much more informative if they were based on detailed processing considerations like these — and this is the essential philosophy behind Perfetti and Lesgold's paper.

D. Summary

This chapter has been discursive, as promised. The aim has been to relate a number of different psychological considerations to the account detailed in Chapter 8.

At the outset, we returned to the argument, introduced in Chapter 1, that discourse has a contractual basis. Just as the participants in a conversation must try to refer to a common situational model, and each participant expects this, so it is with writing. The major difference between the conversational and written methods of communicating is seen not as being one of modality (oral/aural *versus* writing/visual), but as being one of opportunities for interaction. With conversation, interruption by the hitherto silent participant is possible, if necessary, in order to clarify the common discourse model (or domain of reference). With writing, it is not. Beyond that, there is no reason to suppose any major differences in the psychological processes underlying the two.

Apart from the need for the writer to elicit the appropriate model in the mind of the reader, he is faced with the problem of the selection of words to enable primary processing to occur when possible. His efficiency at this was discussed in the section on the considerateness of discourse, which relates to good and poor style. Failures in pronominal reference at the primary level and word repetition are considered as just two cases, although they are undeniably common cases, chosen to show how the present analysis can be used to make sense of commonplace problems in everyday writing. Then the question as to the role of inconsiderate discourse in arguing about human comprehension was examined. Finally, experimental psychologists have begun to investigate the significance of paragraph structure for efficient comprehension, and work on this was described. Each of these issues is ideal material for expansion; here the aim has only been to give the flavour of the possibilities, rather than to enter into detailed, speculative analysis.

The final section made the simple point, by now perhaps all too obvious, that goals in reading may further constrain the nature of focus, and that readers' interests inevitably will. Stepping to the very edge of the territory being mapped out, it was shown how individual differences in reader abilities could possibly be analysed in terms of an information-processing framework like that outlined earlier.

Inevitably, a discursive chapter such as this is both a salutary thing to write and an exciting thing for the authors to contemplate. It is our hope that we may have conveyed the impression that cognitive psychology does indeed make contact with the nature of written language as understood in the everyday world.

CHAPTER 10

Postscript

In this book we have presented an outline of how the component sentences of a piece of written discourse might come to be integrated into a final mental representation. In many respects the account is inevitably sketchy and incomplete, hence our choice of the word 'outline'. The main objective has been to try to draw together various aspects of language-processing into one common framework. So, for example, we have emphasized how memory for text is dependent upon the processes used in understanding the text, and have tried to develop a way of predicting aspects of text memory on the basis of measurements made when people are reading.

The major empirical thrust is the series of experiments in which reading time is the dependent variable. Almost without exception, the results of these were construed as reflecting the mechanisms of reference resolution. From a psychological point of view, the various forms of reference resolution are arguably central to any theory of understanding beyond the level of the sentence. And reference resolution can be thought of as a problem of memory search: if the processor is to find a referent for anything mentioned in a text, then this can be expressed as a procedure for searching memory to find another procedure which will accommodate the thing being mentioned. In order to constrain the search, it was suggested that two devices operate, which together comprise the current focus of the reader. The primary device, *implicit focus*, is thought of as an interpretive system based on knowledge of situations, events, objects, and characters (scenarios). The suggestion was that sometimes sentences search out scenarios of which the sentences themselves provide a partial description. If a sentence can *already* be interpreted in terms of current implicit focus, then a new scenario is not sought. This entails a rule of processing priority: searches for reference resolution are aimed first at the focus system, and only if this fails are they aimed at the broader reaches of long-term memory.

A second device is *explicit focus*. This is conceived of as containing tokens of entities mentioned explicitly in the text, and forms another immediate source of reference resolution. It is assumed to be of limited capacity, or at least to allow for the rapid fade of tokens not mentioned repeatedly, but the advantage arising from this limitation is that it can be used for a special form of anaphor—pronominal reference. We viewed use of a pronoun as a directive to search explicit focus, resolving reference on the basis of a few discriminating feature tests.

Incomplete though it might be, a focus system of this kind enables one to draw another psychological phenomenon under the umbrella of a single theory. A person can say what the *current* gist of a discourse is, or what the current topic is; this should be related directly to the synchronous state of foregrounding of tokens within explicit focus.

There are problems and pitfalls in an account such as this, not the least of which is that somewhat vaguely specified entity, the scenario. Our later discussions of the semantic decomposition of verbs (Chapter 5) ran naturally into discussions of scenarios (Chapter 6), the continuity coming from the way that verb schemata and scenarios allow for the ready resolution of subsequent definite references to entities which they imply. Some problems are indeed common to verb semantics (decompositions) and scenarios; in particular, defining how much information is available at any one time. There is no answer to be found here, but further experimentation on reference resolution may well provide a clearer and more interesting picture. Some writers (e.g. Gentner, in press) suggest that more and more of the information associated with a verb becomes available as it is required, while at least some workers in artificial intelligence consider decomposition to occur primarily by accessing prepackaged modules (e.g. Schank's verb-frames and scripts). Possibly some compromise is more realistic. For a given person, a scenario may contain certain obligatory structures, defaults, and slots, which are very rapidly singled out when the scenario is in use, providing only pointers to other 'related' aspects of the situation. Even these may be graded in accessibility, depending upon how frequently subsidiary aspects are found to be relevant to the main situation stored as a scenario. In essence, such things could be investigated empirically.

To move on to more general considerations, our major aim in describing language has been to express words and other linguistic devices as *mental instructions*. Such an approach (the procedural approach) follows readily from consideration of ways in which one might simulate complex human activities like paraphrasing text or making translations within a computer system. The procedural approach advocated here goes well beyond traditional lexical semantics. All linguistic devices (e.g. topicalization within a sentence, choice of active or passive voice, and other devices of emphasis) may be construed as instructions to the processor. We have also argued (Chapters 4 and 9) that paragraph structure conventions are to be understood in terms of the processing effects upon the reader. This is not a new idea in psychology — it is the inevitable outcome of applying information-processing analyses to language. The problem is rather one of what to include in such an analysis of language-processing. Rather than concentrating on problems of word perception and sentential syntax (see e.g. Foss and Hakes, 1978), we have chosen to concentrate upon the comprehension of sentences in context, and this has led to the view that the way in which a sentence is represented mentally depends upon the current state of context (of the focus system, in our case). The reason for this method of attack springs directly from the observation that sentences are never produced *in vacuo*, just as words are not. They are always produced in some context, and even if the listener/reader does not know what this context is, he will try to supply one. This is not to say that the problems of word perception and applications of the rules of syntax are unimportant: obviously they are important. But it is to suggest that human parsing systems and word recognition procedures may perhaps be understood more clearly if they are analysed within the constraints under which these procedures are normally employed.

As a means of describing language at a general level, our approach may seem limited in other ways. It is essentially psychological, and is based on the outlook that language understanding occurs through the agency of the reader's mind, and so is a proper subject-matter for psychologists to study. Beyond this, however, we might say that natural languages themselves may be thought of as complex sets of symbols, the forms of which reflect psychological constraints as much as they reflect the flexibility of the human mind. This in turn implies that the various, seemingly endless, varieties of natural languages operate within the same set of psychological constraints. Whether adopting a psychological approach to comparing various languages is too limiting or is useful remains to be established.

A further limitation is equally serious, even for a theory which is admittedly psychological: our discussions have been almost entirely concerned with reading. Any adequate psychological model of language must take into account the *production* of language as well as its reception. At present, process-models of dialogue are even more rudimentary than models of reading (however, see for instance Carswell and Rommetveit, 1971). Theoretical analyses of dialogue suggest one thing at least, however: that acts of reference resolution are central in coherent dialogue (e.g. Grosz, 1977). As we have emphasized throughout, and especially in Chapter 9, both conversation and written communications have a contractual basis: the recipient has to assume that the speaker/writer is trying to single out and refer to a particular reference domain, and the recipient has to use this reference domain to interpret the message being produced. Just how the principal acts of language performance (writing, reading, conversing) may be integrated within a unitary system of psychological processes remains to be seen. Many directions are open for exploration, not the least interesting being the analysis of the aims and intentions of writers, compared with the interpretations made by readers.

Finally, one more limitation deserves mention. In common with all information-processing theories, the present theory of comprehension makes little or no contact with the question of affect. Language is used by writers in ways which the reader finds sometimes beautiful, sometimes ugly, sometimes exciting, or boring. It is all too easy for cognitive psychologists to dismiss such things as being epiphenomenal to comprehension. This would be a rather unfortunate outlook, since affect is obviously an important determiner of reader behaviour. Sooner or later, a way must be found to relate cognitive theories to affective variables, and information-processing and affect must be described in some common meta-language.

References

Abelson, R. P., 1975, Concepts for representing mundane reality in plans, In D. G. Bobrow and A. Collins (Eds.), *Representation and Understanding*, New York, Academic Press.

Allport, G. W., 1954, *The Nature of Prejudice*, Cambridge, Mass., Addison-Wesley.

Anderson, J. M., 1971, *The Grammar of Case: Towards a Localistic Theory*, Cambridge, Cambridge University Press.

Anderson, R. C., Pichert, J. W., Goetz, E. T., Schallert, D. L., Stevens, K. V., and Trollip, S. R., 1976, Instantiation of general terms, *Journal of Verbal Learning and Verbal Behavior*, **15**, 667-79.

Austin, J. L., 1962, *How to do Things with Words*, Oxford, Oxford University Press.

Baddeley, A., 1976, *The Psychology of Memory*, New York, Harper and Row.

Baddeley, A., and Hitch, G., 1974, Working memory, In G. H. Bower (Ed.), *The Psychology of Learning and Motivation*, **8**, 47-90.

Bartlett, F. C., 1932, *Remembering*, Cambridge, Cambridge University Press.

Battig, W. F., and Montague, W. E., 1969, Category norms for verbal items in 56 categories. A replication and extension of the Connecticut category norms, *Journal of Experimental Psychology Monograph*, **80**, 1-46.

Berlin, B., 1972, Speculations on the growth of ethno-botanical nomenclature, *Language in Society*, **1**, 51-86.

Bierwisch, M., 1970, Semantics, In J. Lyons (Ed.), *New Horizons in Linguistics*, Baltimore, Penguin.

Black, J. B., and Bower, G. H., 1979, Episodes as chunks in narrative memory, *Journal of Verbal Learning and Verbal Behavior*, **18**, 309-18.

Bobrow, D. G., and Norman, D. A., 1975, Some principles of memory schemata, In D. G. Bobrow and A. Collins (Eds.) *Representation and Understanding*, New York, Academic Press.

Bousfield, W. A., and Sedgewick, C. H. W., 1944, The analysis of sequences of restricted associative responses, *Journal of General Psychology*, **30**, 149-65.

Bower, G. H., 1972, Mental imagery and associative learning, In L. W. Gregg (Ed.), *Cognition in Learning and Memory*, New York, Wiley.

Bower, G. H., Black, J. B., and Turner, T. J., 1979, Scripts in memory for text, *Cognitive Psychology*, **11**, 177-220.

Bransford, J., Barclay, J., and Franks, J., 1972, Sentence memory: a constructive versus interpretative approach, *Cognitive Psychology*, **3**, 193-209.

Bransford, J. D., and Johnson, M. K., 1973, Considerations of some problems of comprehension, In W. G. Chase (Ed.), *Visual Information Processing*, New York, Academic Press.

Broadbent, D. E., 1973, *In Defence of Empirical Psychology*, London, Methuen.

Caramazza, A., Grober, E. H., Garvey C., and Yates, J. B., 1977, Comprehension of anaphoric pronouns, *Journal of Verbal Learning and Verbal Behavior*, **16**, 601-9.

Carpenter, P. A., and Just, M. A., 1977, Reading comprehension as eyes see it, In M. A. Just and P. A. Carpenter (Eds.), *Cognitive Processes in Comprehension*, Hillsdale, N. J., Erlbaum.

Carswell, E. A., and Rommetveit, R. (Eds.), *Social Contexts of Messages*, London, Academic Press.

Chafe, W., 1972, Discourse structure and human knowledge, In J. B. Carroll and R. O. Freedle (Eds.), *Language Comprehension and the Acquisition of Knowledge*, Washington, Winston.

Chafe, W., 1976, Givenness, contrastiveness, definiteness, subjects, topics and point of view, In C. N. Li (Ed.), *Subject and Topic*, New York, Academic Press.

Charniak, E., 1972, Towards a model of children's story comprehension, Tech. Report 266, Artificial Intelligence Laboratory, Massachusetts Institute of Technology.

Chomsky, N., 1965, *Aspects of the Theory of Syntax*, Cambridge, Mass., M.I.T. Press.

Clark, H. H., 1975, Bridging, In R. Schank and B. Nash-Webber (Eds.), *Theoretical Issues in Natural Language Processing*, Proceedings of a conference at the Massachusetts Institute of Technology, June 1975.

Clark, H. H., and Clark, E. V., 1977, *Psychology and Language: An Introduction to Psycholinguistics*, New York, Harcourt Brace Jovanovich.

Clark, H. H., and Haviland, S. E., 1977, Comprehension and the Given–New contract, In R. O. Freedle (Ed.), *Discourse Production and Comprehension*, Norwood, N. J., Ablex.

Cofer, C., 1941, A comparison of logical and verbatim learning of prose passages of different lengths, *American Journal of Psychology*, **54**, 1-20.

Cofer, C. N., 1973, Constructive processes in memory, *American Scientist*, **61**, 537-43.

Colby, B., 1972, A partial grammar of Eskimo folktales, Working paper, School of Social Sciences, University of California, Irvine.

Collins, A. M., and Loftus, E. F., 1975, A spreading activation theory of semantic processing, *Psychological Review*, **82**, 407-28.

Collins, A. M., and Quillian, M. R., 1969, Retrieval time from semantic memory, *Journal of Verbal Learning and Verbal Behavior*, **8**, 240-8.

Collins, A. M., and Quillian, M. R., 1972a, Experiments on semantic memory and language comprehension, In L. W. Gregg (Ed.), *Cognition in Learning and Memory*, New York, Wiley.

Collins, A. M., and Quillian, M. R., 1972b, How to make a language user, In E. Tulving and W. Donaldson (Eds.), *Organization of Memory*, New York, Academic Press.

Concise Oxford English Dictionary, 4th Edition, Oxford, Clarendon.

Conrad, G. M., 1972, Cognitive economy in semantic processing, *Journal of Experimental Psychology*, **92**, 149-54.

van Dijk, T. A., 1975, Recalling and summarising complex discourse, Preliminary paper, University of Amsterdam, Department of General Literary Studies.

Dooling, D. J., and Christiaansen, R. E., 1977, Levels of encoding and retention of prose, In G. H. Bower (ed.), *The Psychology of Learning and Motivation*, Volume 11, New York, Academic Press.

Dooling, D. J., and Lachman, R., 1971, Effects of comprehension on retention of prose, *Journal of Experimental Psychology*, **88**, 216-22.

Dooling, D. J., and Mullet, R., 1973, Locus of thematic effects in retention of prose, *Journal of Experimental Psychology*, **97**, 404-6.

Ehrlich, K., 1979, Comprehension and anaphora, Unpublished Ph.D. thesis, Sussex University.

Ehrlich, K., 1980, The comprehension of pronouns, *The Quarterly Journal of Experimental Psychology*, In press.

Eisenstadt, M., 1979, Schank-Riesbeck versus Norman-Rumelhart: what's the difference? *Proceedings 17th Annual Meeting of Association for Computational Linguistics*, Arlington, Virginia, Association for Computational Linguistics.

Fillmore, C. J., 1968, The case for case, In E. Bach and R. T. Harm (Eds.), *Universals of Linguistic Theory*, New York, Holt, Rinehart and Winston, pp. 1-90.

Foss, D. J., and Hakes, D. T., 1978, *Psycholinguists. An Introduction to the Psychology of Language*, Englewood Cliffs, N. J., Prentice-Hall Inc.

Freud, S., 1940-52, *Gesammelte Werke*, 1-8, London, Imago.

Garnham, A., 1979, Instantiation of verbs, *Quarterly Journal of Experimental Psychology*, **31**, 207-14.

Garrod, S., and Sanford, A. J., 1977, Interpreting anaphoric relations: the integration of semantic information while reading, *Journal of Verbal Learning and Verbal Behavior*, **16**, 77-90.

Garrod, S., and Sanford, A. J., 1978, Anaphora: a problem in text comprehension, In R. N. Campbell and P. T. Smith (Eds.), *Recent Advances in the Psychology of Language*, New York, Plenum Press.

Garrod, S., and Sanford, A. J., 1980, Bridging inferences and the extended domain of reference. Paper presented at 9th International Attention and Performance Conference, Cambridge, England, In press.

Gentner, D., In press, Verb semantic structures in memory for sentences: Evidence for Componential Representation, *Cognitive Psychology*.

Gibson, E. J., and Levin, H., 1975, *The Psychology of Reading*, Cambridge, Mass., M.I.T. Press.

Gilliland, T., 1975, *Readability*. London, Hodder and Stoughton.

Glucksberg, S., Krauss, R. M., and Higgins, E. T., 1975, The development of referential communication skills, In F. D. Horowitz (Ed.), *Review of Child Development Research*, Vol. 4, Chicago, University of Chicago Press.

Gomulicki, B. G., 1956, Recall as an abstractive process, *Acta Psychologica*, **12**, 77-94.

Goodenough, W. H., 1965, Yankee kinship terminology: a problem in componential analysis, *American Anthropologist*, **67**, No. 5, Part 2, 259-87.

Grice, H. P., 1975, Logic and conversation, In P. Cole and J. L. Morgan (Eds.), *Syntax and Semantics, Vol. 3: Speech Acts*, New York, Seminar Press.

Grimes, J. E., 1975, *The Thread of Discourse*, The Hague, Monton, Janua Liguarum.

Grosz, B., 1977, The representation and use of focus in dialogue understanding, Technical note 15, SRI International Artificial Intelligence Center.

Halliday, M. A . K., 1967a, Notes of transitivity and theme in English, Part 1, *Journal of Linguistics*, **3**, 37-81.

Halliday, M. A. K., 1967b, Notes on transitivity and theme in English, Part 2, *Journal of Linguistics*, **3**, 199-214.

Haviland, S. E., and Clark, H. H., 1974, What's new? Acquiring new information as a process in comprehension, *Journal of Verbal Learning and Verbal Behavior*, **13**, 512-21.

Hirst, G., 1979, Anaphora in natural language understanding: A survey, Technical report 79-2, Department of Computer Science, The University of British Columbia.

Hornby, P. A., 1972, The psychological subject and predicate, *Cognitive Psychology*, **3**, 632-42.

Hudson, L., 1970, *Frames of mind*, London, Penguin.

Jacobson, J. Z., 1973, Effects of association upon masking and reading latency, *Canadian Journal of Psychology*, **27**, 58-69.

Jarvella, R., 1971, Syntactic processing of connected speech, *Journal of Verbal Learning and Verbal Behavior*, **10**, 409-16.

Johnson-Laird, P. N., 1977, Psycholinguistics without linguistics, In N. S. Sutherland (Ed.), *Tutorial Essays in Psychology*, Vol. 1, Hillsdale, New Jersey, Erlbaum.

Johnson-Laird, P. N., and Garnham, A., 1978, Descriptions and discourse models, Unpublished manuscript, Centre for Research on Perception and Cognition, University of Sussex, Brighton, England.

Kantor, R. N., 1977, The management and comprehension of discourse connection by pronouns in English, Unpublished Ph.D. thesis, Ohio State University.

Kaplan, R. M., 1975, On process models for sentence analysis, In D. A. Norman and D. E. Rumelhart, 1975, *Explorations in Cognition*, San Francisco, Freeman.

Katz, J. J., 1972, *Semantic theory*, New York, Harper and Row.

Keenan, J., 1978, Infering causal connections in prose comprehension, Paper presented at the American Psychological Association Convention, 1978.

Kennedy, R. A., 1975, Contextual effects in reading and recognition, In R. A. Kennedy and A. L. Wilkes (Eds.), *Studies in Long Term Memory*, London, Wiley.

Kennedy, R. A., 1979, Eye movements and reading, In M. M. Gruneberg, P. E. Morris, and R. N. Sykes, *Practical Aspects of Memory*, Proceedings of the International Conference, London, 1979.

Kieras, D. E., 1978, Good and bad structure in simple paragraphs: effects on apparent theme, reading time, and recall, *Journal of Verbal Learning and Verbal Behavior*, **17**, 13-28.

Kintsch, W., 1974, *The Representation of Meaning in Memory*, Potomac, Md., Erlbaum.

Kintsch, W., 1977, *Memory and Cognition*, New York, Wiley.

Kintsch, W., and Keenan, J., 1973, Reading rate and retention as a function of the number of propositions in the base structure of sentences, *Cognitive Psychology*, **5**, 257-74.

Kintsch, W., Kozminsky, E., Stretby, W. J., McKoon, G., and Keenan, J. M., 1975, Comprehension and recall of text as a function of content variables, *Journal of Verbal Learning and Verbal Behavior*, **14**, 196-214.

Kintsch, W., and van Dijk, T. A., 1978, Toward a model of text comprehension and production, *Psychological Review*, **85**, 363-94.

Koestler, A., 1964, *The Act of Creation*, London, Hutchinson.

Kuhn, T., 1970, *The Structure of Scientific Revolutions*, Chicago, University of Chicago Press.

Kuipers, B. J., 1975, A frame for frames: representing knowledge for recognition, In D. G. Bobrow and A. Collins (Eds.), *Representation and Understanding*, New York, Academic Press.

Lakoff, G., 1972a, Structural complexity in fairy tales, *The Study of Man*, **1**, 128-50.

Lakoff, G., 1972b, Hedges: a study in meaning criteria and the logic of frizzy concepts, *Proceedings of the Chicago Linguistics Society*.

Landauer, T. K., and Meyer, D. E., 1972, Category size and semantic memory retrieval, *Journal of Verbal Learning and Verbal Behaviour*, **11**, 539-49.

Lehrer, A., 1970, Indeterminancy in semantic description, *Glossa*, **4**, 87-110.

Li, C. N., 1976, *Subject and Topic*, New York, Academic Press.

Lyons, J., 1968, *Introduction to Theoretical Linguistics*, Cambridge, Cambridge University Press.

Mandler, G., 1975, *Mind and Emotion*, New York, Wiley.

McKoon, G., 1977, Organization of information in text memory, *Journal of Verbal Learning and Verbal Behavior*, **16**, 247-60.

Meyer, D. E., Schvaneveldt, R. W., and Ruddy, M. G., 1975, Loci of contextual effects on visual word-recognition, In P. M. A. Rabbitt and S. Dornic (Eds.), *Attention and Performance V*, New York, Academic Press.

Miller, G. A., 1969, The organization of lexical memory: are word associations sufficient?, In G. A. Talland and N. C. Waugh (Eds.), *The Pathology of Memory*, New York, Academic Press.

Miller, G. A., 1972, English verbs of motion: a case study in semantics and lexical memory, In A. W. Melton and E. Martin (Eds.), *Coding Processes in Human Memory*, Winston, Washington, D. C.

Miller, G. A., and Johnson-Laird, P. N., 1976, *Language and Perception*, Cambridge, University Press.

Minsky, M., 1975, A framework for representing knowledge, In P. H. Winston (Ed.), *The Psychology of Computer Vision*, New York, McGraw-Hill.

Morton, J., 1970, A functional model for memory, In D. A. Norman (Ed.), *Models of Human Memory*, New York, Academic Press.

218

Morton, J., and Byrne, D., 1975, Organisation in the kitchen, In P. M. A. Rabbitt and S. Dornic, *Attention and Performance V*, New York, Academic Press.

Norman, D. A., and Bobrow, D. G., 1975, On data-limited and resource-limited processes, *Cognitive Psychology*, **7**, 44-64.

Norman, D. A., Rumelhart, D. E., and LNR, 1975, *Explorations in Cognition*, San Francisco, Freeman.

Perfetti, C. A., and Goldman, S. R., 1976, Discourse memory and reading comprehension skill, *Journal of Verbal Learning and Verbal Behavior*, **14**, 33-42.

Perfetti, C. A., and Lesgold, A. M., 1977, Discourse comprehension and sources of individual differences, In M. A. Just and P. A. Carpenter, *Cognitive Processes in Comprehension*, Hillsdale, N. J., Erlbaum.

Propp, V., 1958, Morphology of the folktale, *International Journal of American Linguistics*, Part III, **24**, 4.

Propp, V., 1968, *Morphology of the Folktale*, Austin, University of Texas Press.

Purkiss, E., 1978, The effect of foregrounding on pronominal reference, Unpublished undergraduate thesis, Glasgow.

Quillian, M. R., 1968, Semantic memory, In M. Minsky (Ed.), *Semantic Information Processing*, Cambridge, Mass., M.I.T. Press.

Quillian, M. R., 1969, The teachable language comprehender, *Communications of the Association for Computing Machinery*, **12**, 459-75.

Rieger, C. J., 1975, Conceptual memory and inference, In R. C. Schank (Ed.), *Conceptual Information Processing*, Amsterdam, North-Holland.

Rosch, E., 1973, On the internal structure of perceptual and semantic categories, In T. E. Moore (Ed.), *Cognitive Development and the Acquisition of Language*, New York, Academic Press, pp. 111-44.

Rosch, E., 1977, Human categorization, In N. Warren (Ed.), *Advances in Cross-Cultural Psychology*, Vol. 1, London, Academic Press.

Rosch, E., and Mervis, C. B., 1975, Family resemblances: studies in the internal structure of categories, *Cognitive Psychology*, **7**, 573-603.

Rosch, E., Mervis, G. B., Gray, W., Johnson, D., and Boyes-Brown, P., 1976, Basic objects in natural categories, *Cognitive Psychology*, **8**, 382-439.

Rothkopf, E. Z., 1968, Two scientific approaches to the management of instruction, In R. M. Gagne and W. J. Gephart (Eds.), *Learning Research and School Subjects*, Itasco, Ill., Peacock.

Rubin, D. C., 1977, Very long-term memory for prose and verse, *Journal of Verbal Learning and Verbal Behavior*, **16**, 611-21.

Rumelhart, D. E., 1975, Notes on a schema for stories, In D. G. Bobrow and A. Collins (Eds.), *Representing and Understanding: Studies in Cognitive Science*, New York, Academic Press.

Rumelhart, D. E., 1977, *Introduction to Human Information Processing*, New York, Wiley.

Rumelhart, D. E., and Ortony, A., 1976, The representation of knowledge in memory, In R. C. Anderson, R. J. Spiro and W. E. Montague (Eds.), *Schooling and the Acquisition of Knowledge*, Hillsdale, N.J., Erlbaum.

Ryle, G., 1949, *Concept of Mind*, New York, Barnes & Noble.

Sachs, J. D. S., 1967, Recognition memory for syntactic and semantic aspects of connected discourse, *Perception and Psychophysics*, **2**, 437-42.

Sanford, A. J., and Garrod, S., 1975, Processing class membership information directly and indirectly, Paper presented to a meeting of the Experimental Psychology Society, Cambridge, July 1975.

Sanford, A. J., and Garrod, S. C., 1977, Implicit information in comprehending discourse, Paper presented at the 4th International Salzburg Linguistics Meeting, 1977.

Sanford, A. J., and Garrod, S., in press, Memory and attention in text comprehension: the problem of reference, Paper presented at 8th International Attention and Performance Conference, Princeton, N. J., 1978, In press.

Sanford, A. J., Garrod, S., and Bell, E., 1979, Aspects of memory dynamics in text comprehension, In M. M. Gruneberg, P. E. Morris, and R. N. Sykes, *Practical Aspects of Memory*, Proceedings of the International Conference, London, 1979.

Sanford, A. J., and Garrod, S., 1980, A demonstration of the situational basis of text-comprehension through implicit assignments of roles to entities. Unpublished manuscript, Dept. of Psychology, University of Glasgow.

Sanford, A. J., Garrod, S., and Boyle, J. M., 1977, An independence of mechanism in the origin of reading and classification-based semantic distance effects, *Memory and Cognition*, **5**, 214-30.

Sanford, A. J., and Seymour, P. H. K., 1974, The influence of response compatibility on a semantic classification task, *Acta Psychologica*, **38**, 405-12.

Schank, R. C., 1973, Identification of conceptualisations underlying natural language, In R. C. Schank and K. M. Colby (Eds.), *Computer Models of Thought and Language*, San Francisco., Freeman.

Schank, R. C., 1975, The structure of episodes in memory, In D. G. Bobrow and A. Collins (Eds.), *Representation and Understanding*, New York, Academic Press.

Schank, R., and Abelson, R., 1977, *Scripts, Plans Goals and Understanding: An Enquiry into Human Knowledge Structures*, Hillsdale, N. J., Erlbaum.

Schegloff, E., 1972, Notes on conversational practice: formulating place, In D. Sudnow (Ed.), *Studies in Social Interaction*, Glencoe, Ill., Free Press.

Searle, J. R., 1975, A taxonomy of illicutionary acts, In K. Grunderson (Ed.), *Minnesota Studies in the Philosophy of Language*, Minneapolis, University of Minnesota Press.

Shafto, M., 1973, The space for case, *Journal of Verbal Learning and Verbal Behavior*, **15**, 551-62.

Spencer, N. J., 1973, Differences between linguists and non-linguists in intuitions of grammaticality-acceptability, *Journal of Psycholinguistic Research*, **2**, 83-98.

Springston, F., 1976, Verb derived constraints in the comprehension of anaphoric pronouns, Paper presented at the Eastern Psychological Association (U.S.A.), 1976.

Stenning, K., 1975, Understanding English articles and quantifiers, Ph.D. dissertation, Rockefeller University.

Stenning, K., 1977, Articles, quantifiers and the encoding in textual comprehension, In R. O. Freedle (Ed.), *Discourse Production and Comprehension*, Hillsdale, N.J., Erlbaum.

Sulin, R. A., and Dooling, D. J., 1974, Intrusion of a thematic idea in retention of prose, *Journal of Experimental Psychology*, **103**, 255-62.

Thorndyke, P. W., 1975a, Conceptual complexity and imagery in comprehension and memory, *Journal of Verbal Learning and Verbal Behavior*, **14**, 359-69.

Thorndyke, P. W., 1975b, Cognitive structures in human story comprehension and memory, Doctoral dissertation, Stanford University, Technical Report P-5513, The Rand Corporation, Santa Monica, California.

Thorndyke, P. W., 1976, The role of inferences in discourse comprehension, *Journal of Verbal Learning and Verbal Behavior*, **15**, 437-46.

Thorndyke, P. W., 1977, Cognitive structures in comprehension and memory of narrative discourse, *Cognitive Psychology*, **9**, 77-110.

Trabasso, T., Nicholas, D. W., Omanson, R. C., and Johnson, L., 1977, *Inferences in story comprehension*. Paper presented at the Symposium on the Development of Discourse Processing Skills; society for research in Child Development, New Orleans.

Tulving, E. A., 1972, Episodic and semantic memory, In E. Tulving and W. Donaldson (Eds.), *Organization of Memory*, New York, Academic Press, pp. 381-403.

Wilkins, A. J., 1971, Conjoint frequency, category size and categorisation time, *Journal of Verbal Learning and Verbal Behavior*, **10**, 383-5.

Wilks, Y., 1975, A preferential pattern-seeking semantics for natural language inference, *Artificial Intelligence*, **6**, 53-74.

Wilks, Y., 1976, Frames, scripts, stories and fantasies, unpublished paper presented at NATO Conference on Psychology of Language, Stirling, 1976.

Wilson, G., 1978, On definite and indefinite descriptions, *Philosophical Review*, **87**, 48-76.

Winograd, T., 1972, *Understanding Natural Language*, New York, Academic Press.

Winograd, T., 1977, A framework for understanding discourse, In M. A. Just and P. A. Carpenter (Eds.), *Cognitive Processes in Comprehension*, Hillsdale, N. J., Erlbaum.

Winston, P. H. (Ed.), 1975, *The Psychology of Computer Vision*, New York, McGraw-Hill.

Wittgenstein, L., 1953, *Philosophical Investigations*, New York, MacMillan.

Zangwill, O. L., 1972, Remembering revisited, *Quarterly Journal of Experimental Psychology*, **24**, 123-38.

Author Index

222

Kuhn, T., 34, *217*
Kuipers, B. J., 33, 36, *217*

Lachman, R., 9, 67, *215*
Lakoff, G., 25, 73, *217*
Landauer, T. K., 122, *217*
Lehrer, A., 16, *217*
Lesgold, A. M., 139, 207, *218*
Levin, H., 204, 207, *216*
Li, C. N., 133, *217*
Loftus, 23, *215*
Lyons, J., 5, 136, *217*

McDonald, N. B., 185
McKoon, G., 71, 182, *217*
Mandler, G., 203, *217*
Mervis, C. B., 119, *218*
Meyer, D. E., 99, 100, 122, *217*
Miller, G. A., 16, 18, 19, 27, 36, 47, 60, 156, *217*
Minsky, M., 31, 35, 82, 101, 146, *217*
Montague, W. E., 96, *214*
Morton, J., 195, *217*
Mullet, R., 67, *215*

Norman, D. A., 14, 21, 46, 48, 82, 143, *218*

Ortony, A., 46, *218*

Perfetti, C. A., 139, 207, *218*
Propp, V., 34, 73, *218*
Purkiss, E., 137, *218*

Quillian, M. R., 7, 20, 22, 23, *215*, *218*

Rommetveit, T. R., 212, *214*
Rosch, E., 22, 25, 96, 119, 120, *218*
Rothkopf, E. Z., 204, *218*
Rubin, D. C., 64, *218*
Rumelhart, D. E., 34, 46, 50, 68, 73, 77, 78, 85, 187, *218*
Ryle, G., 18, *218*

Sachs, J. D. S., 64, *218*
Sanford, A. J., 96–98, 100, 112, 115, 120, 121, 122, 166, *216*, *218*, *219*
Schanck, R., 7, 14, 29, 30, 34, 48, 51, 52, 53, 54, 58, 59, 60, 68, 80, 81, 109, 111, 129, 131, 206, 211, *219*
Schegloff, E., 98, *219*
Searle, J. R., 190, *219*
Sedgewick, C. H . W., 28, *215*
Seymour, P. H. K., 96, *219*
Shafto, M., 43, *219*
Spencer, N. J., 195, *219*
Springston, F., 143, *219*
Stenning, K., 95, *219*
Sulin, R. A., 65, *219*

Thorndyke, P. W., 65, 68, 71, 74, 78, 84, 85, 107, 183, 187, 198, *219*
Trabasso, T., 5, 6, *219*
Tulving, E. A., 158, *219*
Tweedie, K., 185

Wilkins, A. J., 96, *220*
Wilks, Y., 59, 142, 196, 197, *220*
Wilson, G., 190, *220*
Winograd, T., 141, *220*
Winston, P. H., 18, *220*
Wittgenstein, L., 17, *220*

Zangwill, O. L., 65, *220*

Subject Index